Germans into Nazis

PETER FRITZSCHE

Germans into Nazis

HARVARD UNIVERSITY PRESS

CAMBRIDGE, MASSACHUSETTS

LONDON, ENGLAND

Sixth printing, 2003

First Harvard University Press paperback edition, 1999

Library of Congress Cataloging-in-Publication Data

Fritzsche, Peter, 1959–
Germans into Nazis / Peter Fritzsche
p.   cm.
Includes bibliographical references and index.
ISBN 0-674-35091-X (cloth)
ISBN 0-674-35092-8 (pbk.)
1. Nationalism—Germany—20th century. 2. Germany—Politics
and government—1918–1933. 3. World War, 1914–1918—Social aspects—
Germany. 4. Germany—Politics and government—1933–1945.
5. National socialism—Germany. 6. National characteristics,
German. 7. Germany—Social conditions—1918–1933. 8. Germany—
Social conditions—1933–1945. I. Title.
DD238.F74   1998
943.085—dc21   97-23453

ACKNOWLEDGMENTS

I am indebted to the University of Illinois at Urbana-Champaign for two Arnold O. Beckman Research Awards in 1993–94 and 1994–95 which funded research assistance by Glenn Penny, who was a great help. Gary Cohen, Gerald Feldman, and David Clay Large graciously read and commented on the manuscript, as did Harry Liebersohn and the German Colloquium. Thanks so much. I am also very grateful for the efforts of the anonymous readers for Harvard University Press and the support of its editor-in-chief, Aïda Donald. This book is dedicated with love to Karen Hewitt and to our children, Eric and Lauren.

Contents

Germans into Nazis

Introduction

Adolf Hitler among the patriotic revelers at Munich's
Feldherrnhalle on 2 August 1914

Photo credit: Süddeutscher Verlag

One of the most famous photographs ever taken of Adolf Hitler perfectly illustrates the rise of the Nazis and the ideal of the Third Reich. It shows patriotic Germans gathered on Munich's Odeonsplatz to hear the declaration of war read aloud from the steps of the Feldherrnhalle on 2 August 1914. Amid the thousand-headed throng was the penniless painter who lived in an attic room on Schleissheimerstrasse. Crowds such as this one in the Bavarian capital had become familiar scenes all across the country in the last, tense week of July as eager patriots assembled again and again to cheer the resolve of the Reich government to support Austria-Hungary in the wake of the assassination of Archduke Ferdinand, heir to the Habsburg throne. But people gathered on the street in recognition of something else as well: the common fellowship of being German and of belonging to a nation. The declaration of war against Serbia and Russia and then France and Britain early the next month was followed by an upsurge of popular nationalism later affectionately remembered as the "August Days," a period in which differences of class, confession, and region seemed erased and the people, the *Volk*, appeared to be all of one piece.

In the first weeks of World War I, a national treasure was steadily accumulated as much by enthusiastic civilians who volunteered for the war effort at home as by dutiful reservists who reported for service on the front. No other previous civic gestures had brought the idea of the nation to life in such compelling fashion as had these huge, spontaneous gatherings in the summer of 1914. Subsequently, the collective activities to survive the war and vanquish the enemy opened up further possibilities for reimagining the future. Both socialists and nationalists felt their political programs justified by the public's war efforts.

Inevitably, the tender sympathies of the "August Days" diminished. As the war dragged on beyond the first winter and into a second, a third, and a fourth, Germans grew weary and disillusioned. Like the inhabitants of other belligerent nations, they lost hundreds of thousands of sons and brothers and fathers and suffered enormously under the deprivations of war. By November 1918, when socialist revolutionaries toppled the German emperor and princes, August 1914 was but a distant memory. Even so, the troubled years of the new Weimar Republic, the unwelcome peace terms at Versailles, the political rancor between Left and Right, the ruinous inflation, and finally the Great Depression insistently coaxed Germans to recall the fabled moment of unity. Over the years August 1914 was embellished as an enchanted counterpoint to the disenchanting terms of the Weimar Republic. Both Left and Right looked back beyond Weimar, and along the horizons of remembrance stretched the exemplary national unity achieved at the beginning of the war.

In ordinary conversations, neighborhood festivals, and war memorial services, Germans repeatedly turned over the memory of August 1914. Fifteen years later a bestseller list of battlefield novels and trench memoirs vividly illuminated this uplifting side to war: the unforgettable experience of the crowds, the heartfelt departures at train stations, the intimate community of the front lines. So it was not by mere chance that one day in 1930 the well-established Munich photographer

Heinrich Hoffmann pulled out the prints he had taken of excited city people on the first day of mobilization back in 1914. Already a locally prominent Nazi (having joined the party in 1920 with the "Number 59"), Hoffmann showed his portfolio to Hitler in a Munich café. Hitler browsed through the photographs and abruptly said: "I, too, stood in this crowd." Hoffmann could scarcely contain his excitement. To connect Hitler—party leader, political hopeful, self-styled redeemer—with the national idealism of August 1914 would be an extraordinary match. Hoffmann laboriously studied print after print, trying to make out each person to see if he could identify his Führer. Several hours later, the story goes, he found Adolf Hitler near the bottom edge of the last photo.[1]

This fortuitously discovered shot caught the precise moment when the Third Reich became possible. An enlargement shows an excited twenty-five-year-old Hitler caught up in the collective exuberance of nationalist celebration. Richard Hanser sets the scene: Hitler's mouth is half open and his "eyes are upraised and fixed. All around men have their hats on, but his head is bare. The hair is uncut and unkempt, adding to his look of intense agitation. The whole attitude is that of a man transported."[2] The new-found photograph corroborated Hitler's recollections in his 1924 memoirs. "Those hours" on the Odeonsplatz, he wrote in *Mein Kampf*, "appeared like a redemption from the annoying moods of my youth." At least figuratively, Hitler fell to his knees and "thanked Heaven out of my overflowing heart that it had granted me the good fortune of being allowed to live in these times."

His good fortune was not the opportunity to serve his Austrian homeland—earlier in the year Hitler had in fact been arrested for evading military service, though a medical examination eventually deemed him unfit. What filled this outcast with "impassionate enthusiasm" was his identification with the cause of Greater Germany, one which would more faithfully represent all Germans inside and outside the Reich. "In my eyes it was not Austria fighting for some Serbian satisfaction, but Germany fighting for her existence."[3] In this Hitler was not very different from thousands of other Germans, who rallied to the flag not to ward off international dangers but to assert national allegiances. Identity rather than duty was at work here. Loyalties were discovered and claimed rather than acknowledged and served. It was with the declaration of war that Hitler first found a wider meaning to his life and a sense of political purpose.

The photograph is also an extraordinary document of the national mobilization that this total war made possible. World War I occupies such a prominent place in modern history because it created new social formations organized around a national identity that was defined in increasingly populist and racial terms. Over the course of the war the massive mobilization of the population challenged older hierarchies of subordination and protocols of deference. At the same time, war reworked traditional gender roles, overruled long-standing class allegiances, and legitimized exclusive ethnic feelings of being German—to produce a fierce new community premised on the struggle for survival in which a whole people stood to win or lose. With an emphasis on nation rather than state, the stakes of the conflict were written in an insistently democratic vernacular. The mobilized crowd on the Odeonsplatz thus provided a glimpse of things to come. For millions of Germans

July and August 1914 constituted a new political point of reference that would remain valid for three decades.

Historians of Germany have tended to pass over the nationalist promise of 1914 to begin their accounts of Nazism with the nation's traumatic military defeat in 1918. Thus they understand Nazism as the outcome of extraordinary hardship more than of popular mobilization, and Nazi voters as more victims of circumstances than willful participants. Yet, to my mind, 1914 is the crucial date because it set in motion tremendous political aspirations. The triumph of National Socialism has to be sought as much in the realm of ideas and loyalties as in the convergence of economic and military crisis. Because the war so thoroughly revised the national imagination and recombined 60 million people in novel and often dangerous ways, 1914 is the appropriate point of departure for an account of why and how the Nazis came to power.

As Hitler himself reported, the declaration of war produced a sense of Germanness that filled him with ecstasy. For the rest of his life Hitler struggled to retrieve the unshakable union based on ethnic-based nationalism and public self-sacrifice. In his eyes the summer of 1914 was truly historic because it had created a new historical subject in world history—the German Volk—one unencumbered by past history and past inequities and finally unified to claim its imperial destiny. Nineteen fourteen always remained a model for what national mobilization could achieve. "More than once" in Germany's history, Hitler could claim, "thousands and thousands of young Germans have come forward with the self-sacrificial resolve freely and joyfully to make a sacrifice of their young lives."[4] For these reasons, 1914 anticipated Germany's national revolution of

January 1933 and its quest for empire in World War II a few years later.

Nazism has to be approached as much in terms of ideas and desires as in terms of traumas and scarcities, and it is the national idea, the satisfaction of upholding such an allegiance, and the social renovations it entailed that Hoffmann's photographs of the summer of 1914 illustrate so well. That so many Germans became Nazis was not an accident, an unlikely result of disastrous economic and political conditions. It should be stated clearly that Germans became Nazis because they wanted to become Nazis and because the Nazis spoke so well to their interests and inclinations. Given the illiberal aims and violent means of the Nazis, this popular support is a sobering, dreadful thing.

However, voters did not back Hitler mainly because they shared his hatred of the Jews. To be sure, many if not most Germans were anti-Semites to one degree or another and most recognized in the Nazis a political force of unprecedented toughness. In 1933 it was not difficult for anyone to imagine an increasingly brutal future for Germany's Jews. But National Socialism's murderous obsession with commonplace prejudices does not explain the wide support it found among Germans of all classes; the so-called Jewish question did not figure in the passionate electioneering of the Weimar Republic.[5] The Nazis out-polled conservative nationalists (who were also anti-Semites) and Social Democrats (who were not) because they were ideological innovators. The Nazis won such decisive pluralities in the 1932 and 1933 elections, not because they provided the operating instructions to carry out what was already on everyone's mind, but because they departed from established political traditions in that they were identified at once with a distinctly popular form of ethnic nationalism and with the basic social reforms most Germans counted on to ensure national well-being. It is this political ensemble that the photographs of July and August 1914 anticipate.

In the four chapters that follow I propose to explore how we get from the anonymous man in the crowd to the Führer of the Third Reich, or more precisely, since this is a collective rather than an individual biography, how we get from patriotic enthusiasm to Nazi revolution, from 1914 to 1933. Each chapter opens with a photograph and a sketch of a crowd scene—July 1914, November 1918, January 1933, and May 1933—and goes on to examine the abundant social and political transformations of German society to offer an explanation of how and why the Nazis assembled such massive and enduring support in a few short years, which are among the most dramatic and terrifying in Germany's twentieth-century history.

July 1914

Berliners gather in front of the Schloss just before the kaiser
speaks on 1 August 1914

Photo credit: Archiv für Kunst und Geschichte, Berlin

Patriotic crowds pushed through the wide streets of the big city, from the Kochstrasse offices of the major newspapers, which around six in the evening had first reported the impending hostilities between Serbia and Austria-Hungary, then up Friedrichstrasse, Berlin's busiest thoroughfare, which connected the new suburbs to the south with the machine shops and railway stations at the city's northern end. At the very metropolitan intersection where the best cafés—Bauer, Kranzler, and the Viktoria—had taken the choice corners, hundreds of excited people (mostly students, clerks, merchants, and other men about town) turned up Unter den Linden, the royal boulevard that swept past hotels, embassies, and museums to the Stadtschloss, the massive, somewhat gloomy palace of the Hohenzollern kings.

As on any Saturday night, pedestrians crowded the city center. Many shops remained open until early evening, and hundreds of cafés, restaurants, and bars made Friedrichstrasse a popular place for entertainment and pleasure after hours. Streetcars crept up and down the streets, which remained brightly lit and well traveled until after midnight. It was not surprising, then, that hundreds of curious browsers became thousands of patriotic revelers eager to cheer on Austria-Hungary, Germany's closest ally in dangerous times. As the last light faded, the drama of events in faraway Belgrade and Vienna enlisted more and more metropolitans. Grabbing extra editions from the hands of newsboys, reading aloud the headlines that reported Serbia's noncompliance with the Austrian-Hungarian ultimatum (which had resulted from the previous month's assassination in Sarajevo of Archduke Ferdinand, heir to the Habsburg throne), furiously debating the consequences of a Balkan war for the German Empire, and standing aside to read the freshly printed columns before rejoining the excited crowds, Berliners quickly filled the busy streets. They blocked traffic, overwhelmed "daily, profane" business, and stretched this peculiar, exciting moment long into the night.[1] Although the favorite activity of city people was usually watching other people do things, on this obviously momentous occasion the mostly middle-class patrons of theaters, vaudeville shows, and cinemas around Potsdamer Platz and the strollers along Friedrichstrasse turned into very active participants.

Reports published the next day varied, but some five to ten thousand Berliners eventually made their way to the Schloss, the palace of Wilhelm II, emperor of all Germans. Singing patriotic songs, first "The Watch on the Rhine," then "Deutschland, Deutschland über Alles," and finally the Austrian national anthem, "God Save Franz the Kaiser," patriots gathered beneath the kaiser's quarters in a remarkable display of allegiance. They looked for some sign from their monarch, whose appearance at the balcony might give a meaningful frame to the surprising events that tumbled into the streets. However, the windows remained darkened, for the kaiser was vacationing on his yacht in the North Sea. After a while, the "impenetrable" crowd broke up and processions of twenty or thirty men, singing and shouting arm in arm, made their way back down Unter den Linden all the way to the Bismarck monument on Königsplatz, in front of the Reichstag. In the shadow of the Iron Chancellor, excited young men milled around in expectation, listened to impromptu speeches, and, all reports agree, sang and sang, verse after verse. Smaller parades visited a string of national sites: the Austrian embassy, where Ambassador Szögyény-Marich made an appearance to thank Germans for their lively support, the Reich Chancellory, the War Office, and, in the end, the Italian embassy. It was nearly dawn on Sunday before the last songs were sung and the last slogans shouted.[2]

That midsummer's night revelers moved back and forth along a classical parade route of kings and emperors. From the palace itself, over Schinkel's Schlossbrücke, past Schlüter's baroque armory, down Unter den Linden, to Friedrichstrasse, across Leipziger Strasse to Belle-Alliance-Platz, which commemorated the victorious coalition against Napoleon one hundred years earlier, and finally to the parade grounds at Tempelhof on the edge of the capital—the kaiser's colorful guards and royal visitors had turned these streets into a familiar corridor of imperial pomp and imperial power. But, year after year, the people of the city had only been spectators to the kaiser's parades—at least until the patriotic carnival of Saturday night, 25 July 1914, when ordinary Germans stepped into the spontaneous parades and when a collective sense of common purpose that transcended differences of class and region and religion seemed to suffuse city streets.

The next day, Sunday, 26 July, crowds reassembled in the city center, anxiously awaiting the extra editions that punctuated and heightened the excitement. According to the newspapers, a general European war appeared more and more likely. The machinery of alliance clicked perfectly as Russia lined up with Serbia, Germany with Austria, and France with Russia. All day long, spontaneous parades swept up and down Unter

den Linden, trawling the ground from Schlossplatz to Königsplatz, from the Hohenzollern palace to the Bismarck monument. In this holiday atmosphere, reporters could not resist
the hyperbole of their profession. They turned hundreds of
youthful paraders into thousands and saw the restless forth-
and-back movements of the crowds as a cumulative declaration
of patriotic resolve. According to the *Vossische Zeitung*, the
regular Sunday summer attractions at the city's edge lay for-
lorn in face of the "mass migration" into the center.[3] For the
monarchist *Kreuz-Zeitung*, the meaning of the demonstrations
was clear: "Germany's youth has arisen" and demonstrated
"strength and duty to the Fatherland."[4]

As news of the previous evening's parades spread, curious
onlookers had indeed wandered in from the suburbs to the city
center; Sunday morning stories generated Sunday afternoon
crowds. Dressed in their distinctive uniforms and outfitted
with flags, banners, and musical instruments, youth groups
from the outlying districts were among the first to gather in
the city, and they dominated the metropolitan picture for the
rest of the day. The Wandervogel, "Young Germany," and
other clubs clustered around statues of Bismarck, Frederick the
Great, and Wilhelm I, struck up patriotic songs, and led numerous parades to the palace. The news from Berlin prompted
similar demonstrations around the country. Hamburg, Munich, Leipzig, Bremen, Kassel, Cologne, Mannheim, and Hanover all reported exuberant activity on Sunday.[5] Although a
few observers admitted that these nationalist tableaux were
mostly middle-class and seemed more animated by rowdy bra-
vado than by earnest patriotism, the main storyline in the
press remained the same: the spontaneous eruption of popular

enthusiasm for the German cause. "The memory of this Sunday," when the nation appeared to come to life, "will remain and will retain its value," the usually sober *Frankfurter Zeitung* pronounced.[6]

Later in the week, as chances for peace faded and after the kaiser returned to the capital, demonstrations in the public square grew more boisterous. Large crowds formed on Friday, 31 July, and, on Saturday, just before mobilization, 300,000 Berliners gathered in front of the palace, declaring their readiness to defend the Reich, singing martial hymns, shouting out their devotion to the Fatherland. When a military band struck up "Pariser Einzugsmarsch"—the "Parisian Occupation March"—the crowd went wild. In the early evening, the kaiser finally appeared on the royal balcony and spoke to his subjects. "I no longer recognize parties or confessions," he proclaimed; "today we are all German brothers, and only German brothers."[7] The cheers were so loud that most patriots never heard the rest of the speech. That night Berlin resembled an enormous "cast party," drunk with the drama of the nation at war.[8]

The celebratory gestures of so many Germans in July 1914 have etched themselves deeply in the history books. No account of the war has failed to take note of them. Whenever we think of the outbreak of World War I, we conjure up the stormy, patriotic crowds that gathered in Berlin and Vienna, and in Paris and Petersburg. As Germans and other Europeans rushed to arms, it became clear that war, which is ordinarily conducted by states and armed specialists, and nationalism, which is the popular business of the people, had become inextricably linked. The patriotic fervor in 1914 symbolized the nationalization of the masses, which not only encouraged the reckless diplomacy of the German Foreign Office in the last days of July but contributed to the cruel duration of the war and came to deepen the resentments harbored by both victors and vanquished in the difficult years that followed the peace. Historians of Germany have returned to the picture of enraptured crowds in front of the palace again and again because the public display there previews so well the tragedies of the twentieth century: the crude nationalism of the war years, 1914–1918, the rise to power of the Nazis in 1933, and the start of World War II in 1939. Everything was in place that appeared wrong with the kaiser's Germany: the unthinking hurrah-patriotism and puerile monarchism of the middle classes, which compensated for their own lack of political power with the expectation that the German Empire be the very best, the most triumphant, and by far the loudest in the world.

Descriptions of the crowd scenes in July and August 1914 became such common fare that they created myths that defined a new political community on the border between history and fiction. During the difficult war years themselves, German military authorities used memories of patriotic union to bolster wavering public morale. August 1914 constituted an idealized community of faith that Germans found extremely difficult to oppose, even as their individual experiences of war no longer meshed with public rhetoric. In the Weimar years (1919–1933), after Germany's defeat, the "August days" provided evidence for a hidden nation that republican misrule and Allied treachery allegedly obscured from view. For the Nazis, the seizure of power in 1933 finally gave sturdy political form to the nationalist sentiments tentatively expressed in 1914. Even after the destruction of the Third Reich, the myth of

August 1914 endured because it fit so well the conceptions of revisionist historians who explained both the onset of World War I and the rise of Nazism as the result of a pervasive and institutionalized illiberalism.[9] In this view, war enthusiasm was the function of an unthinking nationalism nourished by authoritarian traditions deeply rooted in German history.

What is striking about these master narratives is that they all assume that the crowds were unanimous in their nationalist resolve, although each account places a different political value on them. Over the last ten years, however, historians have grown increasingly uncomfortable with this monolithic picture of German nationalism. Did the throngs on Unter den Linden really look forward to combat? Is "war enthusiasm" the right description for the events in July and August 1914? Did the crowds represent all Germans? When Germans came together, did they really leave behind the quarrels of party and confession as the kaiser indicated?

It is easy but not accurate to ascribe the many movements and gestures of those summer days to the bogeyman of German militarism which somehow took hold of its victims and marched them off to war. A closer look at the crowds reveals a more complex picture. In the first place, as many (if not more) Berliners demonstrated against the war as for it. On Tuesday, 28 July, perhaps as many as 100,000 working-class people attended Social Democratic meetings, held mostly in the outlying proletarian neighborhoods of the metropolis. As these ended, around nine o'clock in the evening, smaller parades pressed into the city center in an attempt to "desacralize" the national sites at which patriots had gathered three days earlier.[10] For the most part the marchers were blocked by the police, who were under the usual strict orders to keep what the government considered to be subversive Social Democrats away from Unter den Linden and the Schloss. Nonetheless, several thousand antiwar demonstrators managed to slip through police lines. Their parades up and down Unter den Linden provoked mostly bourgeois merrymakers sitting in cafés into the well-remembered "Sängerkrieg," in which choruses of the workers' anthem, "The Marseillaise," interrupted patriotic renditions of "The Watch on the Rhine" and "Hail to You in Victory's Wreath." It was midnight before the police finally restored order. Peace meetings took place in other cities as well, although these were generally quiet affairs that lacked the color and spontaneity of patriots' gatherings. Once the socialist counterdemonstrations are included in the overall picture, the myth of national community in August 1914 looks less credible.

It was not only Social Democratic workers who were confused and frightened by the turn of events. A glance through newspaper pages from the end of July reveals that the rich descriptions of patriotism were interspersed with terser summaries of restless and nervous behavior. A more sober mood predominated in border areas, for example. But even in Berlin, far away from either Russia or France, anxious savers lined up in the front of banks on Monday, 27 July, and Tuesday, 28 July. It was a week before bankers and municipal officials reassured enough creditors to end the run. At the same time, grocery stores were mobbed; the prices of flour, potatoes, and salt soared as individuals hoarded goods. It is not difficult to imagine members of the same family singing in front of the Schloss, exchanging paper money for coins, and stocking up on basic foodstuffs. Even if we take only the patriotic singers and revelers, and put aside savers and hoarders, it is difficult to know if we are looking at a crowd that is merely excited by startling international events or one that is truly enthusiastic about fighting the French. Newspaper headlines had always assembled curious urban spectators, whether they reported the murder of child in a tenement courtyard, the outbreak of a devastating fire, the arrival of a zeppelin over the city, or, as in this case, an impending war in the Balkans. That the crowd scenes were widely reported in the press and, in a matter of days, even screened in movie theaters indicated the spectatorial pleasure of public commotion. The noise on the Schlossplatz was at least as sensational as it was patriotic.

And if one walked a few steps away from the main tumult on Unter den Linden, one noticed, as did Eugen Schiffer, a liberal Reichstag deputy strolling with his sons on the evening of August 1, "the dead seriousness that had settled down upon the people." The socialist newspaper *Vorwärts* was even less sentimental. "A massive river of people" had streamed into the city center, it conceded, but "the basic mood is serious and depressed." Whenever young people attempted to rouse an ovation, "it peters out sadly."[11] Reports from other cities and other provinces suggested that far from being the brilliant core of popular excitement, war enthusiasm was the brightly frayed margin of a darker, worried mood that disquieted Germany's reservists and the mothers and fathers and lovers they would leave behind. Outside the big cities there was considerably less patriotic enthusiasm. The editor of the cosmopolitan *Schaubühne*, Siegfried Jacobsohn, who took his annual summer vacation on a small North Sea island, found locals there completely uninterested in celebrating a war that would leave so many farms untended. Put a loud-mouthed Berlin patriot among "our fifteen farmhouses here," he claimed, and you wouldn't hear a thing.[12]

The closer historians look the more nebulous war enthusiasm becomes. Many people were drawn to the center of Berlin simply by the high drama of war and the grand spectacle of crowds. And we know that, in the neighborhoods, demonstrations in favor of peace mingled with long lines in front of banks and stores. It is by no means certain that most Berliners were "up and about" because they wanted war. Given this evidence, the familiar nation of patriots gets pushed more and more to the sidelines and our view of the Second Empire accepts other, less well-known Germanies that were peaceable, frightened, uncertain, and, in any case, not hypernationalist. The notion that authoritarian elites could effortlessly mobilize patriotic sentiment for illiberal ends seems doubtful.

What these revisions to the picture of war enthusiasm miss, however, as they reduce the number of patriots by adding Social Democrats, curious onlookers, and frightened housewives, is that the crowds that did form displayed an unprecedented political profile. If one puts aside the overly simplistic question of which Germans were for and which were against the war, and examines how Germans expressed their political conceptions and how they thought about the nation, a very different kind of gathering comes into view.

The public assemblies of July 1914 were nothing like previous nationalist commemorations. Whether on the occasion of Reichsgründungstag, which marked the founding of the Empire on 17 January 1871, or the annual celebration of Kaiser

Wilhelm II's birthday on 27 January, or Sedan Day, the anniversary of the Prussian victory against France on 2 September 1870, or the spectacular events in the "patriotic year" 1913, during which the silver jubilee of the kaiser coincided with the centenary of the Battle of Nations at which Napoleon had been decisively defeated near Leipzig—official patriotism was pretty much officious patriotism and centered around Hohenzollern legacies rather than German achievements. The people played little part in the ceremonies, at which royalty and notables predominated and court protocol prevailed. What was staged at these events was the fidelity of the German princes to the German emperor rather than the common ties that bound the German people to the German nation.[13]

Authorities intermittently attempted to inculcate more community feeling, but their efforts were clumsy. Even the most public occasions emphasized the paternalistic and patrician aspects of German politics. The sumptuous parade through the Brandenburg Gate to mark the kaiser's jubilee in June 1913, for example, was carefully choreographed according to rank and status, and when representatives of the people appeared they did so as protected wards rather than competent citizens, that is, as veterans, guild members, and schoolchildren. Either Berliners marched in exemplary fashion behind the princes or, more likely, they stood along the sidelines to catch a glimpse of court finery. Again and again, social critics lamented the absence in Germany of popular holidays like the Fourth of July or Bastille Day. A great nation required a great people, the argument went. Unfortunately, the German people remained obscured as long as the person of the kaiser dominated displays of German nationalism. The collective surge of emotion in

1914 has to be understood against the background of this troubled, incomplete sense of German identity in which state and nation, and kaiser and people, had yet to find a restful balance.

July and August 1914 also marked a dramatic break with public decorum in the capital. For years, the streets had been carefully regulated. During the annual military parade and the royal visits, the main avenues were rigorously blockaded by the police. On those occasions, traffic was completely snarled and Berliners either had to go completely out of their way to get across town or had to stop in place and watch the parade go by. Anyone who crossed the parade route risked arrest. Berlin's chief of police, Traugott von Jagow, was notorious for keeping not simply Social Democrats but all curiosity-seekers from blocking public thoroughfares. There was no popular right to the streets, he pronounced; streets were for traffic, or for the kaiser and his parades.[14] Of course, Germany's colonial adventures and its oceangoing navy had offered earlier opportunities for the expression of popular nationalism, but these remained limited in scope. Indeed, when nationalists did celebrate the government's victory in the January 1907 Reichstag elections by cheering in front of the Schloss, the police rudely intervened. Seen in this light, the number and size and the spontaneous and exuberant public nature of the patriotic demonstrations which took place in Berlin and in hundreds of cities and towns across the Reich in July 1914 represented something quite new.

For all the highly ritualized aspects of the patriotic scenes— the itinerary up and down Unter den Linden, the standard songbook, the bluster of the speeches, the denunciations of Social Democrats, the demonstrations of allegiance in front of the Schloss—the crowds themselves were a rather novel sight. The very act of exchanging the role of spectator on the sidelines for that of parader in the streets in which mostly middle-class civilians took the places of the kaiser's soldiers was audacious. In the summer of 1914 the crowd was as much the emotional centerpiece of patriotic exuberance as the kaiser, and it is not at all surprising that the press—the *Berliner Morgenpost*, Germany's largest daily; the *Berliner Illustrirte Zeitung*, its largest weekly; as well as their conservative counterparts, the *Berliner Lokal-Anzeiger* and *Die Woche*—tracked this extraordinary creature with such fanfare. Reading newspapers, watching newsreels, or simply walking around the city, Berliners could see themselves constituting a nationalist public with political desires and political weight. They began to reimagine the nation as a more inclusive and less hierarchically bound collectivity.

So unprecedented were the patriotic gatherings that the police reacted with considerable unease: the crowds were not choreographed by the regime. On the first few nights of the demonstrations police officials carefully monitored the processions, noting rowdy behavior and ordering flags to be treated with respect. By the third day the police dismissed the crowds as "rabble," something to be "intercepted, stifled and diverted" much like socialist demonstrations.[15] On Tuesday, 28 July, gatherings in the city center were banned altogether. The kaiser himself appeared uncomfortable in front of the crowds. In his first, very brief public appearance after returning to Berlin on 31 July, he urged the gathered patriots on the Schlossplatz to "go into your churches, kneel before God, and implore his help for our brave army"; in other words, he asked them to disperse and to regroup under the auspices of traditional authority.[16]

The discomfort of the police and the kaiser and the fascination of the press took measure of the same thing: the growing independence of the crowd from the regime. To be sure, the patriots were in no way opposed to the monarch. Schlossplatz filled again and again as Germans acknowledged the central part the kaiser played in the history of the nation. And the kaiser's balcony speech on Saturday, 1 August, provided the emotional high note to the week-long crisis. At the same time, however, the crowd drew on political traditions that the monarchy did not encompass.

The movement back and forth between the Schloss—which was still dark in the first demonstration—and Königsplatz is revealing. At one end of the patriotic corridor stood the palace of Wilhelm II, at the other the statue of Bismarck, who was invoked again and again by the crowd as an exemplary German patriot. Already on 25 July, for example, orators pressed the example of Bismarck on Bethmann-Hollweg. Would the present chancellor prove himself worthy of his predecessor? they asked. Although in his time, Bismarck, the "iron chancellor," had hardly figured as a populist, his memory was cultivated as a way of celebrating the achievements and the unity of the German people. In the last years before the war scores of Bismarck statues were erected on town squares throughout the Reich. It was Bismarck, rather than the kaiser, who was acclaimed as the "greatest of all Germans" and the "forger" of the empire.

This sort of nationalist activity was always more evident in Prussia than in Bavaria, where loyalties to the Catholic kingdom remained strong. Nonetheless a broader, distinctly German sense of identity had begun to take hold. A vernacular, almost kitschy nationalism was identifiable north and south as Germans read about fashions and gadgets in the nationally circulated illustrated magazines such as *Die Woche* and *Berliner Illustrirte Zeitung,* celebrated the gigantic zeppelins that flew over the countryside, and listened to the common repertoire of military marches on Sunday afternoons. The back and forth of the crowds between the Schloss and the Bismarck statue on Königsplatz constituted the first tentative steps toward the people's declaration of political sovereignty. To paint all this as simply feverish war enthusiasm is to miss the increasingly popular dimension of nationalist gatherings. And since crowds gathered in Bavarian Munich as well as Prussian Berlin, they also indicated the robust role that the nation had come to play in the popular imagination.

There was never a simple German identity waiting to be fashioned into an articulate nationalism by the force of great events. Germany always looked very different to Bavarians, Saxons, and Prussians, or, for that matter, to farmers, workers, and schoolteachers or to men and women. Yet in the first years of the twentieth century people in Germany became more and more alike, sharing an incipient consumer culture and poring over the same images in the national press. Their desire for common national symbols, an official anthem or an official holiday, grew more pronounced as well. The consolidation of this unofficial national identity from below is what observers as well as participants thought they were seeing when the crowds assembled so rapidly in July and August 1914. And once the first gatherings were hyped as "national" in orientation in the press and in conversation, subsequent gatherings became just that, a place to dream the nation. Moreover, the national frame fit these local happenings so well because vernacular nationalism expressed populist impatience with the political rigidities of the empire. To talk about the German cause in August 1914 was to entertain the idea of a new polity and to think about new beginnings. In this sense, German nationalism, at least as an unofficial process distinct from the state, is closely intertwined with cultural rebirth.[17]

Over the course of four wartime winters, Germans would mobilize their energies, vitalize public life, and rearrange their political conceptions around the nation rather than the state or the monarchy. More than anything else in the twentieth century, World War I transformed German nationalism by giving it emotional depth and tying it to social reform and political entitlement. Of course, Germans did not experience the war years in unanimous or uniform ways. Indeed, social tensions between workers and employers and between political Left and Right intensified by 1918. But the war provided a national frame in which Germans made sense of their experiences and gave voice to their aspirations. During this public emergency traditional allegiances to the monarchy withered while new conceptions of the national community ranging from utopian socialism to crude Aryan racism proliferated. War-mongering encouraged nation-building. The war would reveal just how decisive was the movement from the castle, where people had watched and waited, to the Bismarck statue, where patriots had sung and spoken up for themselves.

THE AUGUST DAYS

The tumultuous time after the mobilization of the army on 1 August, after the declarations of war against Serbia, Russia, France, and then Great Britain, after the ovations which greeted the unanimous Social Democratic vote in the Reichstag in favor of war credits on 4 August, after the first victory when German troops stormed the Belgian fortress at Liège on 7 August, and after the capture of Brussels on 21 August—this extraordinary period has been remembered as the "August Days."[18] Showered with flowers, reservists gathered at train stations to mobilize to the front, overage merchants and underage adolescents hurried to recruiting offices, and young women from all social strata enlisted in Red Cross courses. A profound sense of national purpose seemed to pull together otherwise disparate political factions. What the kaiser called the *Burgfrieden*, the "peace of the fortress," promised to resolve the divisions between workers and the middle classes, between socialists and conservatives, between Protestants and Catholics, and between Prussia and the smaller German states. For many Germans, the declaration of war in August 1914 finally completed the process of national unification that had been left unfinished and malformed since the official foundation of the Reich in January 1871. For the historian Friedrich Meinecke, the August Days constituted a treasure of the "highest sort." Germans had glimpsed a genuine sense of community: "One perceived in all camps that it was not a matter merely of the unity of a gain-seeking partnership—but that an inner renovation of our whole state and culture was needed."[19]

Ordinary burghers marveled at how the war made "everything seem new." Mobilization had forced twelve-year-old Ernst Glaeser to cut short his vacation in Switzerland. As his train crossed the border, it "rolled between the rich pastures . . . from all the towns and villages rose shouts of rejoicing. I was dazzled. The world lay transfigured."[20] A more intimate Germany had come into view. "You just have to see this," gushed Johanna Boldt in Hamburg: "the patriotism of our building, Number 88 and 86 in the Hoheluftchaussee. Everything covered with flags and banners, over at Hass, Schlömer, Dührkopp, Häfner, Ernst . . . Even our little Edith has stuck out a 10-penny flag." Sedantag, the anniversary of Germany's victory over France in the last war, prompted even more celebrations: "A throng of people, singing, screaming . . . pushing and shoving up and down the streets." Again and again, observers identified the crowd as a completely novel creature. "What enthusiasm!" Johanna reported in letters to her husband, "what a bustle," something, "my dear, you should have experienced."[21] This common fellowship was so remarkable because it was perceived as without precedent. When German victories were reported, patriots were pleasantly surprised to see black-white-red imperial flags flying from the windows of Berlin's roughest tenements, "even in the third and fourth back courtyards."[22] "War, war" had come with an unexpected gift, reflected Kurt Riezler, advisor to Chancellor Bethmann-Hollweg: "the people have risen up—it's as if they did not exist before and are now suddenly here, powerful and heartstirring."[23] Overcoming rigid social restraints and long-standing class divisions, the August Days appeared to work the magic of national unity from below.

But the magic wore off. Every year, on the anniversary of

the August Days, the Viennese critic Karl Kraus fantasized in 1925, someone should gather up all the exalted historians, giddy twelve-year-old boys, and astonished young women who had babbled about Germany's righteous cause. Then they "should be forced to listen to me reread to them what they wrote back then." Given the pointless endurance of millions of soldiers in the trenches, the staggering casualties during offensives "over the top," and the difficult hardships at home, the ebullience of writers such as Hermann Bahr, who thought he recognized "the true Germany on 1 August" and greeted the war as a "blessing," or young Ernst Toller, who described the "magic force" of the words "Germany, Fatherland, War," seemed obscene.[24] For Kraus, the Great War lived on only as a scare-quoted grotesque: the "Great" War.

Although he never was given the opportunity to conduct his annual lesson in civics, Kraus spoke for a postwar generation of intellectuals for whom the grey reckoning of November 1918 had made counterfeit the bright promise of August 1914. For Glaeser, who went on to become a popular novelist, the transfiguring power of the war that had "made everything beautiful" quickly evaporated. After a few months, "a new front" had been created, this time held "by women against an entente of field gendarmes" who tried vainly to keep starved civilians from requisitioning food in the countryside. In 1917 and 1918, the boy remembered, Germans "hardly mentioned the war; all our talk was of lack of food." Indeed, Glaeser concluded, "our mothers were nearer to us than our fathers," an eloquent summary of how the great war of German armies had shriveled into a desperate struggle to find food and coal at home.[25]

To a great extent, Kraus was right. The story of the war could be told as a long tale of disillusionment. From the very beginning private sorrows mediated public celebrations. Johanna Boldt wrote her husband that on "the 3rd. Sunday without my dear man," 23 August 1914, "German cannons thundered at the gates of Namur." This was the occasion for great excitement. "Everybody is enthusiastic," she recounted. But then "the wail and the woe that comes afterward. Yesterday the 6th casualty list with over 800!"[26] The third Sunday in August meant not only absent fathers and sons but also the loss of income as breadwinners mobilized or were laid off when business orders plunged. In some cities unemployment rates in the autumn of 1914 reached 40 percent, a catastrophe completely at odds with the generally prosperous economic climate in the forty years since unification. Without state-mandated unemployment benefits, workers and their families relied on trade-union support (if they were members), municipal funds (not all cities were generous), or, in the most humiliating cases, poor relief. Of course, this hardship generally remained indoors. It was invisible to revelers crowding the streets to celebrate the storming of Liège or Namur. Nonetheless, in tenement after tenement, as a young socialist in Hamburg noted in his diary, "impoverished conditions, crying women, unemployment, despair."[27]

Even when unemployment eased after war production had adjusted to the requirements of a protracted conflict, the families of conscripted soldiers continued to suffer financial hardships which modest government payments to *Kriegerfrauen* could not alleviate. By the end of 1914 increasing numbers of mothers were forced to work, "to stand their man," as the saying went, although they often had to enlist relatives or older siblings to look after young children. At the same time, the price spiral that had begun during mobilization continued, putting more and more ordinary foodstuffs out of the reach of working-class families. According to calculations by Hamburg's construction workers' union, a family of four had to pay 50 percent more for groceries in June 1915 than in June 1914 while wages remained slack. As a result the consumption of cheaper rye bread and the poor person's staple, potatoes, soared. But not even rearranging plates on the table could make up for the consequences of the Allied food blockade and the disastrous harvest of 1915.[28]

No surprise, then, that in the summer of 1915 Hamburg's private charities and municipal offices operated 58 soup kitchens serving 30,000 portions every day. A year later 70 kitchens prepared more than 100,000 meals.[29] At the same time, the Reich introduced rationing, first of bread and eventually of potatoes, milk, meat, fat, soap, and even clothing. Nothing had a greater impact on wartime morale than the deteriorating food situation, which was already serious in 1915 when ration cards and soup kitchens appeared but became catastrophic in the cold winter of 1916–17 when there was little more than turnips to eat.[30] And whether badly provisioned or not, all Germans on the homefront saw the growing numbers of cripples on the street and anxiously scanned the daily casualty lists published in newspapers and posted in public places: 123. Verlustliste, 124. Verlustliste, 125. Verlustliste:

> . . . Augustinus Kliemann, Fritz Bodschwinna, Bruno Rost, Richard Karkutsch, August Kleineberg, Gustav Gerlach, Franz Jux, Martin Liermann, Karl Kleist, Leopold Bensch,

Hermann Voss, Huge Druse, Julian Kortas, Hermann Hack, Fritz Raetschus, Franz Grossien, Emil Mayer, Gustav Albien, Wilhelm Apholz, Ernst Naumann . . .

"The mood is so depressed," confided Johanna Boldt to her husband somewhere along the eastern front at the beginning of October 1914: "no flags, no extra editions."[31]

Soldiers sobered up as well. "This morning I met a young lady I know," wrote an exuberant Walter Limmer, a Leipzig law student, on the second day of mobilization; "I was almost ashamed to let her see me in civilian clothes." Just one month later, however, the uniformed reservist described war as "ghastly" and "appalling." Limmer was killed on the western front a few weeks later, on 24 September 1914.[32] Even before they were exposed to enemy fire, recruits lost enthusiasm as a result of the numbing routines of the drill and the heavy-handed discipline of career officers.[33] The history books had lied, warriors reported back to their loved ones at home. Industrial combat invalidated illusions about the heroics of battle or the "cult of the offensive." "All the hope we can muster," confided one volunteer in April 1915, "all the dreams we have for the future are wrapped up in one single soft word: Peace."[34] Historians of the front tell us that during 1915 war enthusiasm gave way to a hardened sense of duty to comrades and by 1918, after the great spring offensives had failed to budge Allied lines, to utter exhaustion and what one scholar calls a "concealed soldiers' strike" of perhaps one million shirkers and deserters.[35] Along the front and at home, the carnival of August 1914 had given way to four hard years of "Ash Wednesdays."[36]

But Karl Kraus's civics lesson was also skewed, for the story of the war can also be told as a long tale of self-reliance. True, the sentimental verse of war poetry did not last, but civic work to alleviate the hardships continued and its grassroots aspect had far-reaching consequences. War relief cannot be easily dismissed as overwrought pathos. Throughout the war citizens organized to provide social help, collect war materials, comfort wounded and crippled soldiers, and bolster morale and did so well in advance of the government. This unprecedented public-spiritedness carried over to the new collaborative arrangements hammered out between labor and industry and between labor and the army, so that it was possible to envision a more progressive social compact after the end of the war. Even the increasingly female workforce which labored for longer days at a faster pace with fewer calories remained remarkably composed. The industrial strikes and food riots that broke out particularly in the hardship year 1917 were not in sum politically decisive. Radical socialist calls for a unilateral end to the hostilities found little popular support.

On the hellish front lines, soldiers continued to obey orders almost to a man until the last six months of the war. Any reader of the handwritten letters from the front comes away with a vivid sense of the awful conditions and daily privations suffered by the men and also with the strong impression that soldiers fought with a sense of allegiance to the nation. "Great rolling phrases" about honor and duty surely lost their resonance, but as long as soldiers could fit their service in the field to wider frames of meaning they would continue to fight.[37] In fact, they did so even as they found the official versions of why Germany was at war unconvincing. There is no doubt that the experience of front-line conscripts, young mothers, munitions workers, and impoverished civil servants contradicted every day the often saccharine ideals of the Burgfrieden. Nevertheless, even as the gaps between rich and poor, skilled and unskilled, and officers and soldiers widened, Germans expressed their resentments of economic inequities and their hopes for peace in a vocabulary that stressed common goods and public interests. Although mobilization for war did not fulfill the idealistic hopes for a genuine *Volksgemeinschaft*, a national community, it gave those hopes plausibility and legitimacy and thereby prepared the way for the promises of the revolution in November 1918. My point is not to minimize in any way the suffering of the German people during the war, but to argue that moral and political mobilization remained surprisingly strong and that even where it frayed it authorized new conceptions of the polity.

EVERYBODY'S WAR

The war belonged to everyone, and it worked itself into the personal fabric of 66 million individual lives. The war also changed the way Germans looked at one another and thought about the nation. There was no adult German who did not have an intimate connection to the conflagration. Between August 1914 and July 1918, 13,123,011 men served in the German army. Nearly 20 percent of the total population and 85 percent of all eligible males had been mobilized to fight. Of those mobilized, one in three were at the front at any given time. "Willingly or not," writes Richard Bessel, "millions of soldiers had been uprooted from civilian existence and, after a relatively short training period, sent to war. From a world which had been characterized by peace and stability they were catapulted into a world characterized by death and destruction."[38]

At the same time, workers, many of whom the authorities returned to vital war industries, had to adjust to an increasingly volatile labor market. Employment in war-related industry expanded by 44 percent, while employment in other industries dropped by 40 percent, with the net result that workers experienced "an unparalleled degree of fluctuation, mobility, and turnover."[39] The most obvious indication that the conditions of work had been radically altered was the presence of so many women in traditionally male-dominated trades such as metalworking and machine-tooling or in highly visible jobs on streetcars. "Women, everywhere women," wrote Cologne's *Rheinische Zeitung* in mid-1917, though in fact the female proportion of the total workforce rose only modestly during the war.[40]

Under the hard-pressed conditions of the conflict "there was always something going on." Government offices stayed open, factories instituted nightwork so that traffic in Berlin increased by 60 percent: the 28 million annual streetcar riders in 1913 became 44.6 million in 1918.[41] The factory shopfloor was no less sensational. "Almost every night one or more women passed out by their machines," remembered a churlish Karl Retzlaw, who worked in Berlin's Cassirer Cable Factory: "On some days in winter, we had no heat and workers stood around, unable and unwilling to work." And in the canteen "there were almost daily shouting matches and occasional fistfights."[42] While these recollections are hardly testimony to the solidarity among workers or the strength of the Volksgemeinschaft, they confirm that the war dealt millions of Germans a full hand of impressions.

Almost every family had relatives on the front and tales to

tell about fighting the war, procuring food, aiding refugees and wounded soldiers, and toiling in munitions factories. As a result war became what Germans call *Volksgut,* part of the treasury of the people, and as such resisted management by the government. This was an event in which most of the histories were written by ordinary people for ordinary people. Of course, after the war, the German government and the German army put out official histories. Since 1918 there has been a steady stream of history books about major battles and outstanding generals. But this production cannot compare to the millions of letters, poems, songs, and newspaper articles written during the conflict itself.

The people's archive became immeasurably vast during the war. The feelings of patriotism ran so deep that more than 1.5 million poems honoring German soldiers were composed in just one month, August 1914.[43] It has been estimated that some 29 billion pieces of mail were sent back and forth between the battlefront and the homefront in the four years that followed mobilization. Every day some 10 million letters, postcards, telegrams, and packages reached the front, and every day nearly 7 million were sent back home.[44] Many husbands and wives kept in touch daily, prompting comparisons between the drama of the war and the intimacies of love: "Schatzlieb, now we're writing each other more than when we were courting," realized Johanna Boldt.[45] Not only did World War I generate countless individual versions of the conflict but individuals insisted on making sure their version was registered. Military censorship was bitterly resented by millions of wartime writers who were forced to monitor their own impressions to keep them in accordance with official policy.[46] Even so, pastors, mayors, and Reichstag deputies received thousands of pieces of mail that detailed injustices on the front and urged manifold courses of action.[47]

This purely private correspondence made exceptionally strong claims on the public media. Personal experience rather than official versions became the popular currency in which knowledge of the war was exchanged. Illustrated magazines paid notable attention to the way the conflict had changed ordinary lives, following the crowd through the streets of Berlin in July, illustrating the goodbyes in crowded train stations in August, depicting the reading and writing of postcards and letters in the months that followed.[48] From the very beginning of hostilities Germany's major newspapers, including the traditionally antiwar Social Democratic press, published thousands of *Feldpostbriefe* from the front. To be sure, the selection of these letters was often tendentious and reflected literary conventions about honor, bravery, and sacrifice. Nonetheless, editors plainly felt the need to insert popular perspectives into overall understandings of the conflict, precisely what German officialdom had failed to do in prewar celebrations of the nation. By the end of 1918 more than 97 separate editions of war letters had been published, the most famous of which was Philipp Witkop's 1916 *Kriegsbriefe deutscher Studenten*.[49] Feldpostbriefe were republished in newspapers and books and were read aloud at patriotic evenings hosted by women's groups and church congregations.[50] The high command eventually acknowledged the power of these completely ordinary, unauthoritative letters and incorporated them into the patriotic "enlightenment" that the troops received in the last two years of the war.[51]

Newspapers attempted to make every reader a spectator to the war by augmenting the official bulletins that dominated the front page with a variety of back-page feuilletonistic tours to battle sites, staging areas, and field hospitals. Publishers printed millions of postcards, pamphlets, ten-pfennig novels, memoirs, chronicles, and lithographs, often inscribed with the legend "Aus grosser Zeit," for a public eager to assemble their own archives and paste together their own scrapbooks of the national effort. Germans also rearranged curio cabinets in patriotic order. Portraits of heroes such as General Hindenburg and later the popular aces Oswald Boelcke and Manfred von Richthofen appeared on ashtrays, neckties, flags, and other kitschy items. And the German toy industry brought the western front into parlors across the Reich during each of the four wartime Christmases. Writing letters, rereading Feld-postbriefe, selecting postcards, buying patriotic bric-a-brac, the German people took possession of public events and made them their own. It is not so much a question of whether Walter Limmer or Johanna Boldt supported the war enthusiastically or not but of how their intimate involvement in the upheaval and their reflection on its meaning shaped their political attitudes toward the nation. Willy-nilly, an emphatically German identity was being forged by the war.

The people's archive also tended to represent the conflict in explicitly nationalist and even racist terms. Streetcorner rhetoric and patriotic songs made unabashed use of crude nationalist stereotypes. The Germans described the Russians as "Huns" even before the British used the epithet against the Germans.[52] And on both sides war propaganda and rumors fashioned lurid atrocity stories which turned fellow Europeans into horrible

barbarians, although the freer and more adventurous newspapers of the Allies probably were more effective in doing so
than their German counterparts. At the same time, daily in-
teractions on the street enforced the "ethnic cleansing" of
commonplace speech. Germans dropped the pervasive "adieu"
from their goodbyes and deleted dozens of other foreign words
from workaday vocabularies. From Bad Kissingen, Heinrich
Mann reported that idle spa guests fined one another for the
use of enemy words: "for French: 5 pfennigs; for Russian: 10
pfennigs; for English: 15; Italian: 20." Even the socialist paper
Vorwärts urged its working-class readers to substitute "good
German" words for foreign ones. In this atmosphere it is not
surprising that Germans sitting in cafés offered a "sharp three-
times hurra" when learning of the extent of Russian casualties
in the fall of 1914 and broke into cheers to applaud the sinking
of the *Lusitania* the following spring.[53]

The personal scrapbooks of letters, newspaper cuttings, and
postcards that so many German families came to possess were
only physical fragments of a much wider range of wartime
activities. Although the often cited figure of 1.5 million mostly
middle-class volunteers in the first months of the war is too
high, they did number around 300,000 and each one had to go
to the trouble of finding a reserve regiment with openings.[54]
This enlistment of men had similarly impressive corollaries
among stay-at-home civilians eager to join war relief efforts,
attend patriotic assemblies, or support charity drives. After
August 1914 German neighborhoods were charged with unprecedented civic activism which has gone almost unnoticed by
historians.

On Berlin's Weissenburger Strasse, Käthe Kollwitz watched

her son Peter go off to war. A member of the Social Democratic Party, married to a physician who devoted his life to caring for Berlin's poor, and herself a well-known artist of the Berlin Secession, Kollwitz was not likely to be very susceptible to the patriotic hoopla down on Friedrichstrasse. Nonetheless, as she watched her son quietly follow the call to the barracks, Kollwitz reflected in her diary: "I too felt as if I were becoming new, as if the old values no longer held up any more and everything had to be reexamined. I felt ready to sacrifice myself." Four days later, on 10 August 1914, Kollwitz began work in the "Aid Commission" of the Nationaler Frauendienst (National Women's Service). Her duties were to inquire about the needs of wives and children whom soldiers had left behind. At the same time, she found herself distracted by the ubiquitous sight of reservists on the street, which prompted thoughts of her own son.

In these weeks a subtle militarization took place in Kollwitz's life: although she hated the war and lamented the gruesome scenes of devastation in Belgium and Russia, she began reading literature with military themes (Liliencron, for example) and opened her diary entries, at least in the month of August, with the major war news: Liège, Brussels, Namur. She also illustrated for the patriotic weekly *Kriegszeit*, later *Bildermann*, a commitment she maintained for several years. Of course, it would be foolish to suggest that Kollwitz suddenly became a flaming German nationalist. What happened was that the war created new circumstances in which people from diverse political backgrounds suddenly felt "a sense of duty and responsibility toward the Fatherland," as Kollwitz, somewhat astonished at her own high-minded sentiments, put it. Kollwitz took to heart the example of her son Peter, who had put aside personal interests to serve the nation (and was killed in the first autumn of the war). She was surely not alone.[55]

The Nationaler Frauendienst was the first and largest self-help organization to mobilize German civilians. Established by leaders of the prewar middle-class women's movement, and working closely with the Red Cross, the Frauendienst moved quickly to cooperate with its Social Democratic counterpart. In the spirit of the Burgfrieden, socialists, Catholics, and Jews found places on the national and district boards which soon operated Germany's most extensive social welfare administration responsible for aiding those families in which the breadwinner had been mobilized to the front or made unemployed by the rapid business downturn. Occasionally municipalities subsidized the work of the Frauendienst, but for the most part the women collected the necessary sums themselves.

Given the range of its activities and the lack of government support, a genuine sense of exhilaration moved volunteers to get the job done. In the first two weeks after the declaration of war, for example, 40,000 young Berliners crowded Red Cross offices to sign up for First-Aid courses designed for 3,000. By 5 August 32,000 women had attempted to volunteer in Frankfurt.[56] In Barmen, an industrial city of some 172,000 inhabitants, as many as 1,200 volunteers worked day after day and 2,100 more did so on an occasional basis to support the Frauendienst. Many volunteers had been active in prewar groups such as Barmen's Youth Group for Social Work, the Association of Female Postal and Telegraph Employees, the Israelite Women's Union, or the girls' club Joy; a substantial number were also local Social Democratic activists; but other, especially middle-class women became active in public work for the first time in August 1914.[57]

In Barmen as elsewhere, the most important function of the Frauendienst was to staff *Hilfskommissionen*, the welfare aid committees such as the one Kollwitz joined. There was no other place families could turn to resolve the financial worries that came with mobilization. Early on, as many as 26,000 Berliners sought out the committees each week, seeking advice about tax problems, tenant rights, government payments, and the like. By August 1917 committees in the capital had handled a total of 1,730,346 inquiries.[58]

The Frauendienst eventually administered a wartime version of home economics courses that taught housewives the basics of conservation. Demonstration kitchens were scattered throughout urban neighborhoods to give women an opportunity to learn how to stretch food budgets and cook inexpensive and wholesome meals. In addition, the Frauendienst prepared weekly recipes for newspaper supplements and distributed wartime cookbooks such as *Winke für den Kriegshaushalt* (Tips for the Wartime Household) and *Des Vaterlands Kochtopf* (The Patriotic Cooking Pot). Just how important the cook was to the war became clear when the women of the Frauendienst littered the marketplaces of Berlin with invitations to attend lectures on *Krieg und Küche* to be held, as it turned out, in the plenary room of the Reichstag. As many as 1,500 women attended the extraordinary session on the evening of 16 December 1914.[59]

The advice and recipes the Hilfskommissionen handed out in the first months of the war led step by step to the administration of social services and the operation of soup kitchens.

Within a year, Barmen's Frauendienst was running daycare centers, kindergartens, and reading rooms. In addition, sewing circles and craft shops provided employment to as many as 10,000 impoverished people who manufactured more than 435,000 shirts, 50,000 sleeping bags, and thousands of other useful items for soldiers on the front.[60] By the end of 1915 the Frauendienst had recruited volunteers to run soup kitchens in almost every big city. In May 1915, 170 *Kriegsküchen* were serving 50,000 Berliners. Most of the kitchens were located in the proletarian neighborhoods of Berlin O. and Berlin N., but so-called *Mittelstandsküchen* opened as well in the affluent West, on Potsdamer Strasse, on Maasenstrasse, and on Prager Platz, where middle-class "guests," as the *Berliner Tageblatt* politely described them, were charged a little more (35 instead of 25 pfennigs) but were served on tables covered with white linen, graced by flowers, and, at least on one day, heaped with plates of fresh spinach and beef tongue with rice and tomato sauce. On Maasenstrasse it was like "one big family," the *Tageblatt* assured readers, "since the ladies don't just serve their wards food and drink, but help them look for work and listen to their worries, their sorrows, and their hopes." This highly sentimental portrait cannot be taken at face value; it is entirely too harmonious. Nonetheless, the description must be taken seriously as an ideal image of the self-reliance and mutual support that the German people came to cherish.[61]

No domestic activity on the homefront was as visible or involved as many civilians as the great collection campaigns, which are familiar to all Americans who lived through World War II. The fund-raising efforts of the first weeks of the war, such as that of the newspaper house Mosse, which collected

122 million marks in just three weeks,[62] paled beside the annual Christmas offerings and the extensive recycling campaigns of 1915, 1916, and 1917. On this front, the Nationaler Frauendienst served as the "second army of the land."[63] "Almost the entire female world," the police reported with some exaggeration, had joined sewing circles to make clothes for soldiers on the front.[64]

The first concerted collection campaign came early in 1915 (just as the 130. Verlustliste was published), when the Reich announced *Reichswollwoche* (Reich Wool Week) for the week of 18 January. In Berlin huge advertising posters throughout the city urged citizens to donate clothing at any one of 400 separate offices run by the Frauendienst and staffed by high school students.[65] Day after day, huge bundles of clothing were transported across the Königsplatz to the Krolloper headquarters of the collection effort. Newspaper reporters took a peek inside the building. "It is amazing to think how many vests had been put aside," commented the *Berliner Tageblatt* with a smile—"vests from the time when everyone wore those wonderful flower patterns, vests in purple, green, and bordeaux red." Even more astonishing was the sheer number of carpets, throw rugs, and runners that Berliners had lying around on their floors. War was the welcome occasion for aesthetic as well as material economy. In Barmen it took fifty moving trucks to haul away all the donated rugs, blankets, and vests in "purple, green, and bordeaux red."[66]

Statistics for Barmen, a city which put together an extremely thorough and proud account of its wartime activity, indicate that between July 1916 and July 1917 the Frauendienst oversaw three great collections which netted exactly 23,891 items including 11,398 overcoats, 2,434 hats, 1,231 pairs of shoes (in addition to 130 slippers), 2,162 collars, 40 swimsuits, 483 curtains, 16 rugs, 45 suitcases, and 38 suspenders.[67]

Housewives in Barmen as much as in Berlin were called upon by the government, municipalities, and the socialist trade unions to save food scraps. Everything from bones to fruit pits, potato peels, vegetable matter, and coffee grounds could be re-used. And once again it was the Frauendienst that helped staff collection offices. In 1915 and 1916 the city of Barmen contributed 7,815 kilograms of cherry and plum pits that could be crushed for cooking oil. Scavenging Germans collected a grand total of 4 million kilograms of fruit pits in the summer of 1916, which provided 190,000 kilograms of oil.[68] Oil could also be extracted from sunflower seeds, wild fruits, and even the bark of certain trees. It was not long before thousands of school-children were enlisted to collect seeds from sunflowers that grew along railway tracks and the edges of farmers' fields.[69] Other cities organized even more improbable conservation campaigns. It strains credulity but tickles the imagination to consider Lüdenscheid's proud claim that its young people killed no fewer than 47,990 butterflies in an August 1917 *Sonderaktion* to protect the harvest. In any case, children who distinguished themselves by their special efforts received books, toys, or savings accounts.[70]

It must have been these and other *Sondersammlungen* late in the war, which in Barmen could still bring in 25 kilograms of cigar butts and 194 kilograms of women's hair, the last to substitute for the camel hair and mohair used in factory belt-drives, that prompted the agronomist Friedrich Aereboe to reflect in the 1920s that "war psychosis" had truly impaired "rational economic thinking." All the energy spent collecting fruit pits in Bochum could not cover even 1 percent of the city's need for cooking oil.[71] The constant campaigns wasted time and energy that might have been better spent. Schoolteachers, for example, were expected to supplement their official duties with exhausting volunteer work in children's centers, in war bond drives, and on the boards of countless patriotic associations and charity campaigns. They were also called upon to distribute ration cards, organize the agricultural work of young people, and oversee the collection of clothing, paper, and thousands and thousands of fruit pits.[72]

However, to see only the marginal utility of the Frauendienst campaigns is to lose sight of the ways in which they directly connected the majority of the German people with the war effort. For the first year of the war, national and local officials did little to launch propaganda campaigns or provide social services. As a result war relief began as a grassroots affair that had the effect of involving more people from various classes in public life than ever before. The number of volunteers in this period must be counted in the millions. At the same time, the newly founded patriotic, social welfare, and self-help organizations brought a richer texture to public life.[73]

The Nationaler Frauendienst campaigns had a decisive impact on morale. A look at the subscription of war bonds indicates that more and more lower-income Germans invested. The bonds could be bought in units of 100 marks, allowing small creditors to support the patriotic effort, although this investment became less dear thanks to the effects of inflation. For all the ebullience of the August Days, the first war bond drive found only 231,112 people who subscribed 100 or 200

marks, fewer even than the number of wealthier investors sub-
scribing 300 to 500 marks (241,804) or 600 to 2,000 marks
(453,143). Given these figures, "it certainly was an achieve-
ment," writes Gerald Feldman, to increase the number of 100-
and 200-mark purchases sixteenfold to 4,076,649 in the eighth
drive in the spring of 1918.

True, the bond drives sometimes sputtered and the total issues were not fully subscribed. Only 3.8 million Germans subscribed to the fifth war loan in September 1916, down from
5.2 million who invested six months earlier. However, the sixth
war loan in spring 1917 found an estimable 7.0 million sub-
scribers (and this at the height of the food crisis), the seventh
in fall 1917 still 5.2 million, and the eighth in March 1918 6.5
million. (In September 1918 only 2.7 million Germans invested in the final issue of war bonds.) Moreover, after 1916 it
was small creditors who bought most bonds, although the increasingly devalued money they invested remained just a small
percentage of the total 98 billion collected over the course of
the war. The presence of so many investors almost until the
very end is noteworthy. There is also evidence that workers
were no less likely to contribute than other Germans. War had
truly become the people's business. The conservative estimate
of 8 to 10 million investors in German war bonds represents
a substantial proportion of the population and should serve as
a warning to those observers who would too quickly assume
that civilians turned their backs on the war effort.[74]

Nothing symbolized the active participation of so many civilians in what was an increasingly strenuous popular struggle
to win the war better than the homemade wooden Hindenburg
statues scattered across the Reich in 1915. Hindenburg had

rapidly emerged as the people's favorite hero, having repulsed the Russian invasion of East Prussia at the end of August 1914 and advanced into Russia itself in the months that followed. After the deadlock on the western front, it was Hindenburg in the east who most definitively embodied the "suffering, the power, and the victory" of the nation.[75] On 4 September 1915, just a year after the crucial battle with the Russians at Tannenberg, the National Foundation for War Widows placed an immense 28-ton, 12-foot-high wooden statue of Hindenburg in the middle of Berlin's Königsplatz. Overcrowded with 20,000 patriotic sightseers and overflown by an immense zeppelin, the Königsplatz was the site of a remarkable patriotic exercise. For a donation of one mark, Berliners could hammer an iron nail into the statue; silver and gold nails were available for larger donations. The collected funds went to support Germany's war widows. Day after day the tap-tap-tap of hammers echoed across the square. By the end of the week 90,000 common nails and 10,000 silver ones had been driven into what had veritably become an "Iron Hindenburg." Although opening ceremonies included prominent guests such as Chancellor Bethmann-Hollweg and a Hohenzollern princess, the statue invited the participation of ordinary citizens whose personal efforts symbolically forged the national body. This work in progress demonstrated that Germany's iron-clad war effort was not cast in a government smithy but had been manufactured out of the hammer strokes and voluntary actions of thousands of citizens. The "Iron Hindenburgs" that stood on municipal squares throughout the Reich denoted the intimate link between total war and grassroots mobilization, between *Wehrkraft* and *Volkskraft*.[76]

THE PEACE OF THE FORTRESS

As Käthe Kollwitz's diary entries for August 1914 suggest, the highly visible sacrifices of so many soldiers left an impression strong enough to overturn the social and political assumptions of the prewar years. The war revealed the collective goods the German people could achieve by their own efforts and gradually transformed ideas of the German nation. Even working-class Germans reveled in the inclusive sense of nation that came with the war. The very fact that the long-standing political divisions separating socialists and burghers had been at least tentatively overcome gave the quality of the nation even greater value, for it showed what Germans held in common rather than what divided them. Although Germans differed on exactly what the rhetoric of public interest entailed, with trade unionists applauding the end to the self-serving interest politics of conservatives and conservatives, in turn, welcoming the cessation of working-class militancy, there was widespread recognition that prewar political life had been too socially exclusive, too compliant to the interests of economic elites, and too ignorant of the contributions of ordinary citizens. The great opportunity of the war was to recast German politics in a more socially inclusive and self-reliant mold. This meant that the Burgfrieden which Kaiser Wilhelm II had proclaimed was going to be much more than a mere suspension of normal politics for the duration of the war. It would provide the occasion for a thorough renovation of the Reich. Citizens eventually divided bitterly over the nature of the war, but most factions recognized the Volk, the German people, as the true source of political legitimacy. Thus, the significance of the "Peace of the Fortress" is not the patriotic consensus it established, because that frayed soon enough, but the civic activism it authorized.

Mobilization for war was accompanied by an effusive rhetoric of national harmony and a surge in public-spiritedness. Working-class activists, in particular, welcomed the Burgfrieden's recognition of the priority of the common interests of consumers over the special interests of big industry and big agriculture and considered it the first step toward the complete enfranchisement of workers in the "new Germany." The famous SPD saying "not a man and not a penny for this system" was turned on its head with the 4 August 1914 vote in favor of war credits. Socialists agreed to provide men and money in expectation that such a patriotic gesture would lead to suffrage reform, particularly in Prussia, which still recognized three classes of voters, and would open the door to more amicable relations with the military, employers, and state and local governments.[77]

To be sure, many party members were stunned by the failure of socialist efforts to halt the drift toward war in July 1914. But the lack of enthusiasm for the war itself did not immunize socialists from looking forward to the reform that they believed their sacrifices on the battlefront and the shopfloor had finally sanctioned. Indeed, the failure of the party's long-standing internationalist stance may have prompted the Social Democrats to embrace all the more fervently the promise of social acceptability and political liberty at home. Standing on the party's right wing, Konrad Hänisch reflected in 1916 that "we Social Democrats have learned to consider ourselves in this war as part, and truly not the worst part, of the German nation. We do not want to be robbed again by anyone, from the Right or the Left, of this feeling of belonging to the German state." "Worst part," "robbed," "belonging"—this is remarkable pathos that indicates how strong the emotional pull of nation had become.[78] After Germany mobilized, the war was associated with an apocalyptic "new time," which in one stroke had made obsolescent the embittered politics of the pre-1914 period and justified the national solidarism of the Burgfrieden.

The identification with the existing state increased as Social Democrats anticipated imminent reforms and felt the unfamiliar embrace of a society which had persecuted and marginalized them for so long. At the same time, no newspaper reader or tavern bystander could help being caught up in a European war that was invariably cast in terms of "us" versus "them." Thousands of working-class sons and fathers were mobilized to the front (only later would skilled workers be demobilized back to munitions factories on the homefront). Germany's casualties—missing, wounded, or dead men—totaled one million by the first Christmas. "By the end of 1914," estimates Modris Eksteins, "virtually every . . . family had suffered some bereavement."[79] Clearly, personal ties as well as abstract expectations connected more and more proletarians to the fortunes of the nation and its armies. It is not surprising, then, that socialist papers loudly proclaimed the victory of German armies in Belgium and East Prussia. Well into 1916 triumphant headlines screamed: "Victory from the North Sea to Switzerland. The Army is Unbeatable."[80] On the second and third pages articles appeared commending "Trade Unionists as Soldiers," "Social Democrats as Defenders of the Reich," and "Germany's Bebel Uniform" (August Bebel was the acclaimed leader of the socialists until his death in 1913).[81]

At first it looked as if the sentimental attachment to the nation in arms would fade as the war dragged on. The sharp rise in the number of unemployed by Christmas 1914 dampened the celebratory mood. The initial readiness of industrialists to contribute to war relief flagged as well at the end of the year.[82] By February 1915 rising food prices caused so much consternation that Berlin police officials feared the complete breakdown of law and order: "the shops will be stormed and the people will take what is now being denied them," predicted one police official.[83] The mayor of Nuremberg, Otto Gessler, later recalled with horror the time he had gone to the Ministry of the Interior and asked for the official file on "Wartime Provisioning of Civilians." The material consisted only of the file folder itself.[84] An antiquated law provided a few marks a month for soldiers' families (six in the summer, nine in the winter, and four additional marks for each child); otherwise the Reich did very little, leaving the Acting General Commanders who basically administered the country in time of war to seize the initiative in their districts and, more important for our purposes, forcing local officials to work out ad hoc arrangements between the army command, business leaders, trade unions, and the Frauendienst.

This improvisation had the important effect of opening the doors of city hall to Social Democrats, whom liberals and conservatives alike had previously considered dangerous but who now occupied an array of advisory and administrative posts in cities and towns across the Reich and quickly acquired considerable authority. Municipal officials did not accept every Social Democratic proposal, but in the long run they implemented a good many of them, including ordinances restricting milk to small children, prohibiting the baking of cakes and pastries, authorizing butchers to sell only to neighborhood customers, and giving townships the power to set maximum prices on goods. Berlin's mayor, Adolf Wermuth, for example, sought the advice of Hugo Heimann, the leading socialist in the city parliament, at least once a day.[85] The unprecedented local co-operation with socialists gave credibility to the Burgfrieden and laid the foundations for the left-liberal Weimar coalitions in the 1920s. Without this tentative social compact, Social Democrats would not have been nearly as loyal during the war years as in fact they were.

That the nation could successfully wage the war only by reconstituting the roles of citizens and the responsibilities of the state was made clear by the German defeat at the Marne in September 1914, which made a long war inevitable. The setback revealed glaring deficiencies in the mobilization of the homefront and thereby justified federal leadership in a more rationally organized war economy. Raw materials had to be allocated, food prices stabilized, and skilled labor procured. For example, in January 1915 the Reich established a quasi-public Grain Corporation to purchase grain at uniform prices; a few months later introduced ration cards for bread (and eventually for most other basic foodstuffs); and otherwise supervised standards for industrial production and the supply of coal, construction materials, and credit. This orderly regulation of the capitalist market in the public interest the socialists greeted with obvious satisfaction. Social Democrats also gained unexpected allies in regional military authorities, who intervened actively to force retailers to lower unacceptably high prices or employers to raise unacceptably low wages.[86] At least in the first years, the collaborative efforts to solve the food crisis anticipated more permanent social reforms. The widely read and left-leaning *Berliner Morgenpost* took the broad view that the public's interest might actually come to govern public policy: "one of the reasons we have a war," it commented, "is to be able to teach lessons with an iron broom."[87]

Public interest shaped the broad contours of the war economy, as the promulgation of the Auxiliary Labor Law *(Hilfsdienstgesetz)* at the end of 1916 made clear. Originally conceived by the General Staff as a means to transform all Germany into a vast munitions factory, the proposed legislation conscripted all workers between the ages of 16 and 60 into war plants and forbade both strike activity and job switching. But the Germany of 1916 was not the Germany of 1913. It could not be run like a barracks yard; the August Days had sufficiently transformed the relationship between state and society. As a result military leaders were forced to seek the cooperation of trade unions, the Social Democratic Party, and other political groups and to accept compromises allowing workers to look for better-paying work in other designated war plants (which, of course, pushed up wages for skilled labor), recognizing workers' representatives in factory councils, and mandating arbitration procedures. The Auxiliary Labor Law thus laid the foundation for a corporate capitalist order in which the rights of both trade unions and employers were guaranteed and regulated by the state. Given the overwhelming authoritarian conception of the rights of labor before 1914, this legislation was a decisive victory for the trade unions.[88]

Neither the Auxiliary Labor Law nor the war economy in general could be mistaken for socialism. But most Social Democrats acknowledged the extent to which the Reich had departed from the principles of a free-market economy and the practice of prewar special-interest politics and thereby had written the precepts of the Burgfrieden into social and economic policy. Party members welcomed the intervention of the state as a vindication of socialist ideas.[89]

The Burgfrieden was not a sunny place where class conflicts and special interests no longer disfigured the common weal. Even though a great many Germans attested to a more public-spirited mood in 1914, the prosaic relations of a free-market economy still held. There is no reason to believe that Social Democrats or anyone else upheld without qualification the sentiments of the August Days, particularly as economic and working conditions deteriorated and political differences about the internal constitution of the nation reemerged. But the choice was never between realizing a perfectly harmonious social utopia and rejecting ideas of national solidarity altogether. The crucial point is that over the course of the war Social Democrats glimpsed new and compelling versions of the nation in which the administration of economic and social policy not only included working-class representatives but took into consideration working-class interests. World War I authorized the nation as a legitimate vehicle for social reform.[90]

If the government responded with some surprise and great relief to the return of so many workers to the national fold, it had utter confidence in the patriotic rectitude of the middle classes, which had long been regarded as a stabilizing element in German society. Never before had a people gone to war with a greater sense of unity and righteousness, reflected Chief of Staff Helmuth von Moltke. For the kaiser, the bonds of filial duty that tied the people to the person of the monarch were completely manifest. On the balcony of the Schloss on the first day of mobilization he thanked the cheering crowds for "your affection and your loyalty" and forgave "wholeheartedly" those parties who had "attacked me." "I have been forced to draw my sword," Wilhelm II explained a few days later, laying a rhetorical hand on the shoulder of "my people," who were to follow obediently the sovereign's lead.[91] On every street in Berlin the revived authority of the monarchy was plain to see, police officials reported; Sedantag had been a huge success and Germans across the Reich showed the black-white-red imperial flag, hung up the kaiser's picture, and filled to capacity the churches of the almighty "creator of the Empire."[92] August 1914 offered a splendid opportunity to fortify monarchical principles.

At first government and military officials were so convinced that the identification of the people with the monarchy was complete and unmediated that they seriously considered banning political activity altogether. After all, the crowds of July and August 1914 had assembled beneath the Schloss, bypassing the political parties, interest groups, and patriotic organizations that otherwise represented public interests. That thousands of workers, the most discontented element in the German Reich, had stopped attending Social Democratic meetings or reading the party newspaper *Vorwärts* was taken as one more sign of the widespread rejection of routine partisan politics (the real reason for the downturn was that so many workers were fighting at the front). In this light it was easy to read the kaiser's famous declaration "I no longer know any parties" not as a generous promise to put aside political differences of the past in order to embrace the nation in its entirety but as a refusal to legitimate parties at all in order to assert the essential homogeneity of the nation. It quickly became clear, however, that the kaiser's faith in "my people" was misplaced, because the middle classes refused to define the war in the kaiser's terms.

The monarchy was never repudiated, but the kaiser was increasingly forgotten in the midst of a vast public mobilization in which the efforts of the people occupied a central place. Millions of poems, speeches, and letters took as their subject the German people who had demonstrated their love for the fatherland and their willingness to sacrifice themselves for it. The August Days revealed something that had not been very evident before: the German people as an active political actor. Again and again, observers regarded the actions of the crowds as a miracle or a gift that had saved the Reich. In other words, the introduction of the plebiscitary element had renovated the political foundations of Germany. While it was probably true that the people had "never been so close" to the kaiser than in 1914, as Berlin's nationalist *Tägliche Rundschau* reported with gratification, the monarchy was increasingly held hostage to this new, powerful people's union.[93] The Germany for which the patriots cheered and young men mobilized was an unmistakably crowded and public place.

August 1914 was not the first time in modern German politics that the efforts of the Volk were counterposed to the authority of the monarchy. A populist element had long been visible in various radical nationalist groups like the Navy League and the Colonial Society which sought a role for the middle classes in the extension of imperial power. The celebration of German technology and particularly of the ocean-going navy and the great zeppelins honored the middle-class virtues of merit and skill. Nonetheless, 1914 marks a dramatic break in political culture. The universality of the war experience and the extent of relief efforts gave real shape to the ideal of the Volksgemeinschaft. It is clear that Germans did not "stand aside and let those commanding in the war do their duty," as the liberal Albrecht Mendelssohn-Bartholdy later summarized (or as government officials had hoped).[94]

"The people" was a nebulous, largely rhetorical collectivity that obscured substantive political differences, but its reiteration in the media gradually discredited political ideas that checked its full development—the mediating role of corporate estates, the blatantly unjust three-class suffrage system, and the subservient protocols of the monarchy. The more professors and pulp-fiction writers and newspaper editors adored the crowd, lionized the volunteer, and emphasized the subordination to the whole of even the most educated and refined individual, the more credit they gave to the self-organization of civil society which constituted itself alongside if not in opposition to the authority of imperial institutions.[95]

Soldiers themselves insisted that there could be no return to the class-riven, interest-driven politics of prewar Germany.[96] Indeed, it should not be forgotten that the majority of the Prussian army belonged to the third and least influential class of voters who had only a minimal say in regional and local politics. (Prussian votes were counted according to taxes paid, so that, for example, the 1,621 very rich Berliners who in 1907 belonged to the first category of voters carried as much weight as the 33,262 affluent men of the second category or the 346,157 of the third, of whom nearly as many came from plain middle-class as from poorer working-class backgrounds.) Whether front-line troops held the hope "Nie Wieder Krieg" or bathed in the pathos of the Fatherland or thrilled in "the storm of steel," the majority anticipated returning to a more politically open country at war's end.[97] The middle classes demonstrated the ways in which the Kaiserreich's *Klassenkampf* (class war) had given way to a German Volksgemeinschaft not only by reimagining factory workers as patriotic fellows or demanding that the government act to alleviate the hardships of civilians but by staking their own, long postponed claims for political enfranchisement.

From the very beginning of the war the question of reforming the Prussian electoral system was never far from the surface of political discussions. Social Democrats, who had been the most ardent proponents of reform in 1909 and 1910, but also liberal newspapers, including the mass-circulation dailies *Berliner Tageblatt* and *Frankfurter Zeitung,* and influential intellectuals such as Max Weber pressed the issue in the years after 1915. Even if middle-class constituents were inclined to accept the argument that substantial legislation had to be postponed until the end of the war lest parliamentary debates harm battlefield morale, they looked forward to a postwar government that would be more open to talent and more sensitive to the interests of the great majority of veterans and war-relief volunteers. In light of the energetic work of the Nationaler Frauendienst, for example, middle-class women's organizations pressed for the extension of suffrage to women in 1917.[98]

To a remarkable degree, the flowery phrases of German nationalism rested on relatively straightforward declarations in favor of Germany's political and social reformation.

The much-heralded "ideas of 1914" tended in the same direction. A state-directed capitalism that stressed collective organization and social responsibility over the anarchy of capitalistic individualism that had prevailed since "1789" and the French Revolution, and that was extensively publicized by influential wartime writers such as the Münster economist Johann Plenge, the geopolitician Rudolf Kjellen, and right-wing Social Democratic proponents of "war socialism," cannot be dismissed as just one more version of German authoritarianism; concepts like "state socialism," "organization," and "mobilization" implied the enfranchisement of middle-class talent and expertise. Indeed the very word "mobilization" (*Mobilmachung*—"making mobile") suggested a flexibility that clashed with the guiding social, political, and economic presumptions of the Kaiserreich.[99] Both the Left and the Right envisioned an activist state that was premised on the subordination of class and faction to the Volk and thus would be able to prosecute the war more effectively and fulfill popular expectations for social enfranchisement.

The way Germans on the Left and the Right responded to the war was not consistent with political practices before 1914. As the first days of war enthusiasm revealed, the crowds were torn between the kaiser and Bismarck, between Schlossplatz and Königsplatz, between a more deferential and a more populist conception of the German nation. For some patriots who clustered around the Bismarck statue in July 1914, the Imperial Government had in fact done too little to defend and extend

German interests. This opposition from the Right became more vocal and more organized over the course of the war. Considered too conciliatory in his dealings with both the Allies and the Social Democrats, Chancellor Bethmann-Hollweg was the target of particularly vehement attacks from conservative politicians which eventually resulted in his resignation in the summer of 1917. He had not only failed to endorse the annexationist dreams of the extreme German nationalists but encouraged Social Democrats in their reform efforts and compromised on the Auxiliary Labor Law. In other words, the chancellor had failed to promote a German will to victory on both the battlefront and the homefront.

In order to reorient German war policy, nationalist publicists called for a relaxation of censorship and more vigorous public discussion of war aims. At present, in 1916, explained Wolfgang Kapp, director general of the East Prussian agricultural credit banks and a prominent Pan-German (and, incidentally, son of an 1848 revolutionist), "only what is acceptable to the government . . . is printed in the newspapers." "Nowhere does any room remain for the assertion of one's rights or the expression of differing opinions," he continued in a remarkable appeal to public opinion. Kapp, who became an anti-republican putschist in 1920, spoke in the name of the people, whom the chancellor preferred "quiet" and "calm."[100]

By the end of 1916 Kapp had his way: wartime censorship laws were relaxed and vigorous debates on war aims, unrestricted submarine warfare, and suffrage reform followed, revealing more clearly the political divisions of the German people, but also enlarging the parts they played in the political process. From Left to Right citizens mustered themselves in politics: the Independent Socialist Party broke with the Social Democratic Party to call for an immediate end to the war; the great republic of consumers demanded more government intervention in the economy; a left-liberal majority in the Reichstag urged the Reich to take steps to negotiate peace and reform the suffrage, while an increasingly vocal minority on the Right, backed by the General Staff, insisted on a crackdown on allegedly traitorous socialists and on more ambitious war aims. The first casualty of this politicization was the conciliatory chancellor, Bethmann-Hollweg; the final casualty was the monarchy itself.

It is worth taking a closer look at the frantic nationalists around Kapp. In August 1917 they founded the German Fatherland Party with the expressed purpose of preventing the German government from "too quickly conclud[ing] a peace which will destroy the future of our people" for lack of a "united will to victory."[101] The party not only promoted annexationist designs on France, Africa, and Russia but vehemently rejected any version of political compromise at home, reasoning that if the nation did not have something grand to fight for neither soldiers nor their families would continue to endure the hardships of war.[102]

Although the Fatherland Party professed loyalty to the kaiser, it displayed a thoroughly equivocal attitude toward the monarchy. Its references to the people's will to victory, its use of the popular media, and its belief that Germany's manifest destiny lay far beyond the borders of the prewar empire indicated a radically updated nationalist program. It was revealing that the founders of the Fatherland Party gathered in Königsberg, the capital of East Prussia, the province where in

1813 the first generation of German patriots had defied their monarch in the name of the nation. Indeed, supporters of the new party almost announced the creation of the "Bismarck Party," which would have been considered a snub of the kaiser, or the "Hindenburg Party," which would have been just as bad, before settling on the more neutral "Fatherland Party." In any case, the annexationists behind Kapp had moved quite some distance from the shadow of the Schloss.

Still, their numbers remained small. Although a "free workers' committee for a righteous peace," organized by the Fatherland Party and headed by Anton Drexler, emerged in 1918 as the basis of the German Workers' Party, the direct precursor to the German National Socialist Workers' Party, the Fatherland Party cannot be considered the forerunner to the Nazis: its membership remained modest (no more than 200,000 and probably substantially less; the much higher figures that have been cited include corporate memberships) and confined entirely to conservative political currents. Moreover, without a reformist social agenda, it had almost no appeal among workers or the liberal urban middle classes.[103] Even so, the party provided one more indication of the willingness of Germans to organize in the public sphere and engage issues of public concern independently of and even in opposition to the state. It also proved that German chauvinism was much advanced by all this grassroots activity. In a wartime atmosphere increasingly preoccupied with the survival of the nation, pan-German groups such as the Fatherland Party gained a hearing by advancing crude racial stereotypes about Poles and other Slavs and especially about Jews, who were eventually subjected to the notorious "Jew count," which the regime undertook to ascertain whether German Jews were serving (and dying) in great enough numbers (they were).

The effect of the Burgfrieden was paradoxical. The resurgence of patriotism upon which the peace of the fortress was premised was evident, but the compliance that was supposed to follow proved elusive because the patriotism that Germans displayed was of their own making and suited to new conceptions of nation and citizenship which invited rather than discouraged public participation.

THE TURNIP WINTER

Far more troubling to sober German authorities than the adolescent war-mongering of the Fatherland Party was the phantom of the *Grand Peur* that began to stalk towns and cities in 1914. Long lines, high prices, and poor harvests portended the desperate collective unrest that had broken apart the foundations of orderly government in France in just a few weeks in the summer of 1789. A glance at the worried reports of Berlin's policemen in the second year of the war summons up the growing concern: [104]

> The mood can only be described as very bad. Rising prices and irregular deliveries of foodstuffs terrify the population.
> The discontent in the population has reached a new intensity.
> Given the food shortages, people are following the war with less and less interest. The attitude of women toward the war can be summarized as "Peace at Any Price."

On the bleak streets of working-class neighborhoods in the capital the authority of the government appeared to be deteriorating rapidly. Even in middle-class districts high prices, bureaucratic corruption, and rising crime threatened to shred the civic virtues that had been associated with the war effort since August 1914. Given the hardships of four wartime winters, the growing indifference to the outcome of the war, and the bitter, mistrustful mood of the population, the durability of the Burgfrieden seemed questionable.

It was 15 October 1915: after dark, just past six in the evening, several hundred people began throwing stones at the windows of Assmann's dairy at 27 Niederbarminstrasse in Berlin. Two hours later windows at the company's branch store at 24b Boxhagener Strasse were shattered. Not long thereafter the police were called to an Assmann's on Gabriel-Max-Strasse, where three more panes lay smashed. These spare facts led off daily police reports on the mood of Berliners for that day and introduced a new element of danger on the homefront (at the same time the 355. Verlustliste was published). By winter it was no longer unusual to see crowds gathered on the sidewalk, angrily denouncing the "profiteering" of franchise retailers, threatening to plunder the premises, demanding some sort of government action in the name of the beleaguered people.[105] The alacrity with which the government responded to these protests is noteworthy; regulations on the sale of butter were imposed almost immediately by Berlin-area military authorities.[106]

Unfortunately, more extensive rationing did not alleviate the difficulties of high prices. Not only were rations set well below levels of peacetime consumption—so that over the course of the year 1916–17 Germans were allotted less than one-third of the meat, one-seventh of the fat, one-half of the flour, and just under three-quarters of the potatoes they had eaten in 1913—but poor harvests and black marketeers kept even those hunger rations from reaching neighborhood stores. The 1915 harvest had been a disaster, and those in 1916 and 1917 remained little more than half the size of 1913 totals, a catastrophe that made the winter of 1916–17 worse than any other in Germany's troubled twentieth-century history.[107] Long lines began to form every morning and every evening in front of neighborhood stores. Children stayed away from school just to hold places in the densely packed, shuffling, ever longer lines, activity which Germans quickly came to call "dancing the polonaise." When supplies ran out scores of shoppers were turned away, forced to return to empty cupboards, cold kitchens, and crying, hungry children. Increasingly elaborate gradients of rationing were designed to nourish skilled workers, small children, and pregnant women, and careful regulations were drafted to ensure that shops supplied neighbors rather than hoarders, but these simply opened up more possibilities for cheating and left consumers confused and frustrated.

No stretch of the war was as bad as the *Steckrübenwinter* or turnip winter of 1916–17. In the first year of the war the potato had slowly replaced bread, first as a supplement in *Kriegsbrot,* known simply *as K-Brot,* then as a primary staple. Two years into the war, however, even potatoes were hard to find and what was left were turnips. The turnip was a sour, distasteful root that people tired of easily and farmers had hoped to keep as feed for their livestock. But beginning in 1917 turnips appeared as the basis for soup and coffee and reappeared as the main course, vegetable, and even as turnip pudding. Without sugar or fat it was nearly impossible to prepare a flavorful meal, despite a profusion of turnip recipes and turnip cookbooks (Berlin's Nationaler Frauendienst published 200,800 copies of "Turnips Instead of Potatoes," its most popular pamphlet). "Here in Hamburg," wrote one woman to her son on the front lines, "the situation is very sad, already five weeks without potatoes, flour and bread are scarce . . . we go to bed hungry and we wake up hungry . . . all there is is turnips, without potatoes, without meat, just cooked in water."[108] By February 1917 turnips themselves were rationed. The privations of winter persisted into spring and summer. As late as July 1917 shoppers at Berlin-Lichtenberg's Viktoria Market could not buy a single potato or any vegetables, all of which had been diverted to the black market.[109]

If the food situation was not bad enough, the winter turned out to be the coldest in memory. Most Germans warmed themselves with only a few handfuls of rationed coals per day; only the rich had been able to stock up on coal the previous summer. Thirty-five thousand households in Nuremberg simply ran out of coal before the winter ended. For the first time in a century schools closed their doors, announcing *Kälteferien*— cold-weather holidays. A growing incidence of serious illness and premature death due to tuberculosis and pneumonia was the inevitable result of the turnip winter. Public health remained so imperiled that 175,000 men and women died of influenza in the year 1918.

Unable to deliver food, the regime lost authority. There was no more confidence, as there had been in 1914, that "the Fatherland won't let us starve." The crowds that gathered in front of stores and ration offices and around the publicly posted *Verlustlisten* now began to openly criticize the regime. An informal, uncensored public sphere formed as the *Polonäsen* grew longer and longer.[110] Every day "those up there," the rich, the powerful, the profiteers, the generals, and the bureaucrats were the subject of bitter remarks up and down the *Brotschlange* (bread line) or *Kartoffelschlange* (potato line). "This stinks," so the talk went on 6 February 1917 in front of Theodor Ruess's grocery on Munich's Schillerstrasse; "alone we women can't do anything and our men don't dare."[111]

But in fact political attitudes were changing dramatically. Civilians hungered for information, exchanging gossip in food lines, crowding at train stations to read the latest bulletins, buying newspapers a few steps away at a kiosk, retracing their steps to watch for the latest transport trains rolling through town—a restless public bearing that admitted that anything could happen from one moment to the next. What came to prevail was an atmosphere of uncertainty, of doubt, of disbelief. The entire horizon of expectations shifted: not only was the government no longer trusted but the wildest rumors about the miseries of the front, the high life of officers and industrialists, and imminent peace treaties gained credibility.[112] More important, housewives took matters into their own hands. As German men battled the French, the British, and the Russians, German women struggled to guarantee the survival of their families.[113]

If the very rich could afford trips to the black market, where most items were available for many times their prewar price, working- and middle-class families learned to evade the marketplace altogether and go directly to the producer. Beginning in 1916 more and more city people fanned out into the countryside to purchase goods directly from farmers or simply steal vegetables and potatoes from fields, and every evening they returned with pockets and knapsacks filled with butter, eggs, potatoes, and sometimes even a chicken or a duck. Military authorities tried to stop the hoarding, because it diminished the authority of the state, disrupted the supply of food, and only encouraged farmers to hold back more of their produce from government purchasers. (According to one expert estimate, the black market diverted perhaps as much as one-seventh of the total production of cereals, flour, and potatoes, one-third of milk, butter, and cheese, and nearly one-half of eggs, meat, and fruit at the end of the war.)[114] But there was little that the regime could do once the public lost confidence in the ration system and thousands embarked on daily plundering expeditions.

The clandestine journeys that had once been taken under cover of darkness and along out-of-the-way country lanes now resembled weekend outings in which whole families traveled openly by train. "At times, complete anarchy reigned on the railways," reported the second Army Corps in July 1917.[115] Incredible as it may seen, railway officials even added extra trains for those hoarders returning home on Sunday nights as a precautionary safety measure against overcrowding.[116] Policemen were posted at railway stations, but their confiscations made so little difference that they could only be perceived as completely arbitrary by those infuriated civilians unlucky enough to be caught. Hoarding had lost its notoriety. For hard-pressed civilians, the outings were acts of desperation, but also adventurous escapades against uniformed authorities and tenacious displays of self-reliance.

Housewives traveled alone into the countryside and also banded together in collective actions to demand food to keep their families alive. The first food riots were those outside Assmann's in the Berlin neighborhood of Lichtenberg in October 1915, when angry consumers attacked the dairy for price-gouging. By the spring of 1916 the effects of the poor harvest of 1915 made it difficult for shoppers to find goods at any price. Police reported ugly incidents in almost every major city. The scenarios are strikingly similar. In almost all cases working-class housewives, adolescents, and, often enough, soldiers home on leave were the main protagonists; organized interest groups or trade unions played almost no role. Food riots occurred whenever several dozen frustrated citizens stepped out of the long lines in front of Assmann's or Ruess's and reassembled to run in groups from store to store demanding that shopkeepers hand over their produce or to gather in protest in front of the mayor's home or city hall. In Leipzig, where rationed goods were completely unavailable in mid-May 1916, workers went on a rampage that left hundreds of shop windows smashed and dozens of trolley cars overturned. Food riots persisted throughout the summer and autumn as more and more Germans proved willing to take matters into their own hands, to stand up to the police, and even to attack them with refuse, stones, and bottles. What had begun in Berlin as local incidents between consumers and retailers had escalated into a broad confrontation between citizens and the state. It was not long before the calls for "bread" were accompanied by demands for "peace."

The Imperial government worried constantly that food shortages would lead to political protest. Beginning in 1915 the police reported a growing desire for peace in the capital's working-class neighborhoods. Karl Liebknecht, who in December 1914 was the first deputy to abstain from voting for war credits, galvanized the small antiwar opposition. On 18 March 1915 about fifty women waited outside the north entrance of the Reichstag to wave to and greet Liebknecht; several weeks later their numbers had increased to more than one thousand.[117] A year later, at the end of June 1916 (just as the 586. Verlustliste was published) the conviction of Liebknecht on charges of treason prompted "large and small demonstrations in various quarters of the city."[118] Quite clearly, opposition to the war represented a strong undercurrent among Berlin workers.

Since food riots in 1916 and 1917 coincided with the resolve of antiwar activists to break away from the Social Democratic Party and found the Independent Social Democratic Party, it was common to link the two developments. There can be no question that hardships on the homefront contributed to war weariness. By the third year of the war military authorities, mayors, and even Social Democrats were struck by the erosion of authority. In light of weekend hoarding expeditions and violent disturbances on market squares, political legitimacy seemed completely up for grabs. "The word 'enemy' now meant the gendarmes"—in the closing pages of his novel of the homefront, Ernst Glaeser summed up the classic prerevolutionary situation in which the government has become alienated from the people.[119]

For all the hardships, however, surprisingly few Germans actually broke with the Burgfrieden. The partisan appeal of the Independent Socialists, for example, and the extent of popular disturbance was rather limited. Apart from significant strongholds in central Germany, the Independent Social Democratic Party did not enjoy broad support until after the outbreak of the November 1918 Revolution. Most Social Democrats in Berlin and surely the great majority outside Berlin continued grudgingly to support the war and, in any case, to uphold the official Social Democratic line that German soldiers were defenders, not attackers. Even the momentous January 1918 strike, in which hundreds of thousands of munitions workers quit their workplaces and demonstrated for peace, was largely confined to the capital and stands out as a remarkable confrontation without significant sequels. Moreover, the winter of 1917–18 was not nearly as difficult as the one before; rations were more ample; potatoes and bread were actually available; and fewer meals were served in food kitchens. The public mood improved as well with Germany's Spring Offensive in March 1918. Most tellingly, the number of subscriptions to the seventh and eighth war bond drives in the autumn of 1917 and the spring of 1918 remained high. What is extraordinary is how long the German people put up with the hardships of war.

Far more consequential for the future direction of Germany than either the Fatherland Party or the Independent Socialists was the general mood of *Durchhalten*, the resolve to see the war through by self-reliance and strenuous economies. Durchhalten was nothing like the optimistic mood of August 1914 when the kaiser still intended to bring victorious soldiers back home before Christmas. It was a tougher, more skeptical, and more mercurial mood. Arthur Holitscher described "gloomy months spent between being wide awake but totally helpless and being asleep, dreaming of aerial dogfights and other wild battles until these too were interrupted by the nightmare of the official bulletins. Any good news was digested on an empty stomach. A new element had come into our lives: Durchhalten."[120] What the spirit of Durchhalten did was to magnify the efforts of the German people: the endurance of ordinary soldiers, the resolve of volunteers at home, and the spartan virtues of leaders like Hindenburg. This was a recognizable reformulation of the Burgfrieden, though it did not prize the annexationist war aims of the government or celebrate the person of the kaiser. With the turnip winter, German politics had taken on a decidedly populist slant.

Remarkably, the Kartoffelschlangen and Brotschlangen, which had come more and more to dominate the public aspect of German cities, promoted a sense of national unity. Standing in line, assembling in protest, harried working-class women elicited widespread sympathy. As consumers they not only represented broader civilian sacrifices and thereby bridged the social gulf between working class and middle class but also sanctioned Germany's reorientation into a more socially responsible state that had to mitigate the effects of the free market to sustain the health of all Germans. Although the Kaiserreich ultimately failed to assume the guardianship that the public had created for it, and collapsed amid popular recriminations, both the wide scope of welfare activities during the Weimar Republic which followed and the insistent emphasis on Volk (however racially defined) in the Third Reich fifteen years later were legacies of the political reconstitution of the homefront in which "the people" were owed something by the state.[121]

The lesson of Durchhalten was that Germans had to help and organize themselves. It was not always an uplifting lesson. In the face of the government's inability to provide public sustenance, social welfare remained makeshift and purely self-interested efforts had to take up the slack. Thus, for every Frauendienst volunteer there was a weekend hoarder; for every soup kitchen, a black market. If the war advanced the organizational abilities of the German people it did so in part by making social groups keenly aware of what they lacked and what others acquired. Both the turnip winter and the Auxiliary Labor Law deepened social and economic resentments.

In the first place, hunger rations impelled working-class families to organize collectively. The food riots of 1916–17 were only the most dramatic sequences of a process of mobilization which transformed the working class from political pariah into a powerful constituency. Given all the spirited antiwar activity of the Independents, it is often forgotten that the Social Democratic Party and especially the Free Trade Unions emerged from the war stronger than they had entered it. The Social Democrats fought tenaciously for public regulation of the food supply, for extra food allowances for mothers and infants, and for the rights of tenants. Even if its standing among card-carrying socialists was tarnished by its association with the war effort, which is not at all clear, the party earned substantial credit for advocating the interests of consumers. In the last months of the war the socialist press more than made up the number of readers lost in 1914. Party membership was on the rise as well. By contrast, the preoccupation of the Independent Socialist Party with the war left radicals without a social policy or, consequently, much of a social base, although this was to change after the revolution.[122]

At the same time, the Auxiliary Labor Law gave trade unions an indirect but strong voice in factory committees. As a result union membership shot up after 1916. That the Free Trade Unions refrained from participating in political strikes against the regime hardly mattered given the benefits organization conferred. The war had fashioned the Social Democratic Party and the Free Trade Unions into effective and powerful interest groups on behalf of labor.

However, the Auxiliary Labor Law benefited only those workers who had secured well-paying jobs in the munitions factories. A substantial minority of workers—about one-third, employed mostly in smaller artisanal shops—and especially the families left behind by conscripted breadwinners did not enjoy the high wages that in 1917 and 1918 had climbed back to and in some cases exceeded 1913 levels. "Suddenly there was rich and poor within the working class," comments Klaus-Dieter Schwarz in his study of wartime Nuremberg, and they often lived on the same tenement floor: a family in which the father and eldest son earned good money in war industries across from a young wife who was unemployed because she had four small children to look after and lived hand-to-mouth in the most miserable conditions. For the munitions worker war was the opportunity to obtain social recognition and political power. Only in the last year of the war, when efforts to achieve suffrage reform in Prussia faltered and the Reich imposed a blatantly annexationist peace on Soviet Russia, did it become difficult for these more fortunate workers to imagine a happy peacetime transition to a liberal people's monarchy. Across the hall, the war had brought only pain and deprivation. With the chaotic food supply and the inequities of the rationing system, the poor were even more powerless than before the war and more apt to sympathize with the Independent Social Democratic Party.[123]

The Auxiliary Labor Law also knocked down many of the material distinctions between workers and burghers. White-collar employees and civil servants lost nearly half of their purchasing power as a result of wartime inflation, while munitions workers improved theirs. Once income levels no longer expressed status distinctions, they raised fears that society was being indiscriminately leveled and the upright middle classes proletarianized. While the middle classes bitterly resented the privileges of the rich and the powerful, particularly the inequities of the government's contracting system, they also nursed grievances against "big labor." In their view big labor and big industry were equally ominous threats to economic security. As a result middle-class constituencies began to organize interest groups in order to achieve more effective political representation. By the end of the war employees' groups and the white-collar committees the Auxiliary Labor Law authorized had largely abandoned their traditional opposition to unionization and strike activity. Civil servants, farmers, and the "old" middle class of shopkeepers and artisans were slower to organize, but in the last year of the war a more assertive cadre of interest-group spokesmen had begun to loudly extol the virtues of self-reliance.[124] War widows and crippled veterans emerged as vocal constituencies as well.

Under the strains of the war German society appeared slowly to dissolve into angry factions; the sacrifices of the Burgfrieden seemed to give way to the self-interest of Durchhalten at any price. Unprecedented corruption in the bureaucracy, petty vandalism, and crimes against property dramatized the embittered, aggressive mood of the population. A generation of social historians has described how economic shortages, the reallocation of resources, broader government regulations, and new corporate relations between industry and labor sharpened social and economic distinctions and plainly revealed the Kaiserreich to be a brittle class society. Citizens increasingly thought of themselves as members of particular economic constituencies and approached the state through narrowly defined interest groups. This diffuse left-leaning discontent helps explain the sudden collapse of the Kaiserreich in the November 1918 Revolution. As the most organized element, the working class grew increasingly militant in the defense of its interests, while the less organized middle classes turned against an incompetent and weakened bureaucracy. Once it became clear that the Germans could not win the war, the authority of the state crumbled, and the Social Democrats were left to pick up the pieces.[125]

However, heightened self-interest should not be confused with complete disintegration. It is not at all clear that civil society had come apart at the seams on the eve of the revolution. In the first place, the mobilization of social and economic groups was in many ways a derivative of the Burgfrieden's emphasis on the collective abilities of the German people. August 1914 had profoundly changed the relationship between society and state and raised popular expectations about political entitlements that organized interest groups sought to realize. In other words, although the turnip winter raised the economic stakes, the Burgfrieden had the unintended effect of authorizing popular claims for recognition.

Germans continued to invoke the solidaristic ideas of 1914 and the agreeable vocabulary of public interest. Constituencies put forward their own economic and political claims and judged the actions of the state and other political parties in terms of the collective rights and responsibilities associated with the wartime Volksgemeinschaft. Many Germans reported on their disillusions at the end of a war increasingly regarded as "good business" for the lucky few but a rather bad "swindle" for the majority—one only has to glance at poignant letters from the battlefront and angry proclamations on the homefront. "I was mustered up on the third day of mobilization full of ideals, loyal to the German National Union," wrote one white-collar employee in May 1917, "but what I experienced at the hands of our officers killed my idealism long ago."[126] Certain politicians were sure to "get the shock of their lives."[127]

Yet the effect of this sense of betrayal was to reaffirm rather than invalidate the necessity of insisting on a less paternalistic politics organized around the interests of ordinary Germans. The argument that the hardships of war dissolved the "Peace of the Fortress" is simplistic because it focuses on the resentments of citizens and soldiers and overlooks the increasingly republican forms in which those resentments were held. Indeed the revolution, when it came in November 1918, actually increased public interest in the Volksgemeinschaft. The long lines in front of Assmann's dairy had a similar effect. And although socialist Left and nationalist Right had very different ideas about the German future, they conceived politics in the terms of the future tense. Each projected forward from the experiences of the war to fashion a new responsibilities for the state and new, more inclusive categories of citizenship.

Moreover, immediate economic interests did not supersede other civic identities, even in the brutish struggle to find food and purchase coal and negotiate an unforthcoming imperial bureaucracy. Despite the avalanche of special-interest publications and angry testimonials, it is important to remember that interest groups did not speak with complete authority. Ordinary constituents never shared their single-minded concern with labor markets, inflated prices, and government regulations. In the rhythms of social life the Burgfrieden, in which Germans recognized each other as citizens rather than partisans, remained a powerful memory. The German people had gotten a glimpse of themselves as a national compact that existed independently of the monarchy and rested on the achievements of ordinary citizens and soldiers. When one thinks of the upheaval of the war, it is not enough to tabulate the heart-wrenching losses on the front or the difficult deprivations at home;[128] war also fashioned compelling images of national solidarity that would largely determine the politics of the postwar era.

Taken together, the summer of 1914 and the winter of 1916–17, the combination of nationalist crowds and economic interest groups and long food lines, set in motion a "democratic wave" which made the last four years of the Kaiserreich the "most horrible of all revolutions" to conservatives and the necessary foundation for both the Weimar Republic and the Third Reich.[129] The motley groups singing patriotic verses around the Bismarck statue on the night of 25 July 1914 had been transformed by war into an increasingly contentious public that had begun to fashion its national and economic destiny by its own efforts, that had grown more confident in its ability to do so, and that in any event appeared less impressed than ever by the political institutions of the Kaiserreich. The definitive measure of Germany's political future had now become the people, the great curbside republic of soldiers, workers, and consumers.

November 1918

Soldiers, workers, and burghers mingle on Berlin's Potsdamer Platz
on the day of the Revolution, 9 November 1918

Photo credit: Ullstein Bilderdienst

"Get up, Arthur, today's revolution!" With this
extraordinary announcement Cläre Casper-Derfert shook Arthur Schöttler awake and handed him a stack of leaflets to distribute as the early shift arrived at the munitions factory on Kaiserin-Augusta-Allee. A few hours later, at nine o'clock, workers streamed out of the plant and with Cläre and Arthur marched toward the Reichstag.[1] A few miles away, the entire workforce of the Allgemeine Elektizitätsgesellschaft on Brunnenstrasse walked out, hooked up with comrades at the Berliner Maschinenbau on Scheringstrasse, and moved to the center of the city from the north. Work stopped at the Daimlerwerke in Marienfelde, at Borsig, at Siemans & Haske, at Argus-Motorenfabrik in Reinickendorf, and in dozens of other factories. Just before putting the afternoon edition to press, the *Berliner Tageblatt* reported that employees at the Akkumulatorenfabrik in Oberschöneweide, at Mix & Genest, and at Kraussler & Co. had joined the general strike. Columns of workers marched to the city center, which, for the first time, was not sealed off by the kaiser's police. Saturday morning traffic came to a complete halt; if streetcars could still move amid the proletarian crowds they were soon stopped in their tracks by demonstrators who cut the electrical wires.

The same morning, the leader of the Social Democratic Party in Berlin, Otto Wels, won over army battalions stationed throughout the city. At the Alexanderkaserne on Prinz-Friedrich-Karl Strasse he climbed to the top of an old wagon to make his appeal. That no officer of the Naumburg Rifles Battalion intervened to arrest the socialist is noteworthy, since the barracks was considered particularly *kaisertreu* and had been the site of one of the kaiser's most notorious speeches when, in 1901, he told soldiers that they would have to be willing to shoot down their own families in order to defend the authority of the emperor. It was a dramatic turn of events. At stake on the morning of 9 November, Wels argued, were thousands of lives. Only the abdication of the kaiser could forestall the total destruction of the nation. It was time to make peace, Wels urged the soldiers; loyalty for the Hohenzollerns had to be traded for loyalty to Germany. The sensible step was to rally under the banner of the Social Democratic Party in order to avoid civil war and to establish a free "people's state." Wels's ecumenical tone persuaded the soldiers, who poured into the streets, lending the afternoon demonstrations a festive air. Soldiers and workers fraternized along Unter den Linden, exchanged red armbands, and held up placards inscribed "Brothers, don't shoot!"[2]

From Kaiserin-Augusta Allee, from Brunnenstrasse, from Scheringstrasse, demonstrators converged on the city center. Parades of factory workers fell into step with troops of soldiers and smaller groups of revolutionary sailors who had arrived by train from naval stations in Kiel and Wilhelmshaven. Observers pointed out the large numbers of women, who, after all, labored alongside men in war industries, and of children, many of them released from school on account of the influenza epidemic; *Kälteferien* had given way to *Grippeferien*. Handmade red flags contrasted with the drab browns and blues of the marchers. At ten o'clock in the morning, Germany's Imperial Chancellor, Prince Max von Baden, remembered, "the message reached us that thousands of workers were marching in procession" toward the Reichstag. Downtown Berlin was under siege.

Never before had the socialists demonstrated in the government quarter: in front of the Schloss, down Unter den Linden, across Potsdamer Platz. In 1890 during the city's desperate hunger demonstrations, in 1910 during the mammoth suffrage protests, and again in 1914 on the eve of the war, Jagow's police or the kaiser's regiments had always managed to head Social Democratic marchers off before they came in sight of the castle. But on this extraordinary November day in 1918 military authority simply melted away. Bands of workers and soldiers and other young people lingered at the castle, as the crowds had in 1914, and the armed trucks and cars and motorcycles that revolutionaries had commandeered whizzed back and forth between Schlossplatz and Königsplatz, following the route of the colorful processions that had made their way to the Bismarck statue on the eve of war more than four years earlier; most demonstrators, however, gathered around the Reichstag, which housed the offices of the Social Democratic parliamentary delegation and its leader, Friedrich Ebert.

The beleaguered chancellor understood immediately that the popular revolution had triumphed. In order to avoid bloodshed Prince Max dropped his efforts first to secure the kaiser's promised abdication and then to conclude the orderly transfer of authority to Friedrich Ebert and the Social Democrats. Instead, just before noon, the chancellor simply informed the Wolff News Agency of the kaiser's intention to abdicate, thereby creating a fait accompli and generating a flurry of extra editions that broadcast the news to the entire world. A short while later he handed over the offices of the government to

Ebert. Dramatic as they were, the last-minute telephone calls between the chancellory and the kaiser's staff at Spa and the speedy transfer of authority to Germany's leading socialist did not provide the insurrection on the streets the grand gesture of triumph it needed. So when the Social Democrat Philipp Scheidemann was pulled out of the Reichstag cafeteria and hustled up to a second-storey balcony to address the masses gathered on the Königsplatz he very sensibly declared the old regime dead and hailed the new German republic: "The German people have triumphed all along the line."[3] Although Ebert was furious at this unilateral declaration taken without the consent of a democratically elected national assembly, Scheidemann had simply looked out into the crowds and recognized events for what they were.

The Berlin diarist Harry Kessler, a true cosmopolitan who watched these years of German history with a somewhat detached, mournful eye, acknowledged 9 November as "one of the most memorable and dreadful days in German history." In just a few hours the old order had crumbled. In the Reichstag itself Kessler watched a reenactment of the Russian Revolution: "it's like a film . . . a scene from the Tauride Palace" (originally built by Katherine the Great for her lover Potemkin, but in 1917 the seat of the Provisional Government). "Groups of soldiers and sailors stood and laid about on the enormous red carpet . . . Here and there some individual was stretched full length and asleep on a bench." "Waste paper, dust, and dirt from the streets litter the carpets," he ascertained on a return visit to this people's house.[4]

Abandoned by the kaiser, the state rooms of the Schloss were in a similar state of dishevelment and housed units of revolutionary guards. It was from the north balcony that Karl Liebknecht declared Germany a socialist republic to his left-wing supporters, but most of the revolutionaries remained loyal to the Scheidemann and the Social Democrats. (Social Democracy's fraternal slogans—"Kein Bruderkampf!" head-lined *Vorwärts* the next day—appealed not only to the city's imperial guards but also to the great majority of factory workers. By contrast, the angry demand of Liebknecht's Spartakus newspaper, *Rote Fahne*, to sweep out of power so-called government socialists, patriots of August 4 like Wels, Scheidemann, and Ebert, found little resonance.)

The scene at the imposing red-brick headquarters of the police on Alexanderplatz was no less incredible. It was not Social Democrats but the more radical Independent Socialists who stormed the building at half past two in the afternoon, disarmed officers, and named one of their own, Emil Eichhorn, chief of police. Berlin was completely in the hands of revolutionary workers and soldiers, the *Berliner Tageblatt* summed up the next day: "Yesterday morning . . . everything was still there"—the kaiser, the chancellor, the police chief—"yesterday afternoon nothing of all that existed any longer."[5] The revolution secured the first German Republic, although the new democracy always remained compromised by the fact that its leaders accepted the Allies' armistice terms without delay and later signed the Treaty of Versailles in the face of public opposition. Nonetheless, from now on, elections and parliamentary coalitions, lobby groups and political propaganda would determine Germany's destiny.

The November Revolution was certainly one of the most peaceable in history. The monarchy had been toppled but only

fifteen lives lost. This alone would have been cause for celebration, and bourgeois observers gave the revolution credit on
this account.[6] Yet there was little joy in the parades and only
the occasional red flag for a dash of color. Too many lives had
been lost in the senseless war and too much privation suffered
at home for the mood to be anything but sober. There were no
lively processions down Unter den Linden and no songs sung
around the Bismarck statue as had been the case in July 1914.
Whereas patriots in 1914 hoped to raise their voices and volunteer their services for the national cause, the revolutionaries
in 1918 acted to remove illegitimate authority. In 1914 citizens
gathered on the Schlossplatz in acclamation, in 1918 they did
so in defiance. And yet both crowds underscored the popular
nature of modern politics. They showed the extent to which
spontaneous plebiscites on the streets gave authority to twentieth-century institutions. Indeed, the November Revolution
marked a much more complete mobilization of the people than
the August Days. The demonstrations were not confined to the
largest cities; they had been touched off by events in quite
provincial places: Kiel and Wilhelmshaven.

Although Social Democrats had already joined a left-of-
center coalition government under the chancellorship of Prince
Max von Baden in early October, political reforms had stalled,
peace terms remained uncertain, and workers seemed more
and more swayed by the radical Independents who sought
a thoroughgoing revolution. These were dangerous circumstances in which every local incident threatened to have national implications. In the first days of November sailors mu-
tinied in Kiel (refusing to follow admirals to engage the British
fleet in a final clash) and together with workers and reservists

took over a string of port cities along the North Sea: Wilhelmshaven, Lübeck, Hamburg, Bremen, Cuxhaven. On the spot,
local socialists affirmed that the long-awaited moment had arrived: "the revolution is on the march! What happened in Kiel
will spread throughout Germany."[7]

At the same time, revolutionary activists in Berlin made
preparations for a general strike to begin on 11 November,
although it was not clear just how much influence the Independents had or whether enough workers would walk out. The
task that faced the regular Social Democratic Party was difficult
indeed: "as a government party to resist popular pressure, as
a popular party to lead it," in the concise words of one historian.[8] To regain some control over events, the party issued an
ultimatum on 6 November that linked its further participation
in the imperial cabinet to the abdication of the kaiser, immediate parliamentary reform in Prussia, and the easing of martial law. Two days later, however, developments outside the
capital completely overran negotiations in Berlin. The revolution traveled by train from Kiel to Lübeck, Bremen, and
Hamburg. Bands of mutinous sailors followed the timetables
of the Imperial Railways, boarding trains to search and disarm
officers and riding on to reach Cologne, Braunschweig, Hanover, and Frankfurt.[9] For Prince Max the news on 8 November
was all bad. Bavaria and Braunschweig had been declared socialist republics by maverick socialists and, across western Germany, city halls had been seized by local councils of revolutionary workers and soldiers *(Arbeiter- und Soldatenräte)*:[10]

> 9 AM: Magdeburg serious disturbances. 1 PM: unrest threat-
> ens the Acting General Command VII. 5 PM: Halle and Leip-
> zig red. Evening: Düsseldorf, Haltern, Osnabrück, Lüneburg

red; Magdeburg, Stuttgart, Oldenburg, Braunschweig, Cologne red. 7:10 PM: Acting General Command in Frankfurt deposed.

That military authorities in Cologne had been removed was particularly significant because the city served as a bridgehead to the armies on the western front. These astonishing developments were at least partially known to Berlin's workers; factory delegates reported to leading Social Democrats late on the night of the 8th that the rank and file was pressing to get into the streets and waiting only for the party's signal. "Now's the time to take the lead," admitted Philipp Scheidemann to his fellow Social Democrats, "otherwise anarchy will break out." Before dawn the next morning, 9 November, the Berlin party organization convened in the *Vorwärts* building on Lindenstrasse and called a general strike for 9 A.M., right after the mid-morning break.[11] It was then that Cläre woke up Arthur.

A day later, on 10 November, most large municipalities in Germany were in the hands of workers' and soldiers' councils. Pomerania's Wolgast only registered the turn of events on 12 November, when local workers rallied on the market square. As late as the 14th the nearby vacation island of Rügen gave no sign that anything momentous had happened. And in parts of the rural country west of the Rhine the revolution passed almost unnoticed.[12] Nonetheless, travelers would have to go pretty deep into the countryside to find a place that was not touched by the revolution. In Bavaria's predominantly agricultural regions of Schwaben and Mittelfranken, for example, revolutionary councils appeared in 65 of the 119 rather small communities with some 1,500 inhabitants.[13] By the end of the month workers had rallied in the name of the new republic and organized revolutionary councils in hundreds of towns across the Reich. No other popular event in German history, not even the July 1914 crisis, had filled the national stage so completely or had enrolled so many participants as had the November Revolution.

The far-reaching scope of the revolution was only one of its overwhelming characteristics. It also caught most people by surprise. The revolution seemed to arrive all at once, overtaking statesmen. Suddenly, it was "too late"—as Ebert put it— "the ball has been set rolling."[14] Even militants had to run after the long-awaited event which came between one day and the next: "Get up, Arthur, today's revolution!" For nonsocialists, the sudden turn of events revealed a menacing aspect, giving the largely spontaneous uprising the appearance of a well-orchestrated action animated by a single political will. The sheer numbers of people on the streets enhanced the impression that the revolution was a gigantic, unstoppable force. Revolution displayed mass: workers had marched into the center of Berlin from every direction. Rallies, marches, occupations, and later posters, flags, and placards gave the November Revolution an unmistakable public presence. Demonstrations of this sort were still novel enough in Germany to conjure up images of a general "revolt of the masses" that would leave bourgeois society in tatters. The abiding hostility to the Social Democrats, year after year throughout this period, fed off the fear that life would be brutalized once the Left came to power.

"Burghers darkened their windows and bolted their doors," remembered Goslar's small-town newspaper ten years later.[15] Again and again the November Revolution was cast by bourgeois commentators as an alien force that moved suddenly and with great power. In the span of just a few days the arch-conservative Junker Elard von Oldenburg-Januschau had seen "a world cave in and bury everything meaningful in my life." Years later he still could not find words to express his horror at the revolution.[16] Even a liberal such as Harry Kessler found the 9th of November in part "dreadful." Most middle-class Germans, the right-wing paper *Deutsche Zeitung* concluded, had reacted like a "bunch of scared chickens" at the sight of the class predator, unwilling to defend themselves, unable to counterattack.[17]

This was not altogether surprising since Germany's monarchs had abandoned their thrones, leaving counterrevolutionaries without anything to fight *for*. Historians seem to agree; proletarian councilmen and fiery socialist orators rather than blue-smocked artisans or returning veterans are the main actors in their books. The conventional picture of Germany in 1918 shows the nation fundamentally divided, a strong-willed proletariat pushing aside a passive, generally reactionary middle class. This polarization set the stage for civil war in 1919–20, numbed bourgeois sympathies for what was soon called the Weimar Republic (the National Assembly first met in the sheltered town of Weimar to escape turmoil in the capital), and ultimately helped prepare the victory of the virulently anti-Marxist Nazis in 1933.

Yet a closer look reveals much more movement than a basic choice between active Left and anguished Right. In the first place, the position of workers was neither as unanimous nor as radical as suggested by Prince Max von Baden's telegraphic summary: "Düsseldorf, Haltern, Osnabrück, Lüneburg red;

Magdeburg, Stuttgart, Oldenburg, Braunschweig, Cologne red." Events revealed that "red" meant anything from Bolsheviks in the Spartakus League around Karl Liebknecht and Rosa Luxemburg, to more homegrown Independent Socialists who sought to preserve in some form the grassroots structure of the revolutionary workers' and soldiers' councils, to the majoritarian Social Democratic Party, which was focused on enacting democratic reforms within the existing political institutions, namely the parliamentary parties and the Reichstag. From one neighborhood to the next the November Revolution took on different guises. However, few revolutionaries went so far as did Neukölln's Independent Socialists, who proclaimed the tidy Berlin suburb a socialist republic and proposed the socialization of banks and factories before mainstream Social Democrats restored order.

Burghers tended to remember the threats to expropriate private property and the red flags flying the announcement of the socialist millennium and to forget that most workers' and soldiers' councils avoided making sweeping political changes and left municipal administrators in place. The majority of socialists sought equity: a thorough reform of suffrage laws to give each citizen an equal political voice; the institutionalization of collective bargaining and the recognition of free trade unions; and a renovation of municipal and state bureaucracies to give workers or their representatives a hand in administering social services. The majority of November revolutionaries endorsed the Social Democratic position that the final form of the new state had to await the constitution of a democratically elected National Assembly. Whenever council delegates assembled in the capital, from around Greater Berlin on 10 November or from across the Reich between 16 and 21 December, radicals found themselves decisively outvoted.

This moderation helps explain the widespread cooperation of the revolutionary councils with the imperial bureaucracy, not least to ensure the supply of food, coal, and other necessities. Seen in this light, the efforts of workers' councils in November 1918 built on the ad hoc collaborative arrangements between Social Democrats and municipal and military authorities that had been established during the Burgfrieden, although the revolution certainly shifted the balance of power in favor of workers.[18] Listening to the revolution, one could hear exuberant appeals to the Volk and insistent invocations of people's rights, echoes of the rhetoric of the August Days and of wartime service.

At the same time, the employees, civil servants, shopkeepers, and artisans who made up Germany's urban middle classes were hardly inactive. They moved in and out of the picture, organizing their own councils or *Bürgerräte*, establishing interest groups, and reviving political parties. In late November uniformed veterans returning home from the western front added new elements to the political landscape. Military demobilization was followed rapidly by political remobilization. It is a paradox that many middle-class Germans came to repudiate the revolution yet remained its beneficiaries since so many used its appearance to restate claims for political reform and social recognition. In other words, November 1918 provided an opportunity, though under difficult conditions, to finally undertake the renovations that August 1914 had first authorized.

Whether for or against the Weimar Republic, Germans insistently expanded the bounds of participation in the public sphere. Organization was the watchword, stridency the spirit of the times. Middle-class as much as working-class Germans organized and campaigned and demonstrated, but as they did, they invariably saw more and more opponents among their neighbors and approached these in ever more inimical and unforgiving terms. Thus the November Revolution generated as much political meanspiritedness as public-spiritedness. It is the fierce declarations of sovereignty, more often than not out of step with liberal principles and parliamentary procedures but in line with the declamatory style and self-serving pursuits of democracy, that are the most striking feature of Weimar politics and link November 1918 with the patriotic stirrings of July 1914 and the brownshirted mobilization of January 1933. It is worth taking another look at Berlin at war's end.

The events of 9 November generated hectic activity on the sidelines of the workers' revolution. Quite a few bourgeois Berliners joined republican demonstrators in front of the Reichstag. Käthe Kollwitz stepped into one such parade as it passed through the Tiergarten and later watched a young officer walk over to a revolutionary soldier, shake his hand, and declaim that four years on the front had not been as bad as the ongoing struggle at home against all that was "prejudiced and outdated."[19] Contemporary photographs indicate large numbers of well-dressed burghers—who with their hats and ties had obviously not reported to factory shifts that morning—marching among soldiers and workers along Unter den Linden.[20] On the next day, Sunday the 10th, the New Fatherland League, a progressive counterpart to the Fatherland Party which enjoyed the support of liberal intellectuals, rallied thousands of well-

dressed citizens on the Königsplatz. In the evenings, over din-
ner, radical literati such Kurt Hiller and René Schickele hatched
grandiose plans and, in the Reichstag, requisitioned committee
rooms for clubs such as the New Fatherland League and the
New Activists, which proposed to debate the political issues of
the day alongside workers' and soldiers' councils. It was just
like the Jacobin clubs of the French Revolution, thought Harry
Kessler, who passed by on 12 November.

Unfortunately for Hiller, the New Activists had no real
power and after five days found themselves shooed out of the
Reichstag, though not before volunteering their services for
the "world revolution," an ideal which combined a mishmash
of socialism (the replacement of capitalist enterprises with
workers' cooperatives), pacifism (global disarmament), and
elitism (intellectuals as political advisors). Reconstituted as the
Council of Intellectual Workers, Hiller's companions managed
to rent offices in Charlottenburg. But their first public event
on 2 December was a disaster at which Hiller denounced
prominent guests as mass murderers on account of their earlier support for the war. Thereafter, interest in the council
evaporated.[21] What these antics tend to obscure, however, is
how broad support for a new political start was among Berlin's bourgeoisie. A glance at the city's major newspapers such
as the *Berliner Tageblatt* and the *Berliner Morgenpost* indicates that Kollwitz, Hiller, and the young officer were well
spoken for.

While Hiller and his fellow artists and writers were rebuffed
in their efforts to join revolutionary workers, more effective
organizers stepped forward to press middle-class interests in a
less ecumenical fashion. Just three days after the revolution,

on 12 November, the Hansa-Bund, an influential association of liberal businessmen, published a declaration in Berlin's newspapers urging burghers to constitute their own Bürger-räte and hold public meetings to promote their interests and resist Soviet-style socialism. The result was a flurry of activity that has gone largely unnoticed. Neighbors established councils in middle-class suburbs such as Friedenau and Tempelhof, professional groups and voluntary associations signed on, and by 18 November an astonishing 2,000 representatives met as the Bürgerrat Gross-Berlin.

Recognizing that in a "democratic people's state," political power depended on "the size and power of organization," individual trade groups stepped forthrightly into the political fray as well. All at once the most varied interests and inclinations found political expression. On 11 November a *Beamtenrat* spoke for civil servants in the Berlin suburb of Neukölln; a day later lower-ranked officials at the Foreign Ministry set up a council, the first of several in the government district.[22] Lawyers organized on the 13th and journalists four days later. On 16 November as many as 2,000 engineers, chemists, and architects congregated in the huge dinning hall of the Rheingold, a favorite emporium on Potsdamer Platz, signing on as members of the Association of Technical Professionals.[23] Evidently the Rheingold was booked solid throughout these revolutionary weeks. To formally establish a doctors' council to look after local public health issues and protect professional interests, over 800 physicians and surgeons crowded the Rheingold in "an extremely well attended meeting" on 26 November. "No one will look after us if we don't do it ourselves," summed up the pragmatic mood of the delegates.[24] On 17 November more than 10,000 left-leaning white-collar worker filed into Zirkus Busch and when that filled up gathered outside on the Domplatz to lend their support to the revolution. A day later fourteen nonsocialist employee groups reacted to the upheaval, though more warily. In two mammoth meetings in the Deutscher Hof on Luckauer Strasse, they insisted on organizational parity with workers.

The same night, in the Germaniasälen on Chausseestrasse, a stormy assembly of bakers railed against wartime regulations imposed by the government and wage demands put forward by rebellious apprentices. Unfortunately, the meeting broke up without reaching a consensus, the artisans dividing over accusations made against guild members who had allegedly substituted flour intended for dog biscuits for higher grades and over subsequent demands from the floor to elect a new executive committee.[25] Berlin's master bakers were typical. They reflected middle-class resolve to attain effective professional representation in the new democratic order. A confident sense of collective purpose animated these early gatherings in the Germaniasälen and in the Rheingold and the Deutscher Hof. The angry, defensive tone was also characteristic, as constituents denounced corrupt and cliquish leaders, the state's regulation of the war economy, and the emerging threat posed by organized labor. Throughout the next fourteen years, interest groups would lurch from populist, even egalitarian postures to darker, more aggressively antisocialist positions. One thing was clear: over the course of war and revolution, Germans had developed a regular "Redewut," a mania for speaking out, as one beleaguered chairman put it.[26] The fine organization of interest in 1918–19 was unprecedented in German history.

Once elections for the National Assembly were set for 19 January 1919, the bourgeois party leaders who had been almost invisible in the first weeks of the revolution stepped into public places and faced surprisingly large and enthusiastic crowds. Berlin's democrats sponsored a well-attended forum in the Lehrervereinshaus on 17 November. A few days later, 500 neighbors in Steglitz, a solidly middle-class suburb south of the capital, joined the newly founded German Democratic Party, a more robust successor to the small Progressive Party of the imperial era. In well-groomed Friedenau, the town's meeting hall was too small to accommodate all the citizens who arrived to establish a Democratic Party branch. Tens of thousands came to the party's first major event in the capital on Sunday afternoon, 1 December. In fact so many people arrived that organizers had to hold two parallel rallies, one in Zirkus Busch, the other in an auditorium at the nearby stock exchange.[27] Every weekend from late November to the middle of January thousands of Berliners spent time in political meetings. Many of the participants were women, who were determined to continue to exercise the public responsibilities they had obtained during the war.

Politicians and lobbyists were not the only ones scurrying about the capital. One of the things about the revolution that immediately struck observers was how the streets had all at once emptied of officers, who had been such familiar sights in Berlin throughout the war. Word of mouth had spread countless stories about officers who had been harassed on the streets and in train stations. But gradually the shock of military defeat and political upheaval wore off. Always a heedful observer, Harry Kessler saw an officer in dress uniform for the first time since the outbreak of revolution, on 15 November on Potsdamer Platz.[28]

By the end of the month officers and uniforms were everywhere to be seen as the huge army of men on the western front steadily demobilized and made its way home. From early morning until late at night, for a fortnight, 800,000 soldiers passed through Cologne, another 500,000 through Frankfurt. And to their surprise, veterans were welcomed by thousands of citizens, who waved flags, showered them with flowers, and handed out cigarettes and wine. "Never before had Cologne seen such an impressive military spectacle," recalled one city chronicler. Many troops had on nothing more than the tattered uniforms and shoddy boots of active service, which made perfectly clear just how exhausted the divisions had become. The trappings of the new political order—red flags flying over town halls, placards reading "Long Live the Revolution," speeches made by unfamiliar commissars authorized by newfangled Workers' and Soldiers' Councils—added to the strangeness of coming home. Many soldiers surely sympathized with the revolution. But plenty of units marched according to a more defiant step. They wore patriotic ribbons and cockades and decorated their wagons and horses with garlands and the black-white-red flags of the empire. Repeatedly, they forced local authorities to remove the "red rags" from state and city buildings. By the time the first wave of demobilization reached Berlin in early December it was clear that thousands of returning veterans represented an unanticipated political force.[29]

Units from Bavaria, Saxony, Baden, and Württemberg arrived in Berlin for a splendid welcome parade on 10 December.

At the staging ground on Heidelberger Platz in Wilmersdorf, vendors did a smashing business selling black-white-red flags and pictures of the German monarchs who had been deposed. Thousands of children surrounded the artillery pieces, which were decorated with evergreen branches, flowers, and imperial flags. Outfitted in new uniforms, adorned with lilies, accompanied by military bands, men and officers paraded amid the cheers of citizens who lined Berliner Strasse and Kaiserallee all the way to the Tiergarten and Pariser Platz. There, in the shadow of the Brandenburger Tor, Friedrich Ebert, the ranking people's commissar, hailed the soldiers, who, he emphasized, had returned from the front "undefeated."[30] In the days that followed, units continued to stream through the festively decorated city on their way home. Käthe Kollwitz bumped into a parade up Prenzlauer Allee on 12 December. "Canons, horses, helmets festooned with bright paper streamers. It looked so nice."[31]

Across the city, sixteen-year-old Ernst von Salomon watched in fascination:[32]

> Their eyes were hidden in the shadow thrown by the peaks of their caps, sunk in dark hollows, grey and sharp. These eyes looked neither to the right nor to the left. They remained fixed before them, as if under the spell of a terrifying goal ... God! What a look they had, those men! Those thin faces, impassive under their helmets, those bony limbs, those ragged clothes covered with dirt! They advanced step by step and around them grew the void of a great emptiness ... These men were not workers, farmers, students ... These men were soldiers ... united in the bonds of blood and sacrifice. Their home was the Front ...

that is why, yes, that is why they could never belong to us. That is the reason for this stolid, moving spectral return.

Salomon was certainly not the only one for whom the return stirred the imagination and generated a virtual cult of the front soldier and a romanticized aesthetic of danger. Perhaps a more typical reaction came from peripatetic Harry Kessler, who encountered a division marching up Unter den Linden: "All the men wore steel helmets . . . the limbers and guns were garlanded and innumerable black-white-red" flags could be seen, though "not a single red flag." Once again the cheering crowds were thick on both sides of the street. For Kessler the scene was "heartrending": "Crowned with glory," a "courageous host" had been "crushed by misfortune."[33] Just how many Germans shared Salomon's excitement or Kessler's melancholy is hard to say. But clearly the homecomings had stolen some of the revolution's thunder.

The demobilization of the army in late November and early December coincided with growing tensions between the Social Democrats and the Independents over the exact role of the revolutionary councils and the timing of National Assembly elections, and veterans quickly found themselves reenlisted, this time in the revolution's domestic struggles. In Kassel and Bremen, for example, bourgeois councils hoped in vain to use the presence of armed soldiers to disband workers' councils. For his part, Ebert welcomed the presence of reliable troops and the support they gave to his moderate political course, but he disavowed the bizarre right-wing attempts made in his name on 6 December.

It is highly unlikely that a broad conspiracy existed to derail the revolution as the Communists later claimed. Nonetheless, the link between the demobilization of the western front and the mobilization of a nationalist front is unmistakable. Throughout the month of December the capital was awash in black-white-red. Red flags had been pulled down and patrols of bourgeois volunteers marched about the affluent suburbs, in Dahlem and Wilmersdorf. Of course, most soldiers simply wanted to get home by Christmas, private desires that frustrated counterrevolutionary plans to restore some version of the old order. Nonetheless, the deliberate movement of thousands of soldiers through the city streets left the capital tense and on guard. Two days before Christmas, at the corner of Unter den Linden and Wilhelmstrasse, one of the last homecoming divisions was met by a leftist counterdemonstration of crippled veterans who held aloft angry placards reading "Where are the Ludendorff Funds?" and "Throw out the Guilty who have reduced us to Misery and Poverty." The confrontation, a witness reported, "visibly affected the soldiers. Their faces were taut and the atmosphere was tense."[34] Two very different war experiences had suddenly come face to face, a prelude to the gruesome civil war that would unfold in the winter and spring of 1919.

Even before the end of 1918, as it turned out, army generals had circumvented the problem of unreliable reservists and with the support of the skittish Social Democratic government organized the first *Freikorps* or freelance units, ostensibly to protect the fatherland from subversion and plunder, but, in fact, to crush the radical Left.[35] One of the first volunteers was the young, impressionable Ernst von Salomon.

The German Revolution was not composed of one single

movement that swept long-suffering proletarians down Unter den Linden and into power. Workers were divided, and were joined by revolutionary soldiers and mutinous sailors and radical intellectuals who all pursued their own political programs. At the same time, middle-class constituencies adjusted to the new circumstances with astonishing speed, organizing bourgeois councils, special interest groups, and paramilitary formations. While the return of thousands of veterans from the western front did not spell the end to the revolution, it meant that its momentum had slowed and its direction changed. Each new wave of political mobilization in the fall of 1918 revised further the register of revolutionary demands and angry denunciations.

In a brilliant sketch, Berlin's favorite artist, Heinrich Zille, caught this evanescent palimpsest. Along a smudged wall, tattered edges of prerevolutionary texts are still readable: an advertisement for a patriotic war exhibition and an official proclamation signed by Hindenburg, Ludendorff, and Graf von Hertling, the chancellor who had preceded Prince Max von Baden. The names of Ebert and Scheidemann can be made out as well on a poster fragment that must date from the first days of the revolution. It is pasted over with a notice announcing a meeting of the Spartakus League in Moabit's Arminiushallen for 18 December. Two stark graphics, side by side, compose the most recent layer and make very different comments on the revolutionary struggles. One depicts a figure who appeals to Germans not to "strangle" their "young freedom" in senseless internecine conflict, the other conjures up an alien, obviously Slavic-Bolshevik threat to "die Heimat," home and hearth.

Handwritten chalk messages register more spontaneous responses: "Hail Liebknecht! . . . Down with Ebert."

Zille's German autumn is sharp-edged with anger, denunciation, and alarm. It is also quick changing. Patriotic and revolutionary sentiments come and go, the effects of rain and wind have left only traces. There is a melancholic aspect to this revolution which lacked encompassing and generous gestures. And yet Zille has also well illustrated the newly energized public sphere. A vibrant mobilized political landscape has left its marks on the sandstone wall. Even passersby inscribed their own handwritten messages. It is just this self-authorization that makes the German revolution such a significant event for all social groups. November 1918 lacked the unanimity and national purpose of August 1914, but both war and revolution promoted the search for new political forms.

NEW BEGINNINGS

There can be no doubt that the socialist character to the revolution, which was so plain to see in the new workers' and soldiers' councils, the massive street demonstrations, and the ubiquitous red flags, unsettled middle-class Germans. From the very beginning implacable right-wing foes raised the alarming prospect of a dictatorship of the proletariat. Antisocialist feelings gained strength over the course of 1919 as working-class protest manifested itself in militant strike actions and armed rebellions. But it was not simply fear that shaped middle-class attitudes toward the revolution. What is striking about November 1918 is how widely terms such as *Volksgemeinschaft* (people's community), *Volksstaat* (people's state), and *Volks-*

partei (people's party) circulated in the nonsocialist and even nonliberal press. This vocabulary acknowledged that the unity necessary to confront the socialist Left was workable only in a progressive form. There was also a great deal of talk about August 1914, wispy recollections German unity in stark contrast to the fearsome quarrels of November 1918, but also insistent reminders of the new Germany that had been outlined at that time. Revolution offered the opportunity to give a sturdy political shape to the ad hoc solidarities of the Burgfrieden. Indeed, one of the major reasons for the political volatility of the Weimar Republic, in which millions of voters switched parties, was the electorate's continuing susceptibility to the vocabulary of the August Days and to appeals made "above the parties" on the basis of nation and Volk.

The kaiser's abdication, the triumph of the socialists, and the acceptance of the Allies' armistice terms—these rapid-fire events did not close down the way to the future. On the contrary, with the collapse of the Kaiserreich the conservative journalist Max Hildebert Boehm felt "room—the latitude and perspective of political aspiration." Looking ahead he saw "the bright expanse of meadows and fields." Boehm was not alone in tramping over open ground that autumn. In Jena, Eugen Diederichs, the influential publisher, shouted a "joyful 'Yea' the revolution, for we feel that true German spirit was stifled by the narrow, bureaucratic perspectives of the old regime."[36] It has finally come to pass, wrote Wilhelm Stapel, a spokesman for the very chauvinistic German National Union of Commercial Employees: "the path is free to reach the destination announced long ago by our prophets."[37] Different metaphors expressed similar ideas. In Berlin, René Schickele basked in the light of November 1918's sun that would "remain unforgettable."[38] A new day had broken, even if 9 November was cold and grey in Berlin. Even for those who could not endorse the regime's socialist program, there was little sympathy for the Kaiserreich, often remembered as a place that was narrow, rigid, and dark.

Much of the bourgeois press echoed these sentiments, commending, at least in the first hour, the revolutionaries for their sense of order and condemning imperial elites for betraying the German people by serving special interests and thwarting suffrage reform.[39] It was also completely evident to observers that nowhere in the Reich did the revolution encounter opposition. That so many civil servants continued to carry out their duties and, on the whole, cooperated with soldiers' and workers' councils suggests just how rotten the monarchy had become. There were few tears on November 9. Indeed in some middle-class communities a festive atmosphere prevailed. Celle, an administrative center, was perhaps exceptional, for on the first Sunday of the revolution not one but "two bands, one from the local army reserve, the other made up of sailors, played appropriate tunes," and "an airplane, decorated with flags and pennants, circled about the loudly cheering crowd." Even the "long file of demonstrators made a powerful impression." More typical was the university town of Göttingen, where burghers accepted the revolution but showed little enthusiasm. "There was little that was uplifting or stirring about it," concludes a local historian.[40]

Nonetheless the conviction was widespread among liberal and even conservative voters that it made no sense going back. In Bavarian Nördlingen, a National Liberal *Justizrat* expressed the balance of nonsocialist opinion, maintaining that "a truly free referendum" would "decisively reject the monarchy and endorse a people's state."[41] After the revolutionary turmoil of 1919 the lawyer would probably have revised his summary, but it held up at the end of 1918. Fifty-three-year-old Bertha Haedicke, a homeopath's wife in Leipzig and a relative of the Gebenslebens in Braunschweig, an extended family that will continue to provide us with testimony, had little sympathy with the "dumb laws" of the new regime, and yet her anguish in the face of socialist revolution came with the recognition that Germans had to enfranchise themselves. "Everything has depended on the people at the top," she wrote to her older sister at the end of November, "and everything failed at the top, the kaiser, the government, the Reichstag, *die ganze Politik*. If only the German people would finally take its destiny in hand." In this very nationalist family, revolution offered the opportunity to remake "die ganze Politik."[42] No wonder Heinrich Mann's scathing portrayal of Wilhelmine Germany, *Man of Straw*, became an immediate bestseller, with 75,000 copies sold in just one month, December 1918.

Why did so few people miss the kaiser? His hurried departure from Berlin to military headquarters in Spa and then from Germany cost him quite a bit of sympathy. Moreover, the accumulated resentments against the state and the war economy had weakened his authority. Even before the war he had struck many thinking Germans as boorish and unbalanced. But what really undermined popular confidence in the Hohenzollerns and the other German monarchies was the wholesale revisualization of the nation in terms of the Volk. From the very beginning of the war, after all, the "people" were in ascendancy.

In the context of the strenuous wartime efforts of ordinary soldiers, workers, and mothers, the charisma of the monarch faded while a "new radiance" enveloped the people, as Wilhelm Stapel melodramatically put it.[43] Ensconced at military headquarters in Spa, in Belgium, the kaiser himself grew more remote over the course of the war just as new heroes and military leaders—the middle-class ace Max Immelmann, the dashing Oswald Boelke, the unpretentious commander Hindenburg—appealed to popular tastes. Whatever the troubles ahead, the war had legitimized new, more active political roles for ordinary Germans. The vocabulary of Volk and Volksgemeinschaft, which was so pervasive during the war and also in the revolution, acknowledged this basic fact. Indeed, on Tuesday, 12 November, the arch-conservative *Kreuz-Zeitung* dropped its front-page motto "Forward with God for King and Fatherland," replacing it with "For the German Volk." A few days later the *Deutsche Tageszeitung* appeared without the legend "For Emperor and Empire."[44] Conservatives had begun to reimagine Germany without the kaiser.

What did "for the German Volk" really mean? In the first place, it authorized a much more intense engagement in political affairs than had hitherto been the case. Before the war civic life and the parliamentary parties were still very much in the hands of local notables, but wartime mobilization, the growing power of Social Democrats, and the tremulous activity of middle-class interest groups challenged this state of affairs. It is often forgotten that class-based suffrage laws kept not only workers but also many middle-class Germans from voting in local elections, an interdiction widely resented after 1914. Not until the revolution did women participate fully in national

politics. That burghers filled local assembly halls throughout
November and December 1918 to discuss current events, establish Bürgerräte and other professional councils, and organize local party branches signaled the new, increasingly populist
tenor to public life. Politicians recognized this popular aspect
when they inserted the word "Volk" into the renamed liberal
and conservative parties: thus the Deutsche Volkspartei (German People's Party) and Deutschnationale Volkspartei (German National People's Party). Democrats, liberals, and nationalists disagreed about Germany's future, but they welcomed
the opportunity to participate in political life as equals.

As the 19 January 1919 date for National Assembly elections neared, small towns and cozy neighborhoods, which had
rarely seen much political activity before the war, bustled with
electoral activity. Citizens poured into the meeting halls and
tavern rooms, taking every available seat. Discussions prompted
by vocal socialists and monarchists, democrats and liberals
followed the official speeches, so that gatherings often lasted
late into the night. And far from sitting passively, audiences
stomped, hooted, and applauded speakers. Screams, hisses, and
curses were all part of the repertoire. In the days that followed
the debates spilled over into the columns of local newspapers.

This initial interest held firm as party memberships soared
throughout the years 1919 and 1920 and party branches were
established in even the smallest places. The emphasis was on
mobilizing as broad a political base as possible, to include
clerks, typists, grocers, and low-ranked civil servants as well as
lawyers, doctors, and merchants, a combination not usual in
prewar political life, which despite all the changes after the turn
of the century had still been dominated by notables. Whenever

possible, nationally minded workers, Germany's equivalent of Britain's "Tory" workers, were enlisted as well. Moreover, women as well as men attended public meetings and joined parties, a trend explained not just by the formal enfranchisement of women but also by the sweeping wartime engagement of the Nationaler Frauendienst. In contrast to their prewar counterparts, the parties sought a mass base and organized much more publicly, leading demonstrations in the streets and canvassing actively at election time, much like the Social Democrats.

By the summer of 1919 the largest middle-class party, the prorepublican German Democratic Party, claimed 900,000 members organized in more than 2,000 local branches. Over the course of the following year its main rival, the liberal German People's Party, recruited nearly 400,000 members in 2,181 branches. At the same time, the monarchist German National People's Party worked to extend its organizational ambit into cities and towns well beyond the conservative East Elbian heartland. In the January 1919 National Assembly elections the Protestant middle-class parties accumulated about one-third of the vote (the Democrats received 18.6 percent, the German People's Party 4.4 percent, and the German Nationalists, 10.3 percent; in addition to the 19.7 percent share of the Catholic Center Party, this was enough to deny the Social Democratic Party and the Independent Socialists a majority). "The success of the German Nationalists is not overwhelming," conceded Bertha Haedicke, a newly won party member in Leipzig, but it was evidently sufficiently impressive for her to express confidence that "the future belongs to us."[45] For all the red flags and all the talk of socialism, the picture of the

November Revolution is incomplete without recognition of the popular mobilization that swept up men *and* women, workers *and* burghers, city *and* countryside, socialists *and* nationalists.

THE MOBILIZATION OF INTEREST

There is no more impressive statistic from the first year of the German Revolution than the growth of the socialist Free Trade Unions. Between the beginning of October and the end of December 1918, membership very nearly doubled to 2,858,053 workers; three months later the tally stood at 4,677,877 and by the end of the year 1919 at 7,338,132, almost triple the size of the unions before the war.[46] Thanks to the Auxiliary Labor Law of 1916 and the Stinnes-Legien Agreement in October 1918, by which employers recognized labor unions as collective bargaining agents, the Free Trade Unions emerged as the most attractive and competent representatives of the working class. Although trade-union leaders worked hard to channel often violent outbursts of social protest and tried to calm the spontaneous strike activity that roiled Germany in 1919, they were the real beneficiaries of blue-collar activism. Given these numbers, the *vaterlandslosen Gesellen* of 1914—those "fellows without a fatherland"—had been transformed into the musculature of "Big Labor." At the same time, shopkeepers, artisans, civil servants, employees, and farmers achieved their own organizational successes. Indeed, the proliferation of interest groups is the most distinctive indication of the political might that the middle classes had assembled after the November Revolution.

When Germans spoke up for themselves during war and revolution, they did so most loudly as constituents of particular social and economic interests. Public meetings and town squares echoed with the insistent demands made by post office clerks, primary schoolteachers, deliverymen, and tavernkeepers, a grassroots insurgency that recalled workers' tactics and transformed bourgeois politics by giving it a pronounced populist cast. Economic interest groups sprang up in the most unlikely places, a continuation of the *Verrätisierung*, the compulsive self-organization of artists, doctors, musicians, sailors, and even prostitutes that was so visible in the first weeks after the revolution.[47] Every grouplet, from the League of Blinded Warriors to the Association of Newspaper Vendors and the League of German Canteen Leaseholders, required an interest group, an office, a telephone, and a regular publication to obtain social recognition and, with luck, parliamentary protection. Interest groups not only organized more and different kinds of constituents than before the war but used more militant political tactics. This mobilization of interest is one of the most striking features of German political and social life after 1918.

In no other single year in German history did so many people organize themselves into interest groups or revive moribund organizations as in the twelve months that followed the November Revolution. In addition to the nearly 6 million workers who joined the Free Trade Unions, perhaps as many as 4 million employees, civil servants, farmers, and artisans organized afresh. Professions that had previously lacked representation, such as chemists and laboratory assistants or stage hands, established voluble interest groups. In the final weeks of 1918 forty-five new civil service organizations were founded. At the same time, scattered groups consolidated themselves in imposing federal structures. The newly founded Deutscher Beamtenbund or Federation of German Civil Servants claimed a membership of one and one-half million in 1919. Among organized white-collar employees, nine out of ten were represented by one of three cartels, the socialist Allgemeine freie Angestellten-Bund (450,000 in 1920), the Christian Gewerkschaftsbund der Angestellten (300,000), and the nationalist Deutschnationaler Handlungsgehilfenverband (250,000).[48] In what one historian terms the "second agrarian mobilization," thousands of smallholders became active in local agricultural chambers, in Peasants' Associations, and in newer, more assertive groups like the Free Peasantry.[49] In Westphalia alone 130 inactive agricultural chambers were revived by May 1919; at the end of the year membership had increased by 50 percent over prewar levels.[50] Among master artisans, the substantial majority organized in guilds continued to grow in the years after the revolution, from 625,000 in 1919 to 935,000 seven years later. In southern Germany the largely handicraft Verband deutscher Gewerbevereine claimed some 200,000 members in 1919. Much smaller but more strident was the Nordwestdeutscher Handwerkerbund (Northwest German League of Artisans) founded in 1919 with a membership of 50,000.[51]

In hundreds of towns across Germany, middle-class groups assembled, much like Oldenburg's Gewerbe- und Handelsverein von 1840 (Business and Trade Association of 1840), which convened in January 1919 to assess the new political landscape. The era of "kingmakers has passed," asserted the chairman; it was necessary for members to rely on themselves and to join the reorganized political parties in order to influence public policy. "Into the parties," he urged. Oldenburg's leading newspaper agreed, explaining that party policy was the result of a Darwinian contest among interest groups; only the strongest, most insistent gained political influence.[52] White-collar employees pursued the same strategy. Professional organization had to be accompanied by political mobilization. According to the German National Union of Commercial Employees, every member should "advance the principles of the union by working actively in the parties as a member, officer, candidate, or deputy."[53] The slogans of Germany's young democracy are revealing: "Physician, Help Yourself" or "He Who Screams Loudest Accomplishes the Most" or "Every Member Must Take a Stand." Within a year, physicians had indeed helped themselves and bookbinders had screamed and smallholders had taken a stand.[54]

Compared to the prewar years, middle-class influence in the Reichstag was striking. The bourgeois parties owed the balance of their large memberships to the strident efforts of interest groups such as the Agricultural Chambers, the white-collar unions, and the League of Artisans, all of whom gained significant representation on electoral lists in national elections in January 1919, again in June 1920, and in hundreds of regional and local contests. Moreover, appeals to occupation were the primary modes by which the parties addressed voters. This attentiveness reflected the requirements that came with the new business of democratic politics.[55] When someone like Reichstag deputy Gustav Budjuhn could legitimize his claim for renomination in the German National People's Party with a lengthy list of fifty-five often minutely defined groups with whom he had contact, including the Association of German Railway Retailers, the Central Organization of German Watchmakers, the League of German Butchers, and the League of German Brewers, it was clear that middle-class constituents were playing the game well.[56] There is no reason to regard this mobilization of interest as antimodern or as parochialism necessarily inconsistent with democracy.

Constituents also demanded a more combative political strategy. Artisans, for example, had traditionally organized into separate craft guilds and acquired membership in semipublic administrative bodies, the *Handwerkskammer*, or in trade associations as designated representatives of the guilds. As a result, an artisan's identity as a butcher, or a baker, or a plumber was paramount. The newly founded League of Artisans organized individual artisans irrespective of craft and thereby achieved a much broader public base, enhancing its ability to challenge the government, deliver votes, or otherwise mobilize constituents. "Masses rule in the age of democracy," explained the *Nordwestdeutscher Handwerkszeitung:* "If German artisans want to continue to play a role in politics or in the economy, they must bind themselves into a resolute and properly disciplined mass."[57] In similar fashion, in the Rhineland and in Bavaria, the Free Peasantry split with older Agricultural Chambers and the Peasants' Associations, organizing small landowners, ignoring differences between Catholics and Protestants, and defending agrarian interests against government officials with remarkable ferocity.

Both the League of Artisans and the Free Peasantry took the Social Democratic Party as their model: the middle classes not only embraced the militant organization of workers but adopted an increasingly democratic organization in which leaders were accountable to members. And like socialist workers, middle-class groups did not shy away from strikes, weaponry white-collar unions deployed during the rash of walkouts by employees in 1919. Under pressure from its poorly paid members, even the mainstream Federation of German Civil Servants recognized the legitimacy of strike action in the "last resort," as was apparent during the great railway strike of February 1922. For its part, the Free Peasantry won rowdy support among western farmers for threatening the cities with food delivery strikes.[58]

For the individual middle-class German the most practical political consequence of the revolution was his or her newly acquired membership in an economic interest group. In German towns, large and small, revived branches of older organizations competed with more assertive groups, reaching many more people than ever before. Previously mute constituencies such as railway and post office employees, white-collar workers, and craftsmen gained unprecedented influence in bourgeois party organizations. Despite their alarmist rhetoric about the socialist threat, middle-class constituents flexed considerable political muscle, certainly more than they had before the war. In the long run, interest groups acquired such a dominant role in the parliamentary process that Oswald Spengler dismissively described Germany's new democracy as nothing more than a German-speaking pile of interests.[59] For the autodidactic philosopher and for much of the conservative Right, the postrevolutionary polity was composed of self-absorbed economic entities, the so-called *Stände*, artisans, civil servants, or commercial employees who regarded public life only through the prism of particular corporate rights and group entitlements.

The process that the sociologist Emil Lederer had identified back in 1912, whereby "modern economic development" would bring "to life all previously passive interests" and "replace political ideas with economic interests," was accelerated by Germany's infamous inflation.[60] Rapid currency depreciation since the beginning of the war hit social groups unevenly, creating vastly different experiences for creditors, tenants, and salaried employees and thereby justifying their "special interest" perspectives. At the same time, inflation in the early 1920s offered splendid opportunities for farmers to take advantage of food shortages or workers to push the government for wage concessions or civil servants to seek special allowances. In addition, the rigorous fiscal stabilization that followed in 1924 cost thousands of employees their jobs. Blue-collar unemployment shot up to the highest levels since the revolution and only occasionally dropped below 10 percent before the genuine catastrophe of the Great Depression. Moreover, tight credit created havoc for small-business owners and farmers. With every new season, postwar economics validated the extension of interest-group politics.

The net result of the inflation was a political disaster for the main bourgeois parties—the two liberal parties, the German Democratic Party and the German People's Party, and the conservative German National People's Party—all of which were rent by hostile infighting as occupational groups struggled to gain more influence. Local and national elections in 1924 also indicated the growing appeal of the small but rather numerous special-interest parties, which were relentless in their attack on established politicians in Berlin and their ceaseless horsetrading in the Reichstag. Marshaling the support of small property owners, shopkeepers, and artisans, the Wirtschaftspartei, or Business Party, gained 3.3 percent of the vote in December 1924 Reichstag elections. On the local level the party's affiliates did even better (8.3 percent in Braunschweig's 1924 Landtag elections; 10 percent in Saxony's 1926 Landtag elections). At the same time, a jumble of peasant parties, homeowner slates, tenant unions, and employee and civil service lists confounded the ability of established party leaders to manage local politics. Public confidence in their ability to attend to middle-class interests continued to crumble, for the votes of splinter lists increased in every single local, regional, and national election between 1924 and 1930, the year of the Nazi breakthrough.

The inflation was one of the most traumatic events in German history. It made a weak parliamentary system weaker and constrained the future ability of Weimar governments to enact ameliorative social legislation. Even after it subsided in late 1923, German citizens continued to feel as if they lived in a permanent state of emergency. They were suspicious of values that might prove hollow and quick to jettison loyalties that had once gone unquestioned. Republican virtue rapidly deteriorated into what looked like purely solipsistic self-interest.

Yet the pursuit of economic interest was not quite as parochial as it might at first seem. It was on the basis of occupation that millions of Germans learned to articulate common interests, overcome debilitating divisions among the trades, and attain the high levels of organization that survival in a competitive capitalist society required. Corporatism also provided a vocabulary of entitlement. Appeals to occupational interest reflected a middle-class emphasis on work and merit which eroded traditional ranks of hierarchy and Wilhelmine codes of deference. Corporatist imagery was appealing because it resisted both the class exclusivity of Marxism and the big-business culture of capitalism. It was a logical derivative of the idea of the "people's state" that had been current since the beginning of the war.

To associate inflation with a complete breakdown of the polity is, therefore, a mistake. Indeed, the effects especially of the hyperinflation in 1922–23 were so sweeping, the pain it inflicted so general, and its appearance so fused in the public mind with the Treaty of Versailles, that it exposed the national fate that all Germans shared, made apposite national character and national suffering, and thereby spurred programs for national salvation. This transfiguration of conditions of despair into preconditions for renovation is not at all atypical of the interwar years.

COUNTERREVOLUTION

In the spring of 1919, after putting down Communist insurrections in Berlin, Bremen, and Munich and breaking general strikes in Halle, Magdeburg, and Braunschweig, armed right-wing freebooters may very well have been, as the historian Robert Waite suggests, "the most important single power in Germany."[61] Even if the speculation is overdrawn, it is remarkable how quickly forces of counterrevolution had rallied. Once these Freikorps had murdered their way across Germany and finally disbanded, they left behind a loose confederacy of secret organizations, veterans' groups, and riflery clubs which included Hitler's nascent SA or *Sturmabteilung*. At the same time, regional governments promoted the creation of local citizens' or home guards *(Einwohnerwehren)* to maintain law and order, so that more than one million men were enrolled in paramilitary activities in 1919 and 1920. Armories down the road, veterans back in uniform, and rifles under floorboards— all this attested to the mobilization that had taken place in hundreds of communities across the Reich.

Not surprisingly, the remilitarization deemed necessary to protect the German Republic from the Left endangered it even more recklessly from the Right. Just a few years after the establishment of democracy, a nationalist movement had emerged that was vehemently opposed to republican precepts. The long slide down to Hitler's seizure of power in 1933 began just a few weeks after the November Revolution. However, the paramilitary was not the simple creature of reaction that it is often portrayed to be. A closer look indicates the populist tendency to radical nationalism.

In the spring of 1919 the Freikorps were greeted as liberators by burghers in the cities where they smashed the general strikes of militant workers. But they were hardly models for a postrevolutionary politics. As long as opponents of the Weimar Republic operated in the shadowlands of legality the republic itself was not in great danger. What the secret conspiracies, the audacious assassination of prominent republicans such as the Center Party leader Matthais Erzberger (1921) and Foreign Minister Walther Rathenau (1922), and the putsch attempts of the Freikorps in 1920 and the Nazis in 1923 revealed was a basically elitist conception of politics which went against the grain of developments since 1914.

These escapades may have made good reading, but they did not make good politics. The Kapp Putsch misfired from the start in March 1920; Erich Ludendorff failed miserably as a

Weimar-era politician; and even the Freikorps sank mostly into oblivion. It was only in 1933 that Freikorpsmen were widely recognized as fascists *avant la lettre* and publicly commemorated as political heroes. This is why most of the great histories of the Freikorps movement and memoirs of its veterans appeared after 1933.[62] The Freikorps were the "vanguard of Nazism" largely because the Nazis declared them so. Although many Freikorps veterans eventually made their way into the Nazi movement, the political roles the two groups played were quite different. The Nazis were organizers, the Freikorps rebellers, and while the Nazis shared the anti-Marxism and physical brutality of the Freikorpsmen they lacked their swashbuckling contempt for civil society and their self-stylization as outlaws.

The Freikorps were much like the nineteenth-century Romantics described by Carl Schmitt, interesting because of their detachment, yet ineffective because unpolitical.[63] Standing on a Berlin streetcorner, Ernst von Salomon was struck by the hard look of front-line soldiers. It was the way they had been cut by the dangers of war that impelled him to sign up as a freebooter the very next day. Most of the other freelancers must have felt likewise, since aesthetic rather than political considerations seem to have guided their decisions. By their own admission, volunteers sought adventure, not redemption. "I don't ever want to go back home," Friedrich Siebert remembered feeling at the end of the war; "I want to spend my life walking these country roads, staring at this sky, measuring the world according to quadrants and divisions, calculating the time of day by the intensity of the artillery fire . . . my Germany begins where the rockets are fired and ends where the train to Cologne leaves."[64]

For the Freikorps, politics was simply war fought by other means. Indeed the transition from war to civil war was seamless, as Friedrich Wilhelm Heinz's résumé suggests: "Sixteen years old, a volunteer in the Fusilier Guards. At eighteen, lieutenant in the 46th Infantry Regiment. Somme, Flanders, tank battles, March offensive, defensive action, border duty, Ehrhardt Brigade, Kapp Putsch, Upper Silesia, Black Reichswehr, Ruhr Occupation, Feldherrnhalle."[65] And for the large proportion of Freikorpsmen who were young school-leavers, the so-called Generation of 1902, joining up was one way to make up for the action not seen during the war. Engagement was the point, while the political stakes were often irrelevant. During the Kapp Putsch, men from the Hindenburg Freikorps didn't even know on which side they were going to be fighting.[66] When asked by a British officer why his men had marched on Berlin, one "astonished Freebooter captain replied, 'Why, Because I told them to! Wasn't that enough?'"[67] To be sure, most volunteers hated the socialists, but that enmity hardly added up to a political program. Did they want the exiled kaiser back? "A confused Freebooter stammered, 'N-no, no. Not that, not that . . .' 'What was the sense of it all then?' The question embarrassed the Freikorpskämpfer. He repeated it to himself and decided: 'The sense? The sense? There is sense only in danger. Marching into uncertainty is sense enough for us, because it answers the demands of our blood.'"[68]

Hagen Schulze accurately describes the Freikorps volunteers as nihilists.[69] They had no articulate vision of society, had forgotten about the towns they had come from, and were contemptuous of the burghers they "liberated." As such they were simply not a credible political force. In only one aspect were they typical of Germans in the postwar years. The Freikorps were not nostalgic—the men did not speak much about the kaiser. For them war and revolution had fashioned a fantastic, horrible world that blocked any return to 1913. This adventurousness was illustrative of a much broader recognition that the old political forms had outlived their usefulness.

Potentially more consequential than the Freikorps were the far more numerous Home Guards that were established in towns and villages throughout the Reich in response to proletarian plundering expeditions and working-class strikes. Since veterans shouldered the responsibilities for local security in disproportionate numbers, the Home Guards had the makings of a fresh political force that would draw on the experience of the war in order to remake Germany. Self-defense would foster self-reliance and rally patriots under the banner of a selfless struggle for national liberation. Supposedly above parties and beyond social divisions, the guards were designed to serve as grassroots models for the political and social unity of the nation. Berlin organizers intended nothing less than the revival of the Burgfrieden.

Of course, all the talk about national liberation modeled on the experiences of 1813 quickly degenerated into fulminations against the Allies and the sham democracy they had imposed on the German people. As James Diehl summarizes, "the ostensibly 'nonpolitical' program of the Civil Guard was . . . highly political"; and it contained all the characteristics of an authoritarian political order that intended to roll back the gains of democratic revolution.[70] The antidemocratic and antisocialist rhetoric sounded familiar, but the emphasis on local self-reliance distinguished the guards from other right-wing fantasts like Kapp or Salomon. It was a troop of hometownsmen rather than an executive committee of notables or an elite of marauding warriors who constituted the formative unit of the Einwohnerwehr, and this gave the guards a socially inclusive and popular temperament not usually associated with the German Right.

That so many Home Guards were established in 1919 and 1920 indicates just how far the revolutionary balance of power had shifted in favor of the middle classes. At first glance, the one million Germans who enrolled in the guards and were armed with a total of 660,000 rifles constituted an impressive counterweight to revolutionary workers. Yet, as it turned out, the Home Guards were not the strong-armed force that enthusiastic proponents had envisioned. Here and there the guards did have success: for example, in Kiel where the revolution had first broken out, wealthy burghers financed a well-organized *Freiwillige Ordnungsbund* with over 8,000 members. Village guards also successfully warded off the weekend invasions of hungry metropolitans. In many towns workers' and soldiers' councils were forced to surrender their arms to police and military authorities and to disband. Nonetheless, outside Bavaria, the guards generally remained local in focus and their enthusiasm faded once the immediate threat to the home and hearth had receded; their parochialism severely limited their political usefulness. Over time fewer volunteers showed up for guard duty and those who did ached with boredom. In some areas of the Ruhr socialists blocked the arming of the guards or else joined in such numbers that the units no longer served the interests of burghers.[71]

The Home Guards also failed the biggest test of the Counterrevolution. During the Kapp Putsch in March 1920, when Wolfgang Kapp, who had gained great notoriety as a Pan-German in World War I, led Freikorps divisions into the capital and proclaimed a new national government, most guards failed to collaborate or assume local authority. In western and northern Germany artisans, civil servants, and shopkeepers dominated the guards and they had little sympathy for restorationist plots even if they disdained the republic. Elsewhere the putschists, recognized for the dilettantes they were, failed to gain the support of local politicians or sympathetic editors. "The absolute vacuum of moral support . . . could be felt within the first few hours," reported a British observer in Berlin.[72] After a few days the putsch collapsed in face of a general strike.

What was fearsome to burghers was the concerted counteraction of Social Democrats, Independent Socialists, and Communists who shut down metropolitan Germany for several days. Even to liberally inclined burghers it looked as though the left-wing strike committees that had stepped forward to assume local control were about to establish a dictatorship of the proletariat. Throughout March and into April 1920, near–civil war conditions prevailed around Braunschweig, in Gotha, and throughout the Ruhr. Even in towns where relations between the classes had remained amicable, the aftermath of the Kapp Putsch left deep hostilities. According to the local press, "things have always been quiet" in Goslar, but the town "suffered quite a shock during the strikes last week."[73] In the months that followed, food riots, tumultuous workers' demonstrations to protest the murder of Foreign Minister Rathenau in June 1922, and, in Saxony and Thuringia, socialist majorities in the Landtag (1922–23) kept burghers edgy and on the defensive.

Despite the failure of the Kapp Putsch, the opponents of the Weimar Republic appeared formidable in the late spring of 1920, when national elections revealed a strong rightward drift. Nothing endangered the Weimar Republic more than the deep division between Left and Right. In thousands of communities, particularly in the Protestant north, the eighteen months between the outbreak of the November Revolution and the aftermath of the Kapp Putsch had been enough to square working-class socialists and bourgeois nationalists off into mutually opposed and increasingly radical camps. Very little remained of the spirit of the Burgfrieden, although relations between the classes were easier in the Catholic south and west and in the largest cities. Only the German Democratic Party sought to mediate between Social Democracy and the *Bürgertum*, the middle classes, and in the June 1920 Reichstag elections it lost over half its electorate. In the small- and medium-sized towns where most Germans still lived, the Democrats had been decimated.

At the same time, fighting against the socialists became increasingly intertwined with fighting for the nation. The difficult terms of war and peace imposed what Ernst Renan once referred to as the "daily plebiscite" of nationalism in which the abstract state which raised taxes and enacted laws was imagined as a living, breathing, injured collectivity. Given the magnitude of wartime mobilization and the experience of mass death it was not surprising that individuals would feel part of the body of the nation. Peasants, laborers, and clerks, Martin Broszat notes, returned home in 1918 "with changed personalities"; "the war had torn them from the slow-moving pace of provincial life and thrown them into the 'wide world' and onto the stage of fateful national developments."[74]

As a result, veterans' groups played larger political roles in even the smallest towns. Flag consecrations and memorial ceremonies punctuated social life, and war songs—"Siegreich wollen wir Frankreich schlagen" was always a big favorite—augmented choral repertoires. The harsh terms of the Treaty of Versailles and the creation of the Polish Corridor (1919), the partitioning of Silesia (1921), and the French invasion of the Ruhr (1923) were deeply felt by Germans: collections were taken up, young children boarded in rural sanctuaries, and town squares filled with angry protestors of all parties. Increasingly obsessed with the integrity of the nation, which appeared to have been badly mangled, German nationalists thought in increasingly exclusive or racial terms. They honed an apocalyptic rhetoric of danger and redemption and launched vicious attacks on so-called non-German elements—Socialists, Poles, and increasingly Jews—who stood in the way of national renewal.

Dozens of nationalist groups engaged in paramilitary training and circulated lurid antisocialist propaganda. Audiences eagerly visited lectures to hear about Bolshevik conspiracies and Social Democratic misdeeds. Conservative newspapers lavished attention on right-wing libelists who mocked republican officeholders such as Ebert and Erzberger in mammoth court proceedings. An alternative publishing network sprang up from nothing to crank out hundreds of pamphlets, postcards, and picture books detailing the alleged atrocities of revolutionaries. In December 1918 Eduard Stadtler, an effective propagandist for the Anti-Bolshevik League, printed 50,000 copies of *Bolshevism and Its Elimination;* somewhat later, his *Bolshevism and Economic Life* enjoyed a print-run of 100,000. In Munich the future Nazis Alfred Rosenberg and Dietrich Eckart busily distributed 100,000 anti-Semitic leaflets. The notorious racist Theodor Fritsch put out as many as 2 million leaflets between November 1918 and March 1919. In just the single year 1920, the Deutschvölkischer Schutz- und Trutzbund (German Völkisch Defense and Combat League) claimed it had distributed a grand total of 7,642,000 pieces of propaganda. Zille's sandstone wall was papered over and over with anti-Semitic screeds, patriotic declarations, and scurrilous indictments of parliamentary government.

Yet for all this busy activity, the nationalist opposition remained fragmented. Neither the Home Guards nor the Freikorps offered a vision of the future, and hyperventilated attacks on Socialists, Bolsheviks, and Jews did not add up to a political program. The legal battles into which libelous opponents of the republic continuously forced President Ebert made plenty of headlines, but no real headway. While burghers gathered strength in convivial "German evenings," they usually met quietly and privately and they ended up commemorating mostly the past—Founding Day, Sedan Day, Bismarck Day, the August Days. The devastating effects of postwar inflation made this paralysis even more poignant since the loss of economic security gilded the prewar past as much as it confirmed its unattainability. The very rhetoric of postwar nationalism confirmed the aimlessness of counterrevolution in the early 1920s.

When so much had been scandalized and betrayed, it now seemed that anything could happen and that nothing was secured or anchored. A world turned upside down had sent virtuous patriots to defeat and allowed "November criminals" to triumph. The carnivalesque imagery withheld legitimacy from the Weimar Republic, but it also confused nationalists, who were not sure whether or not they were monarchists or whether the world of 1913 should or could be restored.

What all the poster-pasting and lecture-going did confirm was how crowded the public square had become. Since 1914, and even more so since 1918, voluntary associations had sprung up in communities and neighborhoods as never before. For the first time, political parties opened offices replete with part-time staff, regular hours, and telephone numbers, establishing a presence even in small towns that had been unimaginable before the war. Retailers, bakers, and commercial employees also organized into economic-interest groups with hundreds of local branches. Public activity was invigorated by the busy social lives of gymnasts, folklorists, singers, and churchgoers, who founded and revived clubs in record numbers. Nationalist groups of various kinds grew more active, whereas their prewar counterparts such as the Navy League had been mostly big-city affairs. A motley array of self-authorized anti-Semites, populist tribunes, and religious prophets raised their voices as well.

Just a glance at town address books for 1913, 1919, and 1925 reveals the growing density of organizational life in the provinces. Where there had been two clubs before the war, there were three after the war and four by the early 1930s. In Marburg, Celle, and Uelzen, to take examples at hand, the war had spurred burghers to organize relief efforts, prepare patriotic campaigns, and establish self-help groups, a tendency the revolution amended. After the year 1918 the social reach of clubs lengthened to include the postman, the clerk, and the grocer. Senior civil servants, well-to-do merchants, and professionals continued to dominate leadership posts, but not to the degree that they had before the war. All this was testimony to the widespread impact of egalitarian ideas after the November Revolution.[75]

Club life knit burghers closer together just as the "alternative culture" of the socialist movement captured the political allegiances of workers. Summer festivals, club anniversaries, and gymnastic and choral competitions were happy occasions for townspeople from various backgrounds to come together. Again and again opportunities presented themselves for Gifhorn's or Goslar's or Northeim's Men's Singing Society, Men's Gymnastic League, Voluntary Fire Company, and *Schützenkorps* as well as handicraft guilds, retailer associations, and veterans' groups to put on traditional costumes, bring out flags and banners, and parade about town. These motions of bourgeois sociability sustained an embracing sense of civic identity and kept the community from fragmenting completely into social castes and economic factions.[76]

Clubs also organized burghers in opposition to local socialists, as bitter struggles over which songs to sing (patriotic or folksy) and which flags to fly (imperial or republican) at community festivals attested. Almost without exception, social clubs came in pairs, both pursuing common interests, but one gathering workers, another burghers. Communities came with two canoe clubs, two bicycle clubs, two dramatic societies, and, in Goslar, even two volunteer fire companies. More and more burghers came to find their political bearings in the busy life of local clubs, reveling in the more inclusive note and adhering to the pronounced nationalist themes. At the grass roots, it was clear that citizens were organizing with unparalleled energy.

By 1924 there were signs that this social activity was taking on a more coherent political form. The most viable patriotic associations that emerged from among the scattered remnants of the Freikorps and Home Guards were the *Stahlhelm* (Steel Helmets) and the *Jungdeutscher Orden* (*Jungdo* or Young German Order) which emerged as major political forces by embracing rather than rejecting the philistine social life of the provinces. Unlike their predecessors, the Freikorps, the Stahlhelm and Jungdo struck an appealing ecumenical note, offering membership to all patriotic men, whether or not they were officers, veterans, or middle-class. They were also distinctive for being more open to women, who established their own auxiliaries and attended patriotic celebrations.[77] Stahlhelm activism revolved around the black-white-red imperial banner. Flag consecrations were the beat to which Stahlhelmers moved, and they quickly became cherished events in community life. Brass bands and choral societies provided music and regimental associations and gymnastic societies joined in what looked more like a family celebration than a wartime field service.

From Braunschweig, Elisabeth Gebensleben, the wife of an engineer, described the new look to city streets. On 27 April 1924: "A troop of young people is just passing by, singing 'Swastika on the Flag, with a black, white, and red Band.'" Five days later: "this afternoon, Eberhard," her fourteen-year-old son, "is out on the street distributing campaign literature for the German Nationalist People's Party." In midsummer her daughter Irmgard, who was living in Northeim, looked forward to Sunday's flag consecration and dance: "Everywhere there is great excitement . . . all the regimental associations are coming, even the riflery clubs." A few weeks later Irmgard had reportedly danced with "a big blond" at a German Nationalist evening, Elisabeth reveled in Braunschweig's "glorious Stahlhelm celebration," and Eberhard was preparing to go to yet another big meeting.[78]

"German Days" or "Stahlhelm Days" such as the one Elisabeth Gebensleben found so wonderful attracted thousands of patriots to nearby cities. The military deportment—marches, movement, front—gave a politically confident and forward-looking quality to the nationalist sociability. These large public gatherings provided compelling visual affirmation of the cherished Volksgemeinschaft, the romantic-nationalist ideal by which so many burghers took their political bearings. The Jungdo reached the peak of its popularity in 1922 or 1923, with some 100,000 members, while the more imposing Stahlhelm enrolled about 500,000 Germans by the end of the 1920s.[79] Yet these figures only approximate the immense political authority the two groups commanded and the dynamic role they played in mobilizing the bourgeois community. Both their nationalist politics and their easy-going social ties made them heirs to the grassroots solidarities of the wartime Burgfrieden. They were the product of the new, not the old Germany. They were also increasingly anti-Semitic.

Local activism like party meetings, special-interest campaigns, and Stahlhelm marches indicate that the postwar years added up to much more than the establishment of formal democracy. For good reasons or bad, Germans turned indifferent to the Weimar Republic, but they did not remain inactive or apathetic. The real consequence of the revolution was not so much the parliamentary government it secured as the organization and activism of thousands of constituents it made possible. The new Germany can best be found in the humdrum mobilization of interest groups, veterans' associations, and party branches and in the self-authorization of a hundred voices, libelous, illiberal, and chauvinistic as they may have been. It is a sad but compelling paradox that the hostile defamations of the president of the republic were as indicative of democratization as the presidency of good-willed Fritz Ebert himself.

January 1933

Nazi stormtroopers and sympathizers in Berlin's Wilhelmstrasse on
the day of Hitler's appointment as chancellor, 30 January 1933

Photo credit: Ullstein Bilderdienst

Marchers cutting their boots against asphalt streets, growing louder, cheers swallowing up the winter stillness, torchlights and searchlights advancing on the darkness— the *New York Times* later reported on "a gigantic demonstration such as has not been witnessed" in Berlin, at least not since that November afternoon some fourteen years earlier, in 1918, when "Fritz Ebert reviewed the masses."[1] The day was Monday, 30 January 1933; Adolf Hitler had just been named chancellor of Germany and stood overlooking Wilhelmstrasse, reviewing a newer, larger, more threatening version of Germany's masses. That the *Times* story also referred to Communist leaflets, knife fights, and gunshots ensured that American readers would not be left with the impression that the German people stood unanimously behind the Nazis. Indeed, most observers in Germany and abroad predicted another round of rancorous elections and murderous street fights. But no one could overlook the massive size of the fascist assembly.

All afternoon, following the radio broadcast of Hitler's appointment just after one, curious sightseers jammed the Wilhelmstrasse, where the Reichskanzlei and Hitler's hotel, the Kaiserhof, were located. Newsreel trucks parked up and down the street, their cables and spotlights furbishing the big moment with electric excitement. By early evening members of the Nazi paramilitary formations, the SA (*Sturmabteilung* or stormtroops) and the SS (*Schutzstaffel*, the party's smaller security guard), as well as the nationalist Stahlhelm assembled in the nearby Tiergarten for a full-dress parade through the

Brandenburg Gate, down Wilhelmstrasse, and into the old core of Berlin.

What was not anticipated was the sheer number of civilian wellwishers who also gathered. In this ostensibly "red" city, thousands of Berliners stood and cheered Hitler and Hindenburg, the president of the Republic. "Heils" and "Hochs" and "Hurrahs" resounded between the choruses of "Deutschland über Alles," "The Watch on the Rhine," and the Nazi anthem, the "Horst-Wessel-Song." For a better look, boys clambered up trees and statues, spectators climbed onto the walls of the well-positioned British embassy, and a few even mounted the Brandenburg Gate itself. As the parade set in motion at "exactly eight o'clock," according to the smitten *Berliner Lokal-Anzeiger*, the roars of the crowd were deafening.

Ambassador André François-Poncet witnessed the scene from the windows of the French embassy on Pariser Platz. His is the best description:

> The torches [the marchers] brandished formed a river of fire, a river with hastening, unquenchable waves, a river in spate sweeping with a sovereign rush over the very heart of the city. From these brown-shirted, booted men, as they marched in perfect discipline and alignment, their well-pitched voices bawling war-like songs, there rose an enthusiasm and dynamism that were extraordinary. The onlookers, drawn up on either side of the marching columns, burst into a vast clamor. The river of fire flowed past the French embassy, whence . . . I watched its luminous wake."[2]

As the uniformed party members turned into the Wilhelmstrasse their parade was joined by throngs of civilians who cheered Hindenburg and Hitler, both of whom appeared before the crowd, standing in separate windows, swept in the glare of spotlights and the adulation of the public. "Flags and more flags, marches and more marches, forests and more forests of raised, saluting arms. This goes on for hours. For hours and hours the same picture"—Berlin's Nazi newspaper, *Der Angriff*, hardly exaggerated.[3] For once its editor, propaganda chief Joseph Goebbels, groped for words. "Uprising! Spontaneous explosion of the people. Indescribable," he noted telegraphically in his diary.[4] It was after midnight before all the paraders had made their way through the government district to the Schloss, the site of so many cheers in the name of the kaiser in August 1914, less than twenty years earlier.

The next day the *Völksicher Beobachter*'s Herbert Seehofes made the link to the "August Days" explicit: "Then as now, the blazing sign of a national insurrection. Then as now, resistance has been broken, the dams breached, the people rise up." Watching a newsreel of the parade, Elisabeth Gebensleben made the same connection in Braunschweig.[5] The only bit of the monarchy that was still visible amid the brown uniforms and black boots, however, was the kaiser's son, "Auwi"—August Wilhelm—who stood alongside Graf Helldorf, SA chief for the region that included Berlin, outside the Hotel Bristol on Wilhelmstrasse. On the evening of 30 January German nationalism may have triumphed, a sweet vindication against Versailles, but it was a very different, much more revolutionary kind of nationalism than the sumptuous pageantry of Imperial Germany. Nearly one million Berliners took part in this extraordinary demonstration of allegiance to a party that promised to do away with both the sentimental bric-a-brac of the prewar past and the clutter of Weimar democracy and to establish a strong-willed and strong-armed racial state, a very new twentieth-century Germany.

Of course not everybody supported the Nazis. On a streetcar forced to come to a stop in the nighttime traffic, one young man "saw all the people and the big show they were putting on." "Poor Germany," he said; the exclamation "just slipped out." The streetcar motorman turned around, shook the man's hand, and said, "I think so too."[6] Poor Germany because the Nazis would claim so many innocent victims. Indeed, that very night embassies received urgent calls from foreign nationals who had been beaten up for being Communists, Socialists, or Jews.[7] On the proletarian north side of Berlin, a few Communists managed a counterdemonstration and red streetfighters later shot to death SA Sturmführer Hans Maikowski as he returned home from the parade.[8] And just a few days earlier hundreds of thousands of Berliners had rallied on the Lustgarten demonstrating that "Berlin will stay red." Nonetheless, momentum seemed to be with the Nazis; their opponents, by contrast, had been stopped, assaulted, and pushed to the side. The fight for the streets continued for the next several weeks, but after the night of 30 January the brownshirts never lost the offensive.

Among the well-organized political armies of the Left and the Right, the dramatic change in the government announced itself quickly. Those Germans who owned a radio or gathered around one in a tavern could hear for themselves the live transmission of the loud cheers and martial music on Wilhelmstrasse—the new Interior Minister Wilhelm Frick had imposed Goebbels's live broadcast of the "Volksjubel" on reluctant station chiefs. In the broadcast selected party members spoke the scripted reactions of "ordinary citizens" from all walks of life, who welcomed the new chancellor—stage management that gave the seizure of power the apparent acclamation of "the man on the street."[9]

Almost immediately Nazi parades materialized in dozens of German communities; at the end of January 1933 the National Socialists boasted 719,446 members, organized in as many as 10,000 local branches, for whom the appointment of Hitler as German chancellor was the culmination of long years of difficult work.[10] In Darmstadt, for example, it was only a short time before news of Hitler's appointment turned thousands of citizens into the main streets, where they excitedly discussed the turn of events. In the afternoon Communists organized the first demonstration, which was followed quickly by a Nazi parade and a Social Democratic gathering. In Frankfurt crowds brought traffic around the Schillerplatz to a standstill.[11] Nazi torches lit up the night in Braunschweig, Mannheim, and Coburg, which had been a fascist stronghold since 1929.

The next night, Tuesday, 31 January, the Nazis and their right-wing allies in the Stahlhelm rallied in the streets and clashed with Communists and Social Democrats in bloody fights in Breslau, Düsseldorf, Essen, Lübeck, Schweinfurt, Worms, and Homburg. Over the next days, Nazis and Communists attacked each other in taverns (Worms, Harburg, Bonn, Wilmersdorf), threw stones at party offices (Velbert, Düsseldorf, Essen), or plundered newspaper offices (Mörs, Eisleben). Outside an unemployment office in Mannheim, workers attacked Nazis who appeared in uniform. In Halle brownshirts plundered a soda fountain frequented by Communists. Much of the violence occurred under cover of night, as individual Nazis or Communists ambushed their political enemies. One Nazi was murdered as he sat on the toilet in a bar on Hamburg's Beierstrasse.

More typical, however, were small-town victory parades such as the one held in Northeim a few days later, on Saturday, 4 February. It must have been "exceedingly impressive," writes William Sheridan Allen: "In addition to the fife-and drum corps and flags of the Stahlhelm, there were the flags, band and fife-and-drumcorps of the SA." More than a thousand marchers took a quarter of an hour to pass along streets "packed with onlookers." On the marketplace an enormous crowd, "bigger than any heretofore seen," according to the mainstream press, turned out to hear the speechmaking that followed. It was not just smoke and mirrors that gave the impression that the town was overwhelmingly Nazi.[12]

Every day in February brought three or four dead; weekends proved even more fatal. Clandestine attacks felled victims in all political camps, but it was not long before Communists and Social Democrats, in particular, found it nearly impossible to organize public demonstrations. Police prohibited Communist demonstrations (in the states of Hamburg, Thüringen, Braunschweig, and Oldenburg, also in Karlsruhe and Wiesbaden) or the SA broke up antifascist gatherings (as was the case in Braunschweig on 8 February). Moreover, the police colluded with National Socialists by banning Communist newspapers (in Berlin) and searching Communist offices (in Berlin, Halle, and Magdeburg). Nonetheless, a large Social Democratic demonstration against dictatorship did take place on 3 February in Frankfurt and, four days later, another one was held in Berlin. Republicans in small towns in Hessen such as Auerbach and

Bensheim marched under the watchful eyes of the police on 12 February. But these events were the last public manifestations of anti-Nazism in Germany. They depended on the co-operation of police authorities, who tended to sympathize with the Nazis.[13] Once this protection was no longer available public gatherings became impossible. By mid-February more and more local Communists were arrested (50 in Düsseldorf on 12 February), a sure sign that the authority of the state was marching in step with the National Socialists. Police did nothing as SA toughs chased Social Democrats from a meeting hall in Upper Silesian Hindenburg on 22 February.[14] In Wittenberg SA and SS troops simply joined police patrols.

The triumphant Nazis appeared irresistible as they remained in the public eye. On 5 February they put on one of the largest state funerals the capital had ever seen for the slain SA leader Maikowski and Josef Zaunitz, a policeman killed in the cross-fire. On a rainy winter morning 40,000 members of the SA, the SS, and the Stahlhelm stood in formation outside the Berlin Cathedral alongside hundreds of policemen in a new, fateful alliance. All the prominent figures of the week-old regime were in attendance, including Hitler himself. Thousands of spectators crowded the edges of the Lustgarten and the route of the funeral parade along Unter den Linden and up Friedrichstrasse to the Invaliden Cemetery where Maikowski and Zauritz were laid to rest near the great generals of the nineteenth century, Scharnhorst, Gneisenau, and Moltke.

As would become custom, a live radio hookup broadcast the ceremonies throughout the Reich.[15] Just five days later, brown-shirted Nazis seemed to be all about the city—Wittenberg-platz, Gendarmenmarkt, Kleiner Tiergarten, Küstriner Platz,

Spandauer Rathaus—as thick knots of party members crowded busy intersections where loudspeakers broadcast Hitler's radio address from the Sportpalast.[16] Again and again, radio transformed Nazi events, providing a parade, a funeral, or a speech with a vast acoustical backdrop that extended over the entire nation. The impact of radio was enormous and many, many Germans bought radios to participate in the national drama. "One day" around this time, Martin Koller remembered his father "bringing home a box." "He turned some knobs and it began to sputter and crack. All at once the world barged into our living room." A few weeks later, "I followed the events of the Day of Potsdam . . . You could hear the bells ringing, the marching music playing," and then the chants, "the Führer, the Führer."[17]

By contrast, the public space in which Nazi opponents operated gradually shrunk. Socialist ralliers lacked the mediated sense of unanimity, found themselves hemmed in by police and paramilitary forces, and accordingly made much less of a public impression. At the end of the third week of the Third Reich, Nazi toughs were attacking Social Democratic and Reichsbanner members with impunity; "wild" interrogation centers, prisons, and concentration camps meted out a rough political justice. The two-fisted conquest of the streets culminated in the Reichstag fire (set by a lone Communist on 27 February), a fortuitous event which the Nazis used to ban the Communist Party, vastly increase the power of the police, and otherwise choke off access of political contenders to the public sphere in the last crucial week before the 5 March elections which Hitler had called to provide the Nazis with the parliamentary majority they needed.

The Nazis were somewhat disappointed by the election results, which with 43.9 percent of the total vote denied them an absolute majority. Both the Social Democrats and the banned Communist Party did quite well given the atmosphere of intimidation. With 18.3 percent, the Socialists slipped from the 20.4 percent attained in November 1932, while the banned Communist Party managed to hold on to a 12.3 percent share (down from 16.9). As a result the Nazis had no choice but to rely once again on Alfred Hugenberg and his conservative German National People's Party, with 8 percent of the vote, in order to form a majority government. But the slim majority disguised the political authority the National Socialists in fact enjoyed. Influential bourgeois newspapers such as Berlin's *Börsen-Courier* and the *Lokal-Anzeiger* lauded the Nazis for their resolute opposition to Socialism and Marxism and their youthful, disciplined bearing, and the remaining liberal party deputies along with the rightward-leaning Catholic Center Party shamelessly provided Hitler's government with the two-thirds majority necessary to dismantle parliamentary democracy by emergency legislation.

The few bourgeois opponents who did emerge were easily outmaneuvered by the regime's mass support and brutal methods. What was in fact dictatorial scaffolding in spring 1933 looked like healthy resolve to most Germans, who identified with the national revolution, welcomed the end it put to party bickering, and felt these events vindicated the political paths they had long pursued, even if they did not consider themselves out-and-out National Socialists. In fact Nazi violence against the Left in early 1933 significantly boosted the popularity of the regime. As a result Hitler avoided civil war, setting to rest a fear which had dominated political discussions since the November Revolution. "To allay the spectre of civil war," and to unify the nation by dint of sovereign authority, "no injustice and no oppression was too high a price to pay," writes J. P. Stern about the mood in 1933, "especially if others—the Communists, the Jews, the Slavs, eventually the rest of Europe—could be made to pay it."[18] For conservatives and Stahlhelmers, for "Tory" workers and rural protesters, as well as for Hitler's voters, long years of opposition to the Weimar Republic had finally culminated in the victory of January 1933, a moment which overcame the shame of November 1918 and restored the promise of August 1914, when Germans had pulled together for the national cause. In other words, the National Socialists tapped into a more generic "national socialist" consensus that extended well beyond Hitler's party and his electorate.

Over the next months the National Socialists coordinated civil and political life to erect a one-party dictatorship. Political parties and independent trade unions were outlawed while the social clubs and voluntary associations that made up the fabric of neighborhood life were nazified to suit the purposes of the regime, or else they simply dissolved. The press was effectively muzzled as well. By the summer of 1933 organized opposition to the Nazis had disappeared. To be sure, perhaps as many as one in three Germans continued to sympathize with either the banished Social Democratic or the Communist Party, and German Catholics managed to preserve a degree of autonomy. But what is truly startling is the strong, and growing, support the Nazis enjoyed at the grass roots.

These circumstances allowed the Nazis to take the drastic

measures that revolutionized politics as had no other phenomenon in modern German history. From the status of a splinter
party with 2.6 percent of the vote in 1928, the National Socialist German Workers' Party (Nationalsozialistische Deutsche Arbeiterpartei or NSDAP) astounded the nation with a
18.3 percent share in 1930, vaulted over the Social Democrats
to become the nation's largest party by 1931, and rose to 37.4
percent of the vote (a pre-1933 high) the following year. At
the same time, the National Socialists destroyed their political
competitors: between 1930 and 1933 the liberal and conservative parties that had administered the German Reich since
its founding in 1871 vanished from the scene. Once in power
the National Socialists forcibly eliminated the Social Democratic Party, Germany's oldest, from political life. For the first
time since 1848 there were no parties or partisan forums to
inform public policy.

Even more astonishing was the immense popularity of
Adolf Hitler, referred to by the Nazis as "our Führer," eventually acclaimed as "the Führer" of all Germans. In the years
immediately before World War II, that is, after economic recovery and the cost-free *Anschluss* with Austria in March
1938, perhaps as many as nine in ten Germans were "Hitler
supporters, Führer believers."[19] What made the break of 30
January 1933 even more consequential were the urgent preparations the National Socialists undertook to wage new wars
intended to establish German mastery. In less than ten years
the Third Reich would impose tyrannical rule over most of
Europe and organize the murder of millions of civilians as racial inferiors in what were undoubtedly the darkest years of
the twentieth century.

How do we account for the speedy rise of the Nazis and the sudden switch in party allegiances? Between 1928 and 1933 millions of Germans joined a vast political insurrection that seemed to come from nowhere, a drama which utterly confounded seasoned observers. In the aftermath of the initial National Socialist breakthrough in the September 1930 Reichstag elections most commentators reacted in disbelief. It was a "monstrous fact," sputtered the influential *Berliner Tageblatt*, that "six million and four hundred thousand voters in this highly civilized country had given their vote to the commonest, hollowest, and crudest charlatanism."[20] By 1932 more than one-third of all voters had moved into the Nazi camp. Hitler's was Germany's largest party and his claim to the chancellorship correspondingly strong, strong enough in any event that after a year of weak emergency cabinets and mounting political violence it convinced the conservative eighty-four-year old president, Paul von Hindenburg, to put aside his disdain for the Nazis, to recall his preference for fascists over democrats, and to appoint Hitler chancellor in the hope of restoring law and order.

How did Germany get to this awful point? All sorts of political miscalculations were made at the top levels of government in the last year of the Weimar Republic, not least by Hindenburg, but the main factor in the demise of democracy in 1933 was the insurgent strength of the National Socialists and the wide appeal of their political propositions, and this is what has to be explained. To this day, both the popular success of the Nazis and the improbable figure of Adolf Hitler remain something of a mystery. In the public mind, two standard explanations seem to stand out: the harsh terms of the Treaty of

Versailles and the hard economics of the Great Depression. This line of reasoning suggests that, for all the problems in German society, had the Allies been more reasonable or had New York's stock-market crash not robbed the Weimar Republic of its future, then the world would have been spared Adolf Hitler and the destruction he unleashed. Both counterfactuals are familiar, but neither one is satisfactory.

Whether the peace terms drawn up at Versailles in 1919 were really so punitive is something historians have come to question. Germany retained its basic territorial integrity and industrial potential while guarantees for French security proved to be insufficient. It is also hard to argue that Versailles somehow caused the devastating German inflation which in 1922 and 1923 spiraled out of control mainly as a result of reckless wartime borrowing and fiscally disastrous (though politically prudent) postwar expenditures. Nonetheless, the German people felt the Treaty of Versailles and the reparation payments it mandated to be harsh in the extreme. For almost a decade Germany was excluded from the international community. It did not join the League of Nations until 1926 or participate in the Olympics until 1928. Although the final schedule for reparations continued to be a matter of negotiation throughout the 1920s, it was clear that German payments would be made almost to the end of the twentieth century.

The high price to be paid for losing the war was made worse because Germans never quite believed they had been beaten. Even if the public recognized as political hyperbole the "stab-in-the-back" legend proffered by the nationalist Right and endorsed in 1919 by Field Marshall Hindenburg, it continued to exaggerate the effects of the Allied food embargo and of the

American entry into the war, making Germany's collapse appear the outcome of the most extraordinary circumstances. "We didn't win and we didn't lose" summed up the opinion of most Germans.[21] Friedrich Ebert had said as much at homecoming ceremonies on Pariser Platz in December 1918.

On the face of it, Germans were still fuming in the early 1930s, and many expected the National Socialists to restore Germany's international prestige. To America's best reporter, H. R. Knickerbocker, Weimar's citizens talked constantly about the world war, the Treaty of Versailles, and the aggression of France. At an "evening of discussion" somewhere in proletarian Berlin, both Communists and Nazis boasted of their intentions to liberate Germany. "Do you want to know when the Treaty of Versailles will be destroyed?" asked one Communist speaker: "When the . . . Red Army stands at the French frontier." "'The Red Army on the Rhine.' It had a swing to it," Knickerbocker mused. A Nazi countered: "We shall tear up the Versailles Treaty without any Red Army." And he continued: only National Socialism can "win back all that has been taken from us."

Far away in rural Thuringia, Altenfeld's glassworkers blamed the British for imposing tariffs that priced their goods out of international markets. With Hitler, at any rate, "things could not be worse." In a long conversation with a schoolteacher in cosmopolitan Frankfurt, Knickerbocker learned that Hitler would "tear up the Versailles treaty" and "tell France to go to hell." The Nazi sympathizer had already figured on Lufthansa's passenger planes doubling as long-range bombers and enlisted the SA and the Stahlhelm in Germany's avenging armies. Knickerbocker's visit to a student fraternity in romantic

Heidelberg revealed that the most popular drinking song remained "Victoriously we shall conquer France." "All it takes is guts," the youths averred, to "throw off the French yoke." France, reparations, the Reichswehr also dominated Knickerbocker's discussions with ranking National Socialists such as Hitler and Franz von Epp.[22] It did indeed appear that Germans were voting Nazi to avenge Versailles.

Yet in fact there were so few people in Germany who did not condemn the treaty that foreign policy simply was not a major factor in realigning German voting behavior. In a remarkable consensus, Social Democrats joined German Nationalists on market squares across the country to protest the Treaty of Versailles (1919), the partition of Silesia (1921), and French occupation of the Ruhr (1923). The socialist paramilitary group Reichsbanner even made Anschluss with Austria the theme of its big 1925 Magdeburg rally. Of course, the political parties disagreed over the best way to revise the *Schmachfrieden* (the Shameful Peace) of Versailles. The public's indignation pushed moderate politicians to adopt ever more extreme nationalist positions, with the result that illegal operations such as the so-called Black Reichswehr and secret cooperation with the Soviet Union (first broached in the 1922 Rapallo Pact) found political shelter. In 1923 Freikorps terrorists were celebrated as national heroes when they turned their guns against the French and their Rhenish separatist collaborators. Still, the salience of the Treaty of Versailles as an electoral issue diminished. For example, German Nationalists furiously condemned Foreign Minister Gustav Stresemann, who in the years 1923–1929 pursued a policy of accommodation vis-à-vis the French, yet they made little headway on the issue and saw their votes slip alongside Stresemann's. The hardline position of party leaders like Alfred Hugenberg makes it difficult to imagine that Germans voted for Hitler because German Nationalists seemed insufficiently opposed to Versailles.

Moreover, the Versailles explanation is not consistent with the timing of the Nazi breakthrough, which occurred some ten years after the peace had been signed, or with the basically domestic focus of the Nazis' critical 1930 and 1932 campaigns.[23] Indeed, the National Socialists premised national renewal on a thorough housecleaning at home, in a word, on revolution. The much discussed 1929 campaign against the Young Plan (to revise and implement reparation payments) was of secondary importance to the Nazis, who were more interested in scoring well in municipal elections in city halls across Prussia and Bavaria. It was Stresemann's German People's Party, by contrast, that sought political stability in foreign-policy successes and, as a result, took a beating at the polls for its inattention to bread-and-butter issues. Versailles certainly weakened the Weimar Republic by giving political legitimacy to right-wing nationalists who repudiated democracy, but it did not generate the Nazi vote.[24]

A more plausible explanation for the triumph of the Nazis is the calamity of the Great Depression. The lines seem to follow one another with ineluctable logic: lines of anxious men in front of the labor exchange, lines of stormtroopers in parade formation; the graph charting the rising numbers of unemployed from 3.3 million (registered) in the first quarter of 1930 to nearly 5 million a year later and 6.1 million in early 1932, and the figure depicting the rising number of Nazi voters from some 800,000 in June 1928 to 6.4 million in September 1930 and finally 13.7 million in July 1932. At the height of the crisis, in the winter of 1932, more than 40 percent of all workers in Germany were unemployed. Most of these had long since exhausted their claims to unemployment compensation and barely subsisted on the dole. Ten-year-old Gertrud described perfectly the cumulative horror of "Unemployment" in a school essay written in December 1932: "Then men are so unhappy when they don't have work. When there's money for Unemployment," that is, when the unemployed had not yet exhausted their 26 weeks of state-mandated unemployment support, "they all go get stamped at the labor exchange and wait for a few pennies. When they're stamped out, they go on Crisis"—in especially hard times the state added 39, later cut to 32 weeks of "crisis support." "When they're done with that, they go on Welfare," the meager means-tested municipal welfare payments. "And when they're on Welfare, then they've hit bottom. Then a man comes and looks around the apartment. If he finds something valuable, he takes it away." "My father is a mason," she added (the construction trades were hit hardest in the slump); "he has been out of work for one and one-half years."[25]

Long-term unemployment was the scourge of the 1930s, and more and more workers simply wrote down "unemployed" instead of "mason" as their trade. The effects on private lives were catastrophic. Proletarian budgets were stretched to the breaking point. After deductions for rent, only twenty or thirty pfennigs per person were left each day for food. As a result, men, women, and children quickly became malnourished: meat was a luxury reserved for an occasional Sunday; most of the unemployed subsisted on bread and potatoes and substituted margarine for butter. Once again Germans were tasting the bitter rations of the turnip winter of 1916–17, and once again they were losing confidence in the "system."

Although blue-collar workers suffered the greatest hardships and were far more likely to find themselves utterly destitute, the Great Depression cost one in five white-collar workers, mostly older employees of long standing, their jobs. The fate of Hans Pinneberg, depicted so well in Hans Fallada's novel *Little Man, What Now?* (1932), was typical. Anxious to adhere to the rules of the game, Pinneberg becomes a model salesman, but is unjustifiably fired; keeping up appearances with his white collar, Hans finds himself wandering the streets with nowhere to go and is pushed into the gutter by a policeman who represents the very bourgeois order in which he has always believed.[26]

Shopkeepers also suffered as business turnover collapsed. Knickerbocker of the *New York Evening Post* surveyed the scene in wintry Falkenstein, in Saxony's Erzgebirge: "The hotel was open, but we were the only guests ... a few faint lights showed in shops ... but there were no customers. The beer halls were open, but ... a half dozen men sat the whole evening over the smallest sized pots of beer."[27] Foreclosure and bankruptcy rates climbed and thousands of failed business-owners became street peddlers and traveling salesmen— "Luftexistenzen," Theodor Geiger called them—alongside an estimated 400,000 homeless *Landburschen* (vagabonds) who wandered forlornly from town to town.[28] In the countryside chronically low agricultural prices since the mid-1920s ruined the livelihoods of farmers and the businesspeople who depended on rural trade.

The disintegration of the social fabric was the inevitable result of these material hardships. Between 1928 and 1932 suicide rates increased 14 percent for men, 19 percent for women. Indeed, women bore much of the physical toll of male unemployment. If men sat around, listless and confused like Pinneberg, their wives were the "hardest working people" in the country. Knickerbocker, for one, recognized the sixteen hours a day women spent "sparing, scraping, darning, washing in the ceaseless effort to stretch the dole to its uttermost limits."[29] In these circumstances tensions at home mounted: adolescents, who had the worst job prospects of all, sought to escape the authority of harried parents and ran into the streets to join any number of political gangs and criminal adventures. Inside the tenements marriages broke up and tenants came to blows. The "flight into hatred" that so embittered neighbors also scapegoated German Jews as outsiders, liberals, and capitalists.[30]

The political corollary to domestic friction was growing impatience with the government of Heinrich Brüning, the so-called hunger chancellor, in the worst years of the depression. His authority rested on shaky foundations: the grudging toleration of parties from the Social Democratic Party to the German People's Party who feared what might follow the conservative Brüning more than they objected to him. But conditions continued to worsen and Brüning's deflationary fiscal policies did little to alleviate the suffering and a great deal to augment it. Anything but Brüning and this mock democracy, thought ordinary Germans: in Falkenstein evangelical churches filled up; in proletarian Berlin the Communist vote soared; in middle-class towns voters flocked to the Nazis.

The correlation between crisis and the search for political alternatives makes even more sense if one considers that during the worst years of the inflation, ten years earlier, both the Communists and the Nazis won early converts. Then, with the stabilization of the currency in 1924, the Communist advance stalled and the National Socialists expired completely. So were not political extremists such as these simply the parasitical creatures of crisis? Wasn't it possible that once the slump bottomed out, the Nazis would begin to lose votes? In fact that did seem to be the case in November 1932, when a further round of Reichstag elections finally cut the Nazi electorate by 2 million votes. The tantalizing question poses itself: if President Hindenburg had held firm and not named Hitler chancellor in January, would the National Socialist movement have melted away in the gradually improving economic conditions of the spring of 1933?

The link between the onset of the Great Depression and the advance of National Socialism cannot be disputed. Without an agrarian crisis in the countryside, without the unemployment of millions of Germans for two or more years, and without the slump in business revenues that followed it is difficult to imagine the National Socialists exploding on the political landscape with the same force and the same speed as they did in the years 1929–1933. Yet the connection between the faltering economy and the insurgent Nazis is not as automatic as it might at first glance seem. In the first place, the real losers during the Great Depression were the blue-collar unemployed, who tended to vote for the Communists, not the Nazis. Moreover, the overall hardships among the middle classes have been overstated, since white-collar employees stumbled later and recovered earlier

and therefore did not exhaust their claims to more ample unemployment compensation at nearly the same rate as workers.

Shopkeepers and artisans were also not hit uniformly:
whereas retailers in working-class neighborhoods barely kept
afloat, many provincial businessowners continued to do reason-
ably well. In the town of Northeim, which voted disproportion-
ately for the Nazis, there were only a handful of bankruptcies
and these upended what had been marginal enterprises. William Sheridan Allen, the author of a masterly survey of the
town, concludes that "the middle classes were hardly touched
by the depression." What did trouble Northeimers was the
prospect of bankruptcy, which the depression obviously made
very real, and the specter of political revolution posed by the
growing numbers of unemployed on the streets and Communists in office. Northeim's unemployed numbered around
700 in mid-1931, but every day as many as 2,000 claimants
from around the countryside tramped into the city to the district labor exchange, a disquieting concentration of restless
proletarians. Seen in this light, the middle classes, dreading
social unrest, appear to have supported the Nazis for political
reasons not directly connected to material desperation.[31]

At the same time, Germans do not appear to have voted for
the Nazis because they blamed the Jews for their troubles.
While there is no doubt that anti-Semitism became much more
commonplace in Germany after the war (and the day after the
Nazi seizure of power Berlin's university students took to
singing anti-Semitic choruses along Unter den Linden), anti-
Semitism played only a secondary role in National Socialist
election campaigns. It was not the main feature in electoral
propaganda or in the pages of the leading Nazi newspaper,

Völkischer Beobachter. On the whole, Germans "were drawn to anti-Semitism because they were drawn to Nazism, not the other way around."[32]

But the real problem with explanations that emphasize the catastrophic political effects of the Great Depression is that they focus only on the rise of the Nazis after 1930 and generally miss longer-term trends before then. True, the Nazi breakthrough in 1930 coincided with the first big rise in unemployment. Yet the established bourgeois parties that had run Germany's political system since the 1870s were already in an advanced state of disarray, under attack by special interest groups, single-issue parties, and paramilitary associations. From left to right, the German Democratic Party had been losing voters since some time in 1919, the German People's Party had been slipping since 1921, and the German National People's Party made no headway after 1924. In the 1928 Reichstag elections, when the Nazis were still an insignificant splinter group and the economy was stable, the three big liberal and conservative parties collapsed to a 27.8 percent share of the vote, down from 36.9 percent in December 1924 (and 37.1 percent in 1920). Two years later they tumbled all the way down to 15.3 percent.

It seems logical to take this electoral volatility since 1924 in one piece, so that whatever drove millions of Germans into the Nazi party during the depression had driven them out of the bourgeois parties before the depression. Indeed, the electoral foundation that supported Adolf Hitler had been erected once before, in April 1925, in support of the presidential campaign of Paul von Hindenburg. Hitler voters were familiar as former Hindenburg voters, the political mobilization of 1930–1933 had been rehearsed in 1925. What this correspondence indicates is that the formation of the Nazi bloc was not purely circumstantial, although it was made much more urgent by the depression. The steady disintegration of the bourgeois parties since 1924, the insurgent success of splinter parties in 1928 and 1930, and the bellweather Hindenburg election in 1925 indicate that larger political processes were at work during the Weimar Republic. The makings of a "national socialist" insurrection were already apparent before the Great Depression lifted the fortunes of the National Socialists.

HINDENBURG TO HITLER

Voters drawn to the Nazis in the calamitous days of the Great Depression were not a motley collection of protest voters who had little in common but their own resentment against the "system." The Hitler bloc had assembled nearly ten years earlier as a Hindenburg bloc. Evidently a nationalist and antirepublican union could succeed under the proper conditions. Seen in this light, the Nazis might be considered a much more popular party, something more than the creature of extraordinary crisis; rather than uttering the desperate gasps of panicked "little men," the Nazis may have articulated in just the right pitch the aspirations of millions of burghers. It is worth taking a closer look at the political fragments of the 1920s that the Nazis finally pieced together in the early 1930s.

The similarities between the April 1925 presidential campaign of Paul von Hindenburg and the effort by Adolf Hitler seven years later are startling, although the differences between the two men could not have been greater. Born in 1847, Hindenburg was a general of the old Prussian school who had little feel for the German people, felt most comfortable around horses or equestrian aristocrats like the impossibly reactionary Franz von Papen, and had nothing but disdain for the lance-corporal Adolf Hitler. (On 10 October 1931: "This Bohemian corporal wants to become Reich chancellor? Never!" And a bit more equivocally just three days before appointing Hitler: "Surely gentlemen, you would not credit me with appointing this Austrian corporal Chancellor?")[33] Hitler, by contrast, was a lifetime younger (born in 1889) and a virtuoso in the modern politics of rallies, elections, and propaganda campaigns.

And yet the two men were repeatedly thrown together. Hindenburg not only had to run against Hitler in the spring 1932 presidential election but, once reelected, had no choice but to contend with the Nazi Führer, who was leader of the nation's largest party and whom, in the end, with some displeasure, he formally appointed as chancellor. What is more, Hindenburg and Hitler also confronted each other as representatives of the same constituency. In one of the most remarkable twists in German election history, the overwhelmingly Protestant and provincial precincts that had supported Hindenburg in 1925 voted for Hitler in 1932. Indeed, in statistical terms, there is no better predictor of Nazi electoral success in 1932 (in the April presidential campaign and the July Reichstag elections) than the Hindenburg vote seven years earlier. Clearly the 1925 election of Hindenburg represented an important stage in the formation of the Nazi insurgency.[34]

At first glance the close correspondence between the two elections suggests that Hitler simply reassembled those belligerently nationalist and antisocialist Germans who had never made their peace with the November Revolution and had voted for Hindenburg in 1925 as a symbol of the old Germany and abandoned him in 1932 for compromising with the new. Cheered madly by crowds waving black-white-red banners of the empire, Hindenburg appeared to be an "Ersatzkaiser," the next best thing to the exiled emperor. Voters expressed "widespread longing for the 'good old days,'" explains one influential historian.[35] Had not old-fashioned nationalists finally trumped forward-looking socialists and republicans? Drawing on the same forces, Nazism appeared to be a basically counterrevolutionary force that owed its energy to "time-honored nationalist-conservative and even monarchist ideas," as Martin Broszat put it, even if the movement made necessary concessions to the format and rhetoric of mass politics.[36]

The problem with this explanation is that it cannot account for the alacrity with which erstwhile supporters abandoned Hindenburg for Hitler in 1932. Even in the East Prussian district of Neidenburg, where Hindenburg had stopped the Russians at the Battle of Tannenberg, the Field Marshall was trounced by the "Bohemian corporal" two to one.[37] That loyalties to tradition proved so frail suggests that the ideals of the past had lost their conviction. Indeed, a closer look at the 1925 election indicates that voters were not looking for a return to the "good old days" but fashioning a populist nationalism that Hitler ultimately embodied much more plausibly than Hindenburg. Rather than a pale version of the German kaiser, Hindenburg won the presidency in 1925 as a pale version of the German *Volksmann*.

The first round of elections featured a typically confused campaign of seven candidates; but it was the second round, when the republican candidate, the respected Catholic leader

Wilhelm Marx, squared off against Hindenburg, that was the most lively. A remarkably broad coalition of civic groups, patriotic associations, and bourgeois parties carried the April 1925 campaign from below. Hindenburg electioneering resembled civic work: choirs, athletic clubs, riflery societies, artisanal guilds, Christian organizations, and housewives' associations all played active roles. Even Social Democrats, who had the resources of an impressive organization at their disposal and generally entered Weimar elections better prepared than their nationalist opponents, conceded that this time "the bourgeoisie" was linked together in a "great chain of reaction" down "to the last man."[38] One of the strongest links was undoubtedly the paramilitary group, the Stahlhelm, which leafletted neighborhoods and outlying villages, organized weekend parades, and on election day drove voters to the polls. Often for the first time since the November Revolution, burghers found themselves swept up in the passions of public politics. Depending on their political sympathies, neighbors flew the red-black-gold flag of the republic or the black-white-red banner of the empire. In hundreds of German communities, as the novelist Ernst Glaeser describes for his home state Württemberg, the fabric of civic life was torn into two hostile halves, republican and nationalist.[39]

Hindenburg was a dream candidate because of his role as Supreme Commander in World War I. He appealed to Catholics as well as Protestants and drew in voters who had abstained in the first round. Even more significant, however, were the breadth and strength of the coalition that supported him on the local level. At a time when the established parties were under considerable attack from middle-class splinter parties, when patriots disagreed over the direction of Stresemann's conciliatory foreign policy, and when the pro-business policies of Chancellor Luther unsettled dispossessed savers, Christian workers, and small tradespeople, the Hindenburg bloc was an impressive accomplishment. His supporters also demonstrated unprecedented public poise. Quite unlike the furtive mobilization after the November Revolution and the reluctant mustering in the Home Guards, burghers rallied in public and, once their candidate had won, taunted the socialists in an unusually aggressive manner that anticipated the torchlight parades of 30 January 1933 eight years later.

The day after the election, on 27 April 1925, Hindenburg's supporters took to the streets in massive numbers, confident that with Hindenburg's victory the advance of socialism and republican rule had been decisively halted. In Goslar, which had a substantial working-class minority, a victory parade organized by the Stahlhelm, regimental groups, and the Men's Gymnastic League led hundreds of burghers through the narrow streets of the medieval town to the marketplace. There the editor of the local paper, August Wilhelm Silgradt, congratulated Germans for making their way out of the labyrinth of revolution and onto "the straight path of honor." In Helmstedt patriotic associations, riflery clubs, and student fraternities, with flags and bands, marched in "great numbers," followed by enthusiastic townspeople. Across Germany burghers decorated their homes with black-white-red banners and rallied around local war monuments or Bismarck statues to demonstrate Hindenburg's triumph. Elsewhere exuberant Stahlhelmers attacked Social Democrats, setting in motion the descent into political violence that the SA would continue far more ruthlessly in the years to come. In 1925 the German Right was already brimming with confidence. Social Democrats, by contrast, had begun to retreat. In small towns across Germany Stahlhelm attacks on workers went unpunished, republicans had difficulty renting tavern room for meetings, and socialist clubs lost members.[40]

The grassroots combination in support of Hindenburg was not simply a fair-weather coalition that united around a single candidate in a run-off election but broke apart once the daily business of parliamentary politics resumed. Over the coming seasons burghers assembled again and again to display the nationalist union that the Hindenburg campaign had tugged together. Before the war Bismarck's birthday had occasioned patriotic ceremony; during the late 1920s Hindenburg was accorded the same favor. Commemorations to honor the president were held in 1925 and 1926, but when Hindenburg turned eighty on 2 October 1927 bourgeois neighborhoods erupted in festivity.

Once again it was ordinary members gathered in social clubs and patriotic associations who played the leading roles, organizing parades and rallies, putting on athletic tournaments and talent contests, and outfitting the streets in black-white-red bunting. Goslar's organizing committee, for example, composed the very picture of bourgeois unity: local politicians joined Stahlhelmers; the Committee of Guilds and the chamber of commerce worked with the German Civil Servants' League and the German National Union of Commercial Employees; and the Protestant churches cooperated with the Catholic parish. In tiny Esbeck in northern Germany, Hindenburg supporters assembled in the village's largest room, the Nuthmannschen Halle, which was decorated for the occasion with evergreen boughs and imperial flags. Local authorities rose to say a few words, but the focus of the commemoration was on local clubs: one after the other, the village choir sang, the gymnastic association tumbled, and the dramatic society read poems. To honor Hindenburg athletes in nearby Rotenburg on the Wümme formed a human pyramid four levels high on which assistants hung huge blown-up photographs of the president. After this gymnastic marvel Rotenburg's choirs provided less strenuous musical entertainment.

Although the scale of festivity was grander in larger towns, the grassroots spirit remained the same. In Osnabrück, for example, lines of schoolchildren and divisions of the Stahlhelmer, the Jungdo, regimental groups, riflery clubs, athletic associations, singing societies, and guilds arrayed themselves in a huge parade through the city center. Hundreds of thousands of patriots chartered buses to Berlin and clogged the subways of the capital to stand along Unter den Linden and Friedrichstrasse, the route of Hindenburg's motorcade. Stahlhelm, Boy Scouts, the German National Union of Commercial Employees, youth groups, uniformed trolleymen—all formed a colorful chain of associational life in the giant metropolis.[41]

Overshadowed by subsequent events, the scale and reach of Hindenburg commemoration have been largely forgotten. Yet Hindenburg's eightieth birthday was a massive and genuine declaration of political resolution and political accomplishment. It was this unrestrained, all-German, black-white-red spectacle which so impressed observers. Whereas burghers had rarely marched openly in the streets before 1924, leaving public arenas to the proletarian Social Democrats, preferring to assemble indoors under the auspices of traditional party leaders, Hindenburg's election marked a turning point. Crowds burst out of the closed meeting halls into the streets, into public squares, and, finally, in gestures of political conquest, into working-class neighborhoods.

The Stahlhelm was the point around which this exuberant nationalist sociability crystallized. Year after year in the late 1920s and early 1930s, thousands of local consecrations of the imperial flag culminated in the fanfare of regional Stahlhelm Days and reached an annual climax on Front Soldiers' Day when hundreds of thousands of patriots gathered in Magdeburg, Berlin, or Hamburg. Each march, whether along one village's Breite Strasse or down Berlin's Unter den Linden, attracted excited onlookers, recalled the unity of the Bürgertum, and rehearsed the reconquest of the community in the name of nation. Streets were the acknowledged byways of the new politics. Stahlhelmers clashed with Reichsbanner workers in front of local trade union houses and marched through—"invaded"—proletarian neighborhoods and the "red" cities, Berlin and Hamburg. Again and again they broke working-class domination of the public square and thereby succeeded where the Freikorps and the Home Guards in the early 1920s had not. To be sure, the Stahlhelm was embedded in the "philistine" rounds of small-town festivity, yet it also enrolled burghers—men and, to a lesser extent, women—in a national political campaign to reconquer the country. Bremen's *Weser Zeitung* recognized just this on Front Soldiers' Day in 1927: "Germany not only has a mass organization of the Left but also of the Right."[42] Mobilization in public became a vital indication of the political vitality of the Right. As a consequence,

Hindenburg festivity left a palpable sense of strength and unity: "Germany is moving forward again," concluded the editors of the conservative *Deutsche Allgemeine Zeitung*.[43]

In contrast to the officious ceremony of the Wilhelmine era, in which social rank and military protocol dominated even in small towns and villages, Hindenburg Days and Stahlhelm Days revolved around voluntary associations and relied on the energies of private citizens. Parades composed by various clubs and associations and joined by artisans, employees, Christian workers, and women's groups; large market-square rallies; and private gestures such as patriotic window dressing and the display of black-white-red flags—all conveyed the heartfelt jubilation of burghers. These celebrations resembled a gemütlich summer carnival or *Schützenfest* of national proportions, and had little in common with the careful choreography of prewar Founding Day or Sedan Day ceremonies; there were no strict social divisions between invited guests and passersby, no reviewing stands for municipal notables, and no invitation-only fancy dress balls. As in July and August 1914, burghers themselves composed the spectacle. National feeling was as high as it was because Hindenburg festivity gathered and bonded burghers of all social stations at the same time as it presented a united front against the working-class Left. Democratic scale rather than monarchical pomp gave the nationalist ceremonies their populist appeal.

The Hindenburg election provided a compelling model for successful political mobilization. In contrast to the parties, whose partisan politics in far-off Berlin seemed only to divide Germans, patriotic associations such as the Stahlhelm brought burghers together and successfully confronted the socialist Left in public assemblies. Moreover, the emphasis on large turnouts and boisterous activity appealed to many more constituents than the exclusively parliamentary focus of the parties. During the Hindenburg election the parties had already played a subordinate role, and in the years that followed the Stahlhelm, the Jungdeutscher Orden, and other paramilitary formations replaced local party organizations as sponsors of nationalist ceremony. Flushed by its local successes, the Stahlhelm even tried to force the bourgeois parties to cooperate in a more permanent fashion. It won the hearty applause of the press for its vigorous efforts to construct a unity list in regional elections in Saxony in 1927 and in Braunschweig in 1928. When these failed, antiparty sentiments deepened. "Everything is to remain as it was. The parties do not want to endanger their interest by working together," commented a liberal Braunschweig paper in disgust. Politicians might pay lip service to the idea of bourgeois unity, but behind closed doors the "old game" simply continued, seconded a disappointed editor in Saxon Pirna.[44]

Despite its frantic activity, the Stahlhelm proved unable to organize effectively the growing antiparliamentary tide. Over and over again veterans served as brokers, hoping to cajole the bourgeois parties to subscribe to a nationalist program, but ultimately they depended on the cooperation of the politicians they brought together. Although Stahlhelmers provided much-needed footsoldiers to bourgeois campaigns, they remained mostly an auxiliary to parliamentary politics. What the Stahlhelm failed to see was that popular impatience with the parties was fueled as much by their inattention to the economic and social grievances of ordinary constituents as by their inability to unify against the Left. Antisocialism consumed the populist impulses in the Stahlhelm. As a result the Stahlhelm grew more obviously reactionary. By 1929 it had moved closer and closer to the right-wing German National People's Party, evidently mistaking antirepublican belligerence for political radicalism and thereby losing the momentum it had gained since the Hindenburg election to the upstart National Socialists.

For all their failures, however, the activity of the nationalist leagues turned German neighborhoods into very different places. A visitor to a patriotic household would have found little of the despair or nostalgia typical immediately after the revolution. In the mid-1920s young nationalists, many of them veterans, a few former Freikorpsmen, stepped into the town square with confidence and poise. The Jungdeutscher Orden, the Stahlhelm, and a dozen other smaller organizations (Werwolf, Viking, Bayernbund, Tannenbergbund, as well as a wide range of youth groups and cultural associations) all announced the organizational agility of middle-class Germans. They were also surprisingly successful in enrolling workers. Neither the Navy League before the war, the Fatherland Party during the war, nor the Home Guards and the Freikorps after the revolution had been able to mobilize patriots to the same extent. Public demonstrations took place in even the smallest towns. Always more evident in Protestant regions, the political polarization between Left and Right came to divide German Catholics as well. Amid a busy calendar of Hindenburg Days, Stahlhelm Days, and German Days, middle-class Germans came to see their neighborhoods in increasingly nationalist and familiar terms. This was so not only because patriotic rallies and victory marches adorned in black-white-red claimed the public spaces that had once been the domain of Social Democrats but also because burghers participated in patriotic festivity in an easy, informal manner. The result was a correspondence between German nationalism and hometown Gemütlichkeit, a winning combination already in 1914.

The Stahlhelm's Germany was antisocialist but not aristocratic, nationalist but not monarchist, illiberal but not exclusive. In that sense it was derivative of the truly popular nature of the world war. At the same time, the grassroots stress on the virtue of the nation and the perfidy of its enemies—Jews, Slavs, Bolsheviks—saved a place for all sorts of völkisch and anti-Semitic groups, including the Nazis, who made good use of the platform they thereby acquired. In 1929 the National Socialists joined anti–Young Plan committees across the Reich and jostled with elder statesmen of the German People's Party and the German National People's Party on unity lists and in local coalitions (in Thuringia and Braunschweig, for example). Bourgeois associational life provided cover for increasingly militant antiparliamentary politics. In many ways it prized an "integral nationalism" that rejected a plural political order altogether. In this light, the Hindenburg election was not a remnant of another era. It was a harbinger of the fascist fusion to come.

SPLINTER PARTIES AND PEOPLE'S MOVEMENTS

Stahlhelm groups had been founded and flag consecrations solemnly celebrated in the smallest towns, in out-of-the-way places like Oelber and Baddeckenstadt, in Klein-Elbe as well as Gross-Elbe. This was outwardly the most dramatic sign of the remarkable political mobilization that had taken place among previously inactive burghers. Stahlhelm branches were nearly as commonplace as Social Democratic locals. But other sorts of middle-class marchers crisscrossed the countryside as well. Along the ragged northern edge of Germany, where the poor man's sandy soil met marshlands and the sea, farmers were up in arms. On a "wonderful, sun-drenched winter's day," Sunday, 28 January 1928, "the rural people of Schleswig-Holstein stood shoulder-to-shoulder on the streets." Farmers had assembled on market squares, leaning on their *Krückstöcke* (walking sticks), listening to "short, terse" speeches. As many as 140,000 protesters made their way to Husum, Niebüll, Rendsburg, Schleswig, and Flensburg, to Eckernförde, Heide, Neumünster, Plön, Segeberg, Oldesloe, Ratzeburg, and Itzehoe.

In each town speakers furiously condemned the Reich's agricultural policies, particularly trade agreements that reduced tariffs on some goods and opened the way for the importation of frozen meats. At a time when commodity prices were at historic lows, these were dire developments. Tight credit, high taxes, and meager federal aid to this flood-prone region lengthened the list of complaints. Having organized the protests on his own initiative, Otto Johannsen demanded at a rally of some 20,000 sympathizers that Germany become self-sufficient in foodstuffs and dismantle the "completely spendthrift economy" *(hemmungslose Ausgabewirtschaft)*, a domestic housecleaning that would clear the way for repudiating the reparations which had kept Germans in the chains of a *Sklavenvolk*, a slave people.[45]

It was an astonishing sight that Sunday in January. Farmers normally reluctant to put down their tools, except maybe for a weekend game of cards, crowded into town. There they were joined by shopkeepers and artisans anxious to demonstrate against labor laws, high taxes, and the general corruption that seemed to prevail in Berlin. The Sunday protests in Schleswig-Holstein provided a dramatic climax to increasingly turbulent unrest throughout the nation. Earlier, in June and July 1926, Saxon townspeople had marched against fiscal policies that seemed to favor big labor and big industry. More than 7,000 artisans, homeowners, and shopkeepers took to the streets in Plauen, 9,000 in Zwickau, and 8,000 in Chemnitz.[46] A year later 1,000 Oldenburg homeowners protested the tax on the mortgages liquidated during the inflation (a half-hearted effort to redistribute the awful losses of 1922–23).

A few weeks before the Schleswig-Holstein actions, on 5 January 1928, farmers invaded the small district capital of Aurich, in East Frisia, crowding one assembly hall after another, Brems Garten, the Piquerhof, then the local agricultural hall, and finally the more upscale Bürgergarten. The turnout, estimated at 5,000, surpassed all expectations. The same day, peasants in the nearby village of Ahlhorn convened and resolved to demand the suspension of taxes "until the arrival of better conditions," the closing of revenue offices, and, as a final thought, the forced deportation of all civil servants to Canada.[47] On 17 January demonstrations overwhelmed Stollhamm and Westerstede, and on 26 January, Oldenburg, the provincial capital into which some 40,000 protesters streamed from across the flat, wintry countryside. Artisans, retailers, and homeowners from town joined provincial farmers on the city's Pferdemarkt in one of the largest middle-class demonstrations of the decade.

After the Schleswig-Holstein insurrection made national news two days later, farmers and small businessowners across

Germany took to the streets. In early February 15,000 protesters marched on Mecklenburg's capital, Schwerin. On 14 February as many farmers and tradesmen amassed in Hildesheim while 4,000 assembled in Uelzen. Thousands of middle-class demonstrators marched through the streets of Göttingen, Celle, and Marburg in late February. Demonstrations also took place on 12 March 1928 throughout Saxony: in Meissen, Freiberg, Pirna, Döbeln, Zittau, Löbau, Stollberg, and Zwickau. Similar movements flared in Braunschweig, Hanover, Pomerania, East Prussia, and Thuringia.[48] These rallies are all the more impressive since they took place in mid-sized towns with between 25,000 and 75,000 inhabitants. The scale and number of protests and the pointed nature of the political resentments they expressed indicate that more was going on than just a reaction to economic hard times.

Again and again observers reported on their surprise that the middle classes had become so active. "Never had Aurich, had East Frisia, seen such a massive demonstration," exulted the local paper. "Farmers must really be suffering," Holzminden's editors pointed out, "if they are determined to employ the weapons of political revolutionaries."[49] What is even more remarkable is that the demonstrations brought together diverse constituencies on a common basis. It was not just farmers in the market square, but also grocers, bakers, and plumbers who rallied. Whereas in the early 1920s the focus of middle-class political activity had been parochial, concentrated as it was on attaining representation in the bourgeois parties for each occupational group, by decade's end the focus had shifted; the parties found themselves the targets of angry denunciations declared by diverse protesters gathered in the streets.

The angry crowds repeatedly condemned the fiscal policies of the government, but they no longer spared the political parties or the major interest groups. "The fact is," decried Claus Heim, a Schleswig-Holstein radical, "that the state, the government, the parties, and the agricultural organizations, the chambers of agriculture, and the cooperatives have failed. The fact is," he continued in his persuasive cadence, "that for years the peasant has paid his contributions and for years has heard about all the things that have been done for him and yet sees that his situation is getting worse and worse."[50] Despite all the promises, the liberal and conservative parties had acquiesced in tax hikes. While they represented the interests of large landowners and big industrialists assiduously, they had neglected the middle classes, or at least that was the widespread perception. Rural troubles had nothing to do with floods or bad harvests, an angry farmer from Klein-Oldendorf, near Emden, concluded. They had explicitly political origins: "All the deputies who have brought us these troubles should be thrown overboard. We can't use them." And it was not enough merely to pass resolutions or send petitions on to Berlin: "Berlin has large wastepaper baskets for the paper protests of the Volk," one sympathetic writer noted.[51] The time had come for direct action.

Once the regular parties had failed, there was no longer much point in working with agrarian interest groups whose function it had been to broker the votes of constituents into parliamentary influence. Extolling the virtues of direct action by refusing to pay taxes and disrupting forced auctions, farm protesters threatened the very foundation of bourgeois politics. Not surprisingly, interest-group spokesmen tried to temper the grassroots *Landvolk* or rural people's movement, but without success. Protests spread, especially once the movement found martyrs in those activists arrested for failing to pay taxes, interrupting bank auctions, and bombing government offices in Oldenburg, Schleswig, and Lüneburg. On and off in the years 1930 and 1931, thousands of farmers marched on district capitals to lend support to defendants in court or to welcome them upon their release from prison.

Even as farmers repudiated the representation of established politicians, they ably developed an alternative sphere of activity. A network of paramilitary associations such as the Stahlhelm and Jungdeutscher Orden, and smaller neighborhood groups, tavern societies, and extended families supported the protests. Unpretentious, folksy leaders who had previously not distinguished themselves in public moved to the forefront: Claus Heim and Otto Johannsen, for example. At the same time, the Landvolk uprising captured the imagination of political dissidents of all colors. Communist agitators and völkisch speakers, Stahlhelmers and Hitlerites, all made their way to Schleswig-Holstein. There was no radical group that didn't want to rub shoulders with the muddy farmers who had rehabilitated the words of the nineteenth-century cultural critic Paul de Lagarde: "Let Germany remember that authentic life grows from the bottom up, not the top down!" Sung to the tune of the popular sharpshooters' song "I've Shot the Stag," the "Bomb Setter's Song" poked fun at the sudden popularity of the Landvolk:

> Ich leg' die Bomb' im Landratsamt
> Im Reichstag Dynamit,
> Vom Herrscherhause angestammt

Sing ich voll Stolz mein Lied.
Vom Hugenberg hab ich das Geld,
Von Hitler das Gewehr,
Der Ehrhardt hat das Gift gestellt
Und Ludendorff den Spe—e—e—e—r.
(I've set a bomb at the Prefecture
In the Reichstag it's dynamite
True to history's princes
I sing my song with pride
Hugenberg gave me the money,
Hitler the guns,
Ehrhardt provided poison
And Ludendorff the spears.)

For each one—Hugenberg, Hitler, Ehrhardt, Ludendorff—the Landvolk was "the first sign" of "a new spirit" in postwar Germany. It stood for "movement and struggle."[52]

The Landvolk was only the most dramatic example of how middle-class groups demanded greater political voice. Between 1924 and 1930, in elections across Germany, farmers, homeowners, artisans, and civil servants abandoned the traditional politicians to field their own electoral slates. The bourgeois parties were repeatedly accused of cozying up to the rich and powerful and of ignoring the plight of ordinary Germans. A history of German parliamentarianism in the 1920s adds up to this one storyline played out in dozens of settings. On the national level the two liberal parties, the German Democratic and German People's Party, had identified too closely with industrial interests to command more than fleeting attention. First "Tory" workers and white-collar employees, then artisans, retailers, and farmers had left the liberal fold. Even the German National People's Party, which had attracted millions of middle-class and even working-class voters in 1924 thanks to its staunch "anti-system" stand, proved inhospitable to workers and employees once the arch-reactionary Alfred Hugenberg assumed control in 1928.

Each political season brought a new group of secessionists who bolted the party. An unlikely array of parliamentary fragments, often richly hyphenated, emerged to seize power from the party bosses: the middle-class Wirtschaftspartei had competed in national elections since 1920 but emerged as a major irritant after 1924; by 1930 a Christlich-Nationale Bauern- und Landvolkpartei (Christian National Peasants' and Farmers' Party), a Christlich-sozialer Volksdienst (Christian-Social People's Service), a Konservative Volkspartei (Conservative People's Party), a Volksnationale Reichsvereinigung (People's National Reich Association), and a Reichspartei für Volksrecht und Aufwertung (People's Justice Party) had joined the fray. The orthodox fiscal policies of each of the older middle-class parties in the early 1930s compromised even further their ability to help those voters who remained loyal.

At first glance, the German party system appeared to be in a state of near total disarray. This was certainly the view from Berlin. Having failed to cobble together a unified nationalist program and beleaguered at the grassroots both by the incessant activity of the nationalist groups and by the breakaway slates of dissatisfied special interests, party organizations crumbled, party treasuries dried up. Members stopped coming to meetings, volunteers could not be enlisted to distribute propaganda, and speakers faced embarrassingly empty assembly halls. As early as 1926 a liberal in Hildesheim reported that "all nationalist men" eagerly joined patriotic associations but avoided the parties, which were viewed with growing antipathy. "There was nothing worse than a political party"—that summarized the view of locals in small-town Gandersheim, near Braunschweig.[53] Not surprisingly, parliamentarians felt increasingly uncomfortable on the campaign trail. At one point, a Landvolk activist turned to the German Nationalist Reichstag deputy with whom he shared the stage in Aurich and, to the loud applause of the audience, sputtered: "Only by the grace of God are you still tolerated among us."[54]

In this atmosphere local activists could do little more than urge Berlin politicians to "convince the Stahlhelm and the Jungdo," from above, "to assume a more friendly attitude toward the parties." Unfortunately for the parties there were few remedies. More than 300 branches of the German People's Party in Braunschweig in 1920 had shriveled to 100 in 1925 and only 33 in 1929. The collapse of the German Democratic Party was even more drastic; except in southwestern Germany, all that was left of the party in 1930 was regional executive committees. The German National People's Party maintained a local presence, but party activists reported declining memberships and lack of interest. "Our party is slowly dying out," lamented one German Nationalist in the party stronghold of Potsdam; the older prewar generation remained loyal, but younger people had drifted to the more active programs of the nationalist leagues or the National Socialists.[55] On the campaign trail in the weeks before the 1930 Reichstag elections, which were widely regarded as a turning point in the long-term fate of the parliamentary government and generated above-average voter turnout (81.5 percent versus 74.6 percent just two years earlier), the established bourgeois parties were nowhere to be seen. They published incendiary advertisements in the paper but only rarely held public meetings.[56] In this case, the medium was the message.

The dissolution of the liberal and conservative parties was only one part of the story, however. The very forces that had weakened the major parties also emboldened and enlivened a wide range of middle-class constituencies and "Tory" workers who insisted on influence and representation. Landvolk protests and breakaway slates attested to the organizational capacities of the very farmers, artisans, and small shopkeepers whom the parties had treated in such patronizing fashion. Since 1918 middle-class groups had acquired growing political power, and both their lobbying efforts inside the big parties and their independent lists outside the parties reflected growing strength, not powerlessness. It would also be misleading to regard the proliferation of splinter parties simply as the material egoism of occupational groups. To be sure, many Germans sought more effective representation of their particular interests in single-issue parties. But more often than not they expressed general disgust at political parties, lobbying efforts, and parliamentary horsetrading. The new parties proved to be attractive to voters because they expressed public outrage at the narrowly pro-business politics of the big bourgeois parties. It was splinter formations which embellished a political rhetoric that stressed constitutional rights and public goods and represented a refreshingly moral vision of the nation.[57]

What the appearance of the Landvolk signaled was that successful middle-class politics had to recognize the demands of previously muted groups such as small farmers, white-collar employees, and artisans for a political voice. Protests in the street, where individuals came together in an undifferentiated crowd, expressed the same anti-elite sentiments. Parties that did not adhere to this populist sentiment fell apart, as was the case of the so-called postwar people's parties, the German People's Party and the German National People's Party, as well as the German Democratic Party. Even the Stahlhelm lost some of its considerable political authority because it opposed splinter parties in the name of nationalist unity. To rally around the flag was not enough to hold on to voters who since 1914 judged their political surroundings according to the standard of the Volksgemeinschaft. German voters were looking for social reform as well as national pride, the classic populist combination.

In the end, however, the Landvolk protests remained merely an episode in German history. Relations between farmers in the countryside and businessowners in town deteriorated when the Landvolk tried to strike at Berlin and Hamburg by boycotting retailers in Husum and Aurich. Moreover, single-issue movements like the Landvolk were caught in a basic paradox. Although they invoked the common weal, they did so on a rather narrow political platform. Splinter parties expressed impatience at the rule of special interests by proliferating single interests. As a result they did not represent a lasting resolution to the widespread resentments of voters. In the late 1920s voters flocked to the small parties to express popular anger at the established ones, but they readily abandoned them once the inability of new groups to rebuild the political community or resist the socialists became apparent. Nonetheless, as middle-class voters moved around, casting ballots for special interest parties, joining the large party of nonvoters, marching with the Stahlhelm, auditing the speeches of political radicals such as the Nazis, there was one place to which they never returned: the established bourgeois parties, which at no point recovered their losses in the 1920s. For all the volatility of German politics, the traditional parties did not revive.

ENTER THE NAZIS

Stahlhelm marches and Landvolk protests were the two counterpoints of middle-class radicalism during the Weimar Republic. On the one hand, provincial burghers cherished the nation and identified with its fate. In homespun festivals and ceremonies, they not only honored the war effort and the grand imperial destiny it had unveiled and denounced infringements on German sovereignty but enforced nationalist unity against a supposedly unpatriotic, treasonous Left. Patriotic activity throughout the 1920s sought to retrieve the national solidarity of August 1914. In light of this, it seems clear that millions of voters were looking for political identities more encompassing than that of occupation. On the other hand, more and more Germans insisted on democratic political forms in which all groups had a place of honor and social interests were considered. Even if middle-class activists detested the republic, the demonstrations they led and the independent lists they cobbled together built on the popular legacy of November 1918. Citizens made good use of the newfangled constitutional rhetoric of rights and entitlements. It was obvious that there was no going back to the deferential politics of the prewar era.

That German politics remained so volatile during the 1920s was due to the different emphases both voters and candidates put on the idea of the Volksgemeinschaft. There were plenty of groups giving ample voice to patriotic sentiments, to anti-socialist fears, and to anti-elite resentments, but few struck the right balance. Hugenberg's German Nationalists proudly hoisted the red-black-white banner of the German Empire, but too often dismayed voters by their reactionary stance on social issues. Although Freikorps veterans won accolades for smashing the Communists, they fit poorly into the rounds of small-town social life. The Landvolk made the right populist noises, but proved too parochial. Stahlhelmers worked hard to create nationalist unity and had grandiose visions of Germany's political future, yet remained fixed on the traditional parties. What most burghers, and a great many workers besides, were looking for was a political movement that was unabashedly nationalist, forward-looking, and socially inclusive, that recognized the populist claims of constituents without redividing them on the basis of occupation. The party that adhered most closely to this formula was Adolf Hitler's National Socialist German Workers' Party.

The Nazis were familiar fixtures in nationalist politics even before their electoral breakthrough in September 1930. Since the November Revolution racist groups of one sort or another had existed in most Germans towns, cranking out cheap and scurrilous anti-Semitic pamphlets, spinning dark apocalyptic tales when economic times turned bad, sponsoring speakers such as Ludwig Münchmeyer, a defrocked minister from the tiny island of Borkum who entertained thousands with his stories about the government's attempts to prosecute him. But for the most part these groups eschewed electoral politics and preferred the boozy intimacy of weekly *Bierabende* (beer nights).

They remained trapped in a prewar world that was as anti-urban and anti-industrial as it was anti-Semitic.

Adolf Hitler, a habitué of Vienna's men's hostels before the war, moved easily in these circles. But Hitler, who had grown up politically during the world war, had greater ambitions. His vision of a racially pure, economically productive, and militarily powerful Germany led him to seek larger and larger audiences, to engage socialist workers, and to slowly build the machinery of a mass political movement. He joined Anton Drexler's minuscule German Workers' Party in Munich in 1919 but quickly tired of the clubbish atmosphere into which a few angry men had retreated. A skilled activist and a superb orator, Hitler emerged as a charismatic leader in the renamed National Socialist German Workers' Party, though he alienated many of the older "pioneers," as Joseph Goebbels later dismissively labeled them, in his relentless drive to transform a debating society into a disciplined party.[58]

Hitler was a revolutionary who prized authority and organization. His political skills made him "the king of Munich" in 1922 and 1923, the most incendiary right-wing orator in the very polarized Bavarian capital. Nonetheless his basic miscalculation in the Beerhall Putsch of November 1923 nearly wrecked the Nazi movement. An amateurish production that rested on a stunning exaggeration of Hitler's sway over other people's troops, namely Kahr's Bavarian police units and Seekt's Reichswehr soldiers, the putsch ended in a melodramatic trial that gave the Nazi unparalleled publicity. Previously an exclusively Bavarian personality, Hitler generated headlines across Germany, earning a measure of admiration by taking full responsibility for his actions and declaiming the nobility of his treason against what he regarded as a corrupt republican system.

More important, the putsch prompted Hitler to reorient the Nazi movement away from Freikorps conspiracies toward mass politics. It was not so much Mussolini's March on Rome in October 1922 but the German Revolution in November 1918 that provided Hitler with a working model for political insurgency. In his view, National Socialists had to replicate the accomplishments of Social Democrats, who had organized on a massive scale and, as a consequence, acquired the ability to paralyze the Reich (just as Hitler believed they had done in 1918). After his release from Landsberg Prison in December 1924, Hitler worked systematically to create a disciplined movement that would overwhelm rather than overthrow German democracy.[59] Hitler therefore had two great resources: the sympathy of thousands of disaffected voters thanks to the wide publicity of his headline-fetching trial, and the resolve to organize that support in a broad-based political campaign.

Hitler returned to political life to find the Nazi party in shambles. It took two years to reassert his authority and rally wayward members. More favorable economic conditions after the stabilization of the currency also worked against Hitler's apocalyptic political pronouncements. But it would be misleading to summarize the period 1924–1929 as "years in the wilderness."[60] The Nazis may have languished at the polls, but they achieved remarkable success reorganizing the party and arousing the curiosity of voters. In these five years more than one in every five German voters switched party allegiances, doing so even as the economy recovered and Germany's international position improved as the result of the Dawes Plan and the Locarno Treaty. Thousands continued to declare their hostility to the Weimar Republic by voting for splinter parties, crowding Stahlhelm rallies, and, it turns out, listening to National Socialist speeches.

In just the first year of reorganization (1925), Nazis managed to hold more than 2,370 public meetings across Germany.[61] Hitler's first public appearance after the putsch was scheduled for eight o'clock on the evening of 27 February 1925. The first people gathered in Munich's Bürgerbräukeller in mid-afternoon and by six the police closed the hall, which was filled to capacity with 4,000 visitors. Two thousand more had to be turned away.[62] In Braunschweig, one of the few states where Hitler was not prohibited from making public appearances in the years before 1927, special trains had to be pressed into service to bring thousands of citizens from outlying towns into the provincial capital to hear the racist rebeller speak in November 1925. In Oldenburg Nazis held almost monthly meetings throughout the mid-1920s. Turnouts exceeded 1,000 people when well-known personalities such as Hitler or Goebbels spoke. On two occasions in March 1927 Oldenburg's largest hall, the Unionsaal, was jammed to capacity hours before National Socialist speakers arrived.

A correspondent for *Deutsches Volkstum,* a nationalist but nonpartisan monthly, gave a breathless description of a 1927 rally in Hamburg:[63]

> Half an hour before the beginning of the meeting, hundreds of people pressed against the entrance to the hall . . . thanks to popular demand, the meeting had been switched to one of the largest halls in Hamburg. It was already was difficult to get tickets at 3 marks; all the 1 mark tickets had already

been snapped up. The assembly grows quieter from minute to minute. Whispered conversations indicate the growing excitement of the masses. Many people are standing on chairs in order to see Hitler arriving. Ushers announce that hundreds are still standing outside and ask that those standing move closer together to give room to those waiting . . . Perhaps only a third of those present are connected to the party; most came out of curiosity.

Nazis enjoyed big receptions in small towns as well. A full Kaisersaal, Goslar's largest assembly hall, welcomed local National Socialist orators in September 1925. Moreover, bourgeois newspapers usually reported on these events sympathetically.[64] All this commotion stirred middle-class neighborhoods long before the onset of economic hard times. By 1928, writes Karl Dietrich Bracher, a phalanx of 100,000 National Socialists had constituted "tightly knit cadres" in all parts of Germany. A year later the party counted 3,400 party branches, more than half as many as organized by either the German Democratic or the German People's Party at their high-water mark in 1919–20. Between April 1929 and May 1930 the Nazis trained an astonishing 2,000 speakers to canvass precincts across the Reich. Despite an unimpressive 2.6 percent showing in the 1928 Reichstag elections, it does not seem appropriate to refer to the National Socialist German Workers' Party as a small, irrelevant political entity.[65] Germans may have refrained from voting for the party, but they were listening.

The Nazis have sometimes been mistaken for marginal types, World War I veterans who failed to complete their university studies, young men who drifted from one job to another, maladroit loners who discovered in the party's uncompromising stance a cause and an identity. This outsider status is certainly true to the extent that early Nazis worked outside the clubby framework of bourgeois politics. But it would be erroneous to think that Hitler's men looked or acted different or were generally alien to bourgeois sociability. National Socialists participated in local club life and joined patriotic ceremonies, certainly far more so than Freikorpsmen had in the early 1920s. Before the party's electoral breakthrough in 1930, 46 Nazis in the Hessian town of Marburg belonged to 73 other organizations, mostly church groups, choirs, and interest groups. Obviously not all Nazis used every social occasion to talk up the party, but discussions at the regular's table at the tavern, between shifts at the workplace, and during the congenial rounds of club meetings undoubtedly passed along the party's message.[66] Like other club members, the Nazis sought to appear hospitable and neighborly, sponsoring band concerts, Founding Day celebrations, and Christmas parties. In Bavarian Günzberg, for example, the Nazis adhered to local custom and erected a maypole each year. In Lower Saxony they held "Hermann Löns Evenings" to commemorate the popular poet, a native son.[67] Embedded in provincial social life, Nazis could easily draw a crowd if they had the right issue. For example, local Nazis took quick advantage of small-town tempests: a school board election that areligious socialists contested in Northeim; the suspension of antirepublican teachers in Goslar.

For millions of burghers who in the mid-1920s marched with the Stahlhelm, abandoned the established parties, and cast their votes for dissident slates of one kind or another, the National Socialists were not a forbidding presence or an extremist party. It is not so much a question of Germans moving to a well-defined but previously distasteful Nazi position. Rather, Nazi activists, over the course of the reconstruction of the party after 1925, appeared more and more frequently in neighborhood settings, and neighbors became more and more aware of the Nazis' organizational talents and the party's political resolve. Nazis did not take over innocent townspeople in some sort of audacious invasion; they gave sharp political definition to imprecisely held affinities and frustrated expectations. Suddenly the road ahead seemed clear. For German Nationalists such as Elisabeth Gebensleben, the wife of Braunschweig's deputy mayor, politics became all-consuming—"reading the newspaper, I turn first to politics, then the features"—and political rewards were increasingly tied to the forward movement of the National Socialists, who had picked up such "magnificent momentum" by 1930.[68]

The finely spun organizational efforts of the Nazis paid off in just a few years, though beginnings were always modest. "I made my debut in Andernach, a small town in southern Germany," remembered one Nazi. "In the evening we marched from village to village . . . often we had to run around a week before we could obtain the use of a hall. Once we had the meeting place, we had to start looking for a speaker."[69] In Northeim it was four young men who took the initiative in spring of 1929, organizing weekly meetings at the Cattle Auction Hall. Only a handful of curious townspeople attended the first discussions on "national socialism" and the party program. But each Monday more and more visitors took seats; attendance soon averaged around forty. It was not long before the party enrolled fifteen new members.[70] All at once, in Andernach, in Northeim, the party seemed to come alive—not as an interloper prowling about a bucolic small-town setting, but rather as a familiar competitor in a place already roiled by socialist revolutionaries, Landvolk agitators, and Stahlhelm marchers.

Despite a disappointing 2.6 percent share in the June 1928 Reichstag elections, the Nazis improved their showing over the course of 1929. Historians have generally assumed that Adolf Hitler's participation that year in the anti–Young Plan effort, the *Reichsausschuss für das Deutsche Volksbegehren*, alongside such political bigshots as the German Nationalist Alfred Hugenberg and the Stahlhelm commander Franz Seldte gave the party desperately needed funds, free publicity, and political legitimacy. Without the effort of conservatives against Weimar's policy of international reconciliation, the argument goes, the Nazis would have remained a fringe group. But on closer analysis it seems that very little money flowed to the Nazis. Hugenberg's press empire hardly reported on Hitler's speeches, and National Socialists spent most of their time fighting for votes in local elections rather than drumming up signatures against the Young Plan.

Indeed, Hitler's appearance in the Reichsausschuss was probably a result of his growing authority, from which Hugenberg hoped to profit. After all, every election since 1924 indicated that Hugenberg and his party were in trouble. By 1929 the Nazis were the primary beneficiaries of German Nationalist defections. In contrast to the more patrician leadership of the bourgeois parties, which did not feel compelled to fight for votes despite mounting evidence of voter dissatisfaction, the Nazis held 1,300 meetings in the last thirty days before Saxony's May 1929 Landtag elections and doubled their vote share to 5 percent. In October the party leaped to a 7 percent share in Baden (up from 2.9 in 1928) and two months later to over 11 percent in Thuringia (up from 3.7). Municipal elections in Prussia told the same story. German Nationalists were trumped in Hanover and Wiesbaden. Even in left-wing Berlin the National Socialists garnered nearly 140,000 votes, a personal success for Berlin's *Gauleiter* Joseph Goebbels, for whom the tally was nothing less than an "overwhelming victory."[71] By the end of 1929 political momentum was with the National Socialists, whose gains came mainly at the expense of the traditional nationalist parties.

Basic elements of the Nazi message spoke to the political aspirations that burghers had held for more than ten years. In the first place, the Nazis were unmistakably opposed to the Social Democrats, whom they accused of betraying the German people and trafficking with corrupt Jewish-tainted "big capitalists." Like Stahlhelm marches, Nazi events demonstrated the power of young nationalists and their willingness to take on and beat up the socialists. "Radiating determination and self-discipline," exulted one of Saxony's small-town papers, the *Waldheimer Tageblatt*, the SA "marchers made a good impression." According to the liberal *Chemnitzer Allgemeine Zeitung*, a Nazi rally in June 1930 proceeded with "exemplary order"; "above all, the party's struggle is aimed against Marxism."[72] Again and again the Nazis attracted support by "generating an image of a young, virile, uncompromising political movement—an image which was embodied in the SA," the violent stormtroopers who attacked and conquered "red" taverns, "red" neighborhoods, and "red" citadels such as Berlin and Braunschweig.[73] Violence against alleged enemies of the nation, most obviously Social Democrats and Communists but later Jews and also Slavs and other non-Germans, was central both to Nazi tactics and Nazi ideology.

At the same time, the National Socialists tried hard to fit into the folksy sociability that burghers had created since the end of the war. More convincingly than other right-wing groups, the Nazis welcomed participants from all social classes, especially workers. Moreover, the growing cadre of National Socialist speakers made themselves expert in the most local farm or tax issues as they traveled around the countryside and demonstrated an ability to discuss bread-and-butter issues with just about anybody, a tactic designed not so much to better represent material interests but to win credibility as ordinary fellows who understood the proverbial "man on the street." Wandering speakers like Oldenburg's Jan Blankenmeyer, who spoke in Plattdeutsch or low German, and Hinrich Lohse, Gau leader in Schleswig-Holstein, had a genuine populist touch that was probably much more important than the specific proposals they made to occupational groups. Versed in the customs of tavern sociability, open to sympathizers without respect to status, the Nazis appeared to millions of Protestants and Catholics as representatives of a genuine people's party. In any event they seldom made the German Nationalist mistake of holding political meetings in the best hotel in town.

Just a look at the activity of stormtroopers indicates how appealing the Nazi social message might have been. In hard economic times when the social welfare programs of the state were being cut back and proved woefully inadequate, the Nazis erected a "rudimentary shadow welfare state" for their supporters, responding to the crisis in a concrete way. During the autumn 1930 Reichstag campaign, for example, Berlin's police noted that "food was collected energetically and distributed to stormtroopers," a provision that continued after the election to "long-serving SA men in larger units." During a metalworkers' strike, striking party members were fed three times daily in Nazi pubs. Women's groups associated with the party were particularly active. Königsberg Nazis sang their praises in a revealing summary of local political life:[74]

> The twelve female party members of 1931 would not have been able to cope with the steadily growing volume of welfare work for jobless party members and SA men and their families, however much they tried. However, it went without saying that the Nazi Women's Group included the wives and daughters of party members, even if the former were not themselves members. Thus the countless tasks: organizing the SA hostel, food and clothing collections, Christmas gifts, care of the ill and the imprisoned, first aid duty at meetings etc. could always be mastered with a larger body of helpers.

The robust activism of members reiterated the message that the party was committed to bettering the lives of ordinary Germans; by contrast, the established bourgeois parties simply reinforced their reputation for immobility since their campaigns lacked dynamism. Here was a genuine people's party, remarked the *Werdauer Zeitung* about a Nazi rally in March 1930: "The worker, the master artisan, the civil servant, the farmer, they were all present, and not," the editors added, "as representatives of this or that interest group."[75] The party's commitment to organize even the most isolated valleys underscored the same point. To be sure, the Nazis failed to get their message into every small town, but in the months before the 1930 Reichstag elections they got a lot further than any other party, save perhaps for the Social Democrats. Saxony's National Socialists, for example, held an astonishing 2,000 meetings in September 1930 alone.[76] Compared to the established bourgeois parties, which remained aloof, the Nazis sought out Germans where they were to be found: in taverns, soccer fields, and market squares. These appearances lent credibility to Hitler's repeated rhetorical identification with the tribulations of ordinary Germans.

For all the neighborliness, however, the Nazis insisted that theirs was a political movement with a national purpose. National Socialist speeches and propaganda repudiated the narrow politics of the "reactionary" bourgeois parliamentarians and the proliferating interest groups and splinter parties. In speech after speech Hitler was quite clear about this. Throughout the countryside his followers tended to address voters as citizens at mass rallies, rather than as blocs or constituents of interest groups, and hammered in again and again the need to solve local problems by liberating the entire nation from republican misrule.[77] National solidarity was the answer to Germany's vexing problems: social reform, economic productivity, the shameful peace. There was a deliberate attempt to enroll Germans in a collective destiny and to present Hitler as a national savior rather than a solicitous politician.

Nazi propaganda very effectively portrayed political choices in utopian terms: here was a party that stood inalterably opposed to the present "system" and, once in power, would rebuild the nation. "Der Schritt auf die Strasse"—the sights and sounds of party members marching in the streets, rallying in the assembly hall, canvassing a neighborhood—all delivered the same message of dynamism and movement. Party instructions urged local activists to build up their organizational efforts toward a "big German evening," which would feature the SA and the SA band and thereby make "a big impact" with banners, flags, symbols, uniforms, songs, and the "Heil Hitler" greeting. Whether in small assemblies in the village "Cattle Auction Hall" or the mass spectacles in Berlin's Sportpalast, the party repeatedly rehearsed its seizure of power.[78]

This aesthetic of mobilization very effectively declared a state of emergency in which sides had to be chosen, decisions made, sacrifices accepted, strong-armed actions undertaken, all of which revealed the new nation in formation. "There was a feeling of restless energy about the Nazis," remembered one woman. "You constantly saw the swastika painted on the sidewalks or found them littered by pamphlets." This housewife in Northeim, and many others besides, was "drawn by the feeling of strength about the party, even though there was much in it which was highly questionable."[79] On the day after a big Hitler rally in Braunschweig, in which burghers had decorated the city in patriotic colors and thousands of Nazis marched on the castle grounds and later marauded proletarian districts, Elisabeth Gebensleben wrote to her daughter in Holland: "You wouldn't believe *what* has happened to Braunschweig, our quiet old city . . . we are living as Germans, proud and free. Germany is really awakening."[80] Specifics did not matter as much as the willingness of the Nazis to turn over a new page in the history of the nation. Better than any other political movement, the Nazis choreographed Germany's new beginning.

THE NAZI REVOLUTION

In the late 1920s German middle-class neighborhoods were at the center of a full-fledged populist insurrection. The extended Haedicke-Rauch-Gebensleben family illustrates the politicization that had taken place. Bertha's concern at the end of 1918 that burghers would not take matters into their own hands had given way in 1924 to Eberhard's exuberant activity on behalf of German Nationalists and the Stahlhelm, and, finally, in 1931, to Elisabeth's delirious enthusiasm for the Nazis. In these circumstances the republic and the democratic parties which supported it enjoyed precious little legitimacy. Struggles over which flag to fly, the red-black-white banner of the empire, under which so many men had died in the war, or the venerable red-black-gold colors of 1848, consumed daily politics. Over time these struggles turned increasingly dangerous. Political movements of all sorts made effective use of the streets, creating ever more compelling visual and acoustic propaganda. Social Democrats, organized in the Reichsbanner, and the Stahlhelm confronted each other as armed paramilitary formations. So many citizens had joined political armies of the Left and Right that the novelist Ernst Glaeser could refer to his alienated Weimar-era hero as "the last civilian."[81] At the same time, the established parties had fallen apart, particularly on the local level, giving way to an array of dissident groups. All this had already taken place before the first electoral successes of the Nazis in 1929 and 1930.

Yet it was the National Socialist German Workers' Party and not another "national socialist" group which startled political observers by amassing 18 percent of the vote in the late summer of 1930 and consolidating the populist rebellion of recent years. And it was the Nazis who emerged as Germany's largest party in 1932 and 1933 and thereby acquired the strongest formal claim to lead the government. Why did the Nazis accomplish what the Stahlhelm, the Landvolk, or even Hugenberg's quite strident German Nationalist People's Party could not? In other words, how did the Nazis distinguish themselves from other movements; in what way were they a more innovative or effective political force? To answer this question is to propose the appeal of the Nazi phenomenon.

Two important matters have to be kept in mind. In the first place, splinter parties and single-issue campaigns could not help being part of the very political immobility they decried. As middle-class constituents lost faith in the representation of occupational interests through the established bourgeois parties, they retreated from thinking in *ständisch* (or corporate) terms altogether. Speaking a morally drenched language of corruption, betrayal, and virtue, they came to identify their own interests and needs with national political renewal. A substantial minority of workers came to similar conclusions about the Social Democratic Party, which seemed more and more tied to the government in Berlin and became associated more and more with the economic calamities of the early 1930s. As a result the major parties, which had approached voters mostly as constituents of particular occupations; the interest groups, which had been among the most active voluntary associations after the revolution; and even the splinter parties, which had served as vehicles of protest of first resort—all these faltered and lost influence.

By contrast, the Nazis, with their mass rallies and apocalyptic rhetoric, created a political forum in which the nation could be reimagined as a nationalist whole in which every (non-Jewish) German regardless of status had a place of honor and was accordingly enrolled in a dazzling, prosperous future. They developed an image of themselves as a party that was constructive, that would move forward and bring Germans together in a militant Volksgemeinschaft reminiscent of August 1914.[82] It was a populism that promised to go beyond liberal institutions to recover an essential and enabling national identity. No other party appeared as opposed to special interest politics or as open to lower-middle-class and working-class Germans, and no other party recreated the spectacle of the resurgent nation in mass rallies and marches in such compelling fashion.

The insistent invocation of Volksgemeinschaft also appealed to middle-class women, who believed that the project of national salvation would provide them with the public roles and responsibilities they had enjoyed during the war. In the years that followed the war the progressive ideal of independence remained unfulfilled while the traditional parties ended up neglecting the women they had solicited so eagerly in the first campaigns of the Weimar Republic. While the Nazis regarded themselves as soldiers of the Fatherland first, the party's emphasis on youth, sports, and community work seemed to leave room for women to play a substantial role in the national revolution.[83]

In the second place, the Nazis also profited from the increasingly reactionary politics of the German Nationalists and the Stahlhelm. The German National People's Party probably had a fair chance to transform itself into a genuinely popular party of opposition. With more than one-fifth of the electorate in

1924, its social base was not so different from that of the Nazis eight years later. The party had been rather successful in garnering votes from "Tory" workers and white-collar employees. In fact working-class Berliners gave the German Nationalists most of the votes the party collected in the capital; nationally, only the Social Democrats had a larger proletarian electorate in 1924.[84] However, the German Nationalists squandered their opportunity by pursuing what voters saw as excessively probusiness policies in the years that followed. "I had some regard for the parties of the right on the grounds of their 'nationalism,'" recalled one early convert to the Nazis, "but I missed the right attitude toward the people—the willingness to help."[85] German Nationalists were also very much tied to the past, going so far as to refer to the post-1918 period in exclusively prewar terms, as a "kaiserlosen Zeit," an interregnum.[86] Alfred Hugenberg, Ruhr industrialist, press baron, and notorious Pan-German, gave the party a radical jolt after he assumed leadership in 1928, but his rise offended as many people as it inspired. He was a determined politician but, born in 1865, could hardly be mistaken for a messenger of the new Germany. Hugenberg simply did not appeal to large numbers of young voters, the veterans of the war and the prewar baby boomers who were now reaching adulthood. In a word, the German Nationalists were greying. And it was to Hugenberg that the Stahlhelm linked itself, thus sealing its fate.

The onset of the Great Depression in 1929 only made the reasons not to vote for the special interest parties or the German Nationalists more persuasive. The truly drastic scale of the national emergency highlighted the pettiness of the splinter groups; neither frozen meat nor mortgage taxes could compare to the crisis of millions of unemployed. Against this background the Nazi insistence on radical change rather than more effective representation of interests appeared to make sense. At the same time, the massive numbers of unemployed Germans made the deflationary fiscal policies promoted by the German Nationalists distinctly unattractive. Compared to Hugenberg, Hitler spoke in a pronounced future and active tense.

Nothing better revealed the National Socialists' success in linking themselves with the idea of the Volksgemeinschaft and in distancing themselves from reactionary forces than their efforts to attract German workers. From the very beginning the inclusion of the word "workers" in the party name set the National Socialist German Workers' Party apart and gave it cachet among young Germans for whom the icons of worker and soldier symbolized the wartime contributions of ordinary Germans. "National socialism" conjured up the collaborative efforts of the war. And it was not only workers in "low-tech" industrial regions where firms were small and widely scattered and where the socialist activists had trouble finding a foothold but also many one-time Social Democrats who found the Nazi invocation of the Volksgemeinschaft attractive. Recent research has shown that nearly one-third of Nazi members and Nazi voters were workers, many of them industrial workers. In the 1932 elections the Nazis made significant inroads into the Social Democratic camp—one of every ten Nazi voters in the summer was an ex–Social Democrat—although the bulk of the party's labor support came from Protestant, churchgoing workers who had never considered themselves socialists.[87]

How do we make sense of the surprisingly large working-class vote for the Nazis, which until recently scholars have simply missed? In an age of mass mobilization, class came less and less to determine political allegiances. The long war turned out to be a fundamental experience, even for Social Democrats, who in the main cherished their inclusion in the national community and who commemorated the endeavors and sacrifices that qualified them as full citizens. The Reichsbanner, the Social Democratic counterpart to the Stahlhelm, honored the war effort, if not the war, and played an active role in patriotic politics, demonstrating in favor of Anschluss with Austria at its annual rally in Magdeburg in 1925 and celebrating the Allied evacuation of the Rhineland in Cologne in 1930. At the same time, many workers found attractive the Nazi message that national solidarity, economic productivity, and imperial aspirations could deliver the good life to all Germans. For them a genuine Volksgemeinschaft made class separatism unnecessary. As long as the Social Democrats were unable to speak to the national allegiances of workers, who as much as other citizens were tied to the landscape, the customs, and the history of Germany, their broad support remained vulnerable.[88] Even the Communists, who were much more closely identified with proletarian internationalism, played the nationalist card to rally support against the imperialistic peace of Versailles and the French occupation of the Ruhr.

The Nazis also profited from the strategic mistakes of the Social Democrats, who, during the Great Depression, seemed more intent on protecting the benefits of (still) employed workers than on offering radical solutions to the general crisis. Despite its revolutionary pedigree, the party looked increasingly like a big special interest group. By contrast, it was the Nazis who exuberantly adopted the socialist-inspired work-creation plan which Social Democratic leaders rejected as irresponsibly inflationary. Particularly in the July 1932 elections, the Nazis trumpeted the slogan "Arbeit und Brot." "Work and Bread" was also the title of Gregor Strasser's widely publicized Reichstag speech on 10 May 1932 (reprinted in a run of hundreds of thousands of copies) in which the left-leaning Nazi spoke up for the "anticapitalist yearnings" of three-quarters of the nation and the emancipatory struggle of "the people" against "the state" and promised food for "everyone" and the organization of "national work." Hitler echoed these sentiments in the 1932 campaigns, backpedaling his racialist objectives, appealing instead to the widespread desire to overcome partisan and class differences.[89]

Better than any other party, the Nazis were able to insert the desire for social reform into a national frame, and the more frantic their outbursts the more resolute and uncompromised they appeared. Young people, housewives, and even industrial workers perceived the Nazis to be on the side of "social justice"—these exact words appear again and again in oral histories and contemporary interviews.[90] The Nazi message was brutal, and to many observers it appeared self-serving and propagandistic; nonetheless, it has to be remembered that thousands of Germans were drawn to the movement out of idealism and enthusiastically responded to the task of renovating the nation. As for the Social Democrats, they failed to respond with positive demands of their own. Over and over, "their Marxism deterred them from tinkering with capitalism,"[91] and yet their rigorous rationalism kept them from elaborating their indisputably humane social values into a more compelling utopian vision. As a result, at least half a million

German workers, including many old Social Democrats, voted for the Nazi party by the end of 1932.

At the same time, only the most disciplined Social Democrats comprehended the party's toleration of Heinrich Brüning, the so-called Hunger Chancellor. And, again, it was the Nazis who promised to break with the undemocratic "system" and did so with a dynamic political style. In their view both Social Democrats and social reactionaries had failed the nation by adhering to the caste mentalities that National Socialism would finally overcome. In the minds of more and more Germans, workers as well as burghers, Protestants as well as Catholics, the Nazis stood for renewal, their opponents for reaction and compromise; they spoke for the people, their opponents through corrupt interest groups, inept bureaucracies, and a distant, distracted chancellory.[92] The system seemed so broken, its defenders in such disarray, and the brownshirts so vigorous and well organized that many people, whether sympathizers or not, simply took the Nazi seizure of power for granted.[93]

At the end of 1932 the Nazis were the only acceptable party for the non-Marxist and non-Catholic voters who constituted the majority of German voters. That none of the other rightwing parties came close to challenging the National Socialists indicates just how insistently voters seemed to want fundamental change. The Nazis did not win by being similar to but by being different from their competitors in the bourgeois fold. As Hitler stated again and again: "The nationalists on the right lacked social awareness, the socialists on the left lacked national awareness."[94] This position reflected a genuine break with Germany's established political institutions. The Stahlhelm had at first tentatively and the National Socialists later much more successfully broken the confines of bourgeois politics not only by organizing in a public manner which addressed Germans as individuals and citizens rather than members of corporate entities but also by opening up their ranks to lower-class citizens, conscripts as well as officers, workers as well as shopkeepers, uniformed clerks as well as professionals. They reimagined the nation as the decisive subject in history and responded both to nationalist yearnings and to the social reformist impulses that wartime experiences had legitimized. National Socialism was thus the culmination of a process of popular mobilization going back to 1914 and beyond and cannot simply be seen as the outgrowth of economic catastrophe and political trauma. While National Socialism was not the inevitable culmination of political trends since World War I, it was a recognizable legatee.

The National Socialists constituted Germany's largest and most socially diverse party on 30 January 1933. However, Hitler did not sway all voters. Indeed a majority of German voters did not cast their cast ballots for the Nazis. In July 1932 the Nazis received 37.4 percent of the vote; in the not-so-free elections of March 1933, still only 43.9 percent. Three political cultures proved more or less resistant to National Socialism: the Social Democrats, although they suffered serious incursions over the course of 1932; the Communists; and the Catholic Center Party. In large cities, especially, a well-developed socialist culture kept working-class communities politically intact. In many smaller towns, where farmers and workers constituted two clearly separate milieus, Social Democrats resisted the Nazis as well. Nonetheless the tendency was clear: Social Democrats were losing supporters both to the Communists on their Left and to the Nazis on their Right. The Communists resisted the National Socialists as well, not least because their electorate was drawn so strongly from the long-term unemployed and other marginalized economic sectors. Most immune to the Nazis, however, were provincial Catholic voters in Upper Silesia, Lower Bavaria, and northern Westphalia. But even here the Nazis made gains among Catholic smallholders and workers.[95] No party was as successful in breaking the social pattern of electoral behavior than the National Socialists, who in 1932 had a presence in almost every electoral precinct and were almost surely better represented than the "red" machine of the Social Democrats, their strongest competitor. The Nazi insurgency was broader than the spontaneous celebrations that greeted the war in July and August 1914 or the grassroots uprising against the Kaiserreich four years later. Modern German history had never before seen such an immense people's movement.

It has been a commonplace to regard the Nazi vote as reflecting basically lower-middle-class resentments and frustrations. Yet the notion that upper-class voters in affluent urban districts remained immune to Nazi appeals does not hold water. In fact the richer the precinct the higher the Nazi vote.[96] Even though a number of educated professionals privately disdained Hitler and his lower-middle-class followers, they supported the broad outlines of the national revolution. The vast majority of the bourgeois opponents of the Nazis did not rally to the republic (a figure like Thomas Mann is the exception) and continued to hope for its demise. For this reason modest Nazi losses in elections in November and December 1932 cannot be taken as serious indications of a relaxation of political tensions: Hugenberg's German Nationalists were the primary beneficiaries, and they were hardly defenders of the constitution; in any case, they were not likely to hold on to these newly acquired voters, who would have gone on to search for more congenial "national social" alternatives of one sort or another. At the same time, the Social Democrats continued to lose votes, and other credible republicans, so-called "decent Germans," were hard to find.[97]

Given the political cavalcade of the year 1932—five exhausting election campaigns; on-again, off-again negotiations between Hitler and the successive Brüning, Papen, and Schleicher governments; erstwhile toleration of the government in June, a humiliating interview with Hindenburg in August, collaboration with the Communists in the Berlin transport strike of November, and the defection of Gregor Strasser in December—the party held together rather well. To be sure, the National Socialists were not unbreakable. Electoral support for the party was brittle and membership rolls turned over at a high rate. Yet it is worth noting that ex-Nazis neither became goodhearted republicans nor withdrew from politics, so the demise of the National Socialists would not have saved the Weimar Republic. Besides, disenchanted Nazi voters ended up offering the party their enthusiastic support after the seizure of power. Whether or not nationalists counted themselves as Hitlerites in 1933, they welcomed the Nazi Revolution as the culmination of their own varied efforts for political renovation, which they had pursued in a variety of arenas since the war.

In the most dramatic scenario—the collapse of Hitler's movement, which some historians believe was near at hand, or simply Hindenburg's refusal to appoint the Führer chancellor—stability would not have returned to the Weimar Republic because partisanship was based not on Nazi propaganda or on economic despair but on highly emotive images of the virtuous nation. Ideology mattered and was not about to go away. Of course, this is not to say that the world might not have been spared the brutality of National Socialism in power: there was nothing necessary about Hitler or the Holocaust. Nonetheless, all the efforts to define the contingent nature of Hitler's seizure of power in 1933 do not fundamentally alter the picture of the popular political dynamics outlined here.[98]

With the exception of Social Democrats and Communists, those who still did not vote for the Nazis in March 1933 agreed with those who did on the following points, expertly summed by Ian Kershaw: "virulent anti-Marxism and the perceived need for a powerful counter to the forces of the Left; deep hostility towards the failed democratic system and a belief that strong, authoritarian leadership was necessary for any recovery; and a widespread feeling, even extending to parts of the Left, that Germany had been badly wronged at Versailles."[99] Step by step, "Hitler won over that 'majority of the majority' which had not voted for him in 1933."[100]

However, one key plank in Hitler's world view was neither wholeheartedly shared nor completely understood by most voters; the racial vernacular of his Social Darwinism, his all-embracing anti-Semitism, and the stern eugenic administration such convictions implied may have moved true believers, but not party sympathizers.[101] Anti-Semitic prejudices were common currency among German Christians, certainly among the Gebenslebens, who routinely distinguished Germans from Jews in the belief that they were sorting out the good from the bad, but this did not dispose them to vote for Hitler over Hu-

genberg or do much to inspire their political enthusiasms.[102]
To say that Germans voted for the Nazi Party because it best
expressed a pervasive anti-Semitism in Weimar society is to
miss entirely the ways in which the Nazis set themselves apart
from other parties and thereby gave the electorate reasons to
vote for them. A majority of Germans exchanged party loyalties over the course of the Weimar Republic; anti-Semitism
had little to do with this volatility. To suggest otherwise is to
drain the Nazi phenomenon of all ideology. Nonetheless, the
brutal terms in which all nationalists regarded the enemies of
Germany and the correspondingly imperious way they defined
its future made most Germans complicit in the crimes of Nazism, leading them to accept Hitler's fully articulated racial
state after 1933 and to avert their gaze when the regime's an-
tipathies turned murderous.

The National Socialists did not win votes because they were
similar to the traditional middle-class parties, but because they
were so dissimilar. Nazis shared the anti-Marxism and hyper-
nationalism of the German Right, to be sure, yet they also
talked about the Germany's social and collective responsibilities, and they welcomed workers in their ranks. As a result
they offered a compelling vision of the nation as a solidaristic
entity that had little in common with the deferential hierarchies of the Second Reich, the hot-headed annexationism of
wartime Germany, or the interest-group entitlements of the
Weimar Republic. What was appealing about the Nazis was
their vision of a new nation premised on the Volk, which corresponded both to the populist nationalism of the middle
classes and to the socialist sensibilities of workers and which
left room for both individual desires for social mobility and

collective demands for social equality. That the collectivity was strictly defined in terms of race did not seriously impede its popular resonance and may have made it seem more substantial and more viable.

Although Hitler's appointment to the chancellorship at the end of January 1933 hinged on the closed-door negotiations of unrepentant reactionaries and out-and-out monarchists such as Paul von Hindenburg, Alfred Hugenberg, and especially Franz von Papen, Hitler would never have figured in their calculus had he not been the leader of Germany's largest party. Much as local elites such as landowners, merchants, and clergymen worked with and in due course legitimized the National Socialists, Nazi success rested on a broader populist uprising that had challenged and undercut the power of conservative notables throughout the 1920s. Already the Stahlhelm and the Landvolk had organized the community in more resourceful ways and thereby propelled more Germans into the public arena. The war effort had had similar consequences a decade earlier. Thus the National Socialist seizure of power in 1933 was the triumph of a "right-wing Jacobinism" in which a variety of working-class and middle-class groups sought political voice and policies of change in the name of the German nation.[103]

To regard, as so many observers still do, the Nazis as conservatives or reactionaries or the "petit-bourgeois" shock troops of big capital is to miss the destruction they wrought on the traditional parties and the insurgent forms of political legitimacy they validated. Their aggressive nationalism and virulent anti-Semitism and their elitist conception of leadership did not erase their populist and anti-capitalist appeal (nor does Nazism's broad appeal exculpate the racism, violence, and intolerance it promoted). Unfortunately, our view of how Weimar politics worked is still very much outlined by the savage pens of Kurt Tucholsky, John Heartfield, and George Grosz, who depicted Germany as *Teutschland,* a swastika-emblazoned preserve of stiff monarchists, bloodthirsty generals, monocled industrialists, and saber-scarred academicians who somehow combined to produce the horror of the Third Reich. Again and again, historians of the Weimar Republic quote Tucholsky's satires, reproduce Heartfield's photomontages, and put into words Grosz's etchings. Take the reminiscence of Hannah Arendt, for example: "George Grosz's cartoons seemed to us not satires but realistic reportage: we knew those types; they were all around us."[104]

Yet these observations completely obscure the essence of National Socialism, which amounted to a grassroots repudiation of Teutschland in the name of a renovated nation, the Third Reich. That Nazism appealed to the utopian yearnings of many German workers was just as incomprehensible to the Social Democratic daily *Vorwärts,* which headlined its ignorance of Nazism's popular support the day of Hitler's assumption to power: "Hitler-Papen Cabinet. 'The Well-to-Do' and Three Nazis—A Government of Big Capital."[105] Whatever compromises the Nazis made in the eyes of sympathizers, they were powerful only because they were perceived to be a basic alternative to Brüning and Hugenberg. It follows, then, that we cannot explain the appeal of National Socialism by merely pointing to German militarism, German nationalism, or even German authoritarianism. Familiar trajectories such as Luther to Hitler or Bismarck to Hitler fall short because they do not account for the key element to the Nazi rise to power, namely the unprecedented activism of so many ordinary Germans in the first three decades of the twentieth century and the legitimacy of that activism to attain political rights in the name of the German people.

The National Socialists embodied a broad but extremely vague desire for national renewal and social reform that neither Wilhelmine nor Weimar Germany had been able to satisfy. It is certainly true that disparate social constituents with a variety of pressing social and economic concerns made up the Nazi electorate. With this in mind, Martin Broszat argued that Nazism was "broad-based, not deeply rooted."[106] In similar fashion Thomas Childers describes support for the party as "a mile wide," but "at critical points an inch deep." Most voters, he concludes, were attracted to the Nazis out of "dissatisfaction, resentment, and fear."[107]

These explanations make sense in light of the chaotic conditions of the Great Depression, in which anguished voters bounced from one political messiah to another and were both attracted to and frustrated by the fury behind Hitler's denunciation of the Weimar Republic. But I find the assumption that hard times tossed about a basically self-absorbed electorate unsatisfactory. An examination of the National Socialists in the wider context of political insurgencies in the twentieth century, from July and August 1914, to November 1918, to Hindenburg's election in April 1925, suggests that German voters acted more coherently and more ideologically. Those voters who abandoned the National Socialists did not, by and large, return to the old middle-class parties. They remained sympathetic to the "National Opposition" whether articulated by

Hitler, by the Stahlhelm, or by other radical groups. In other words, they remained "national socialist" in orientation even if they were no longer National Socialists. Support for or opposition to the Nazis should not obscure the primary dynamic of German politics in the twentieth century, which was the formation of a radical nationalist plurality that repudiated the legacy of German conservatism as thoroughly as it rejected the promise of Social Democracy.

Over the course of the Weimar Republic, nationally minded Germans repeatedly sought out a politics that propounded an emphatically "national socialist" world view, one that promised Germany's economic and military resurgence as well as social reconciliation. The real fears of the Great Depression gave urgency to this search, but they did not initiate it. Throughout the 1920s both middle-class and working-class Germans mobilized to recreate the nation-state as a social compact, and they did so with considerable agility and confidence. For all the economic traumas of the Weimar period, the mind-boggling hyperinflation of 1922–1923 and the corrosive business collapse of 1930–1933, the figure of the desperate German voter has been exaggerated. Particularly on the Right, Germans proved much more resourceful and ideologically committed than the imagery of catastrophe would suggest.

National Socialists captured the political imagination of almost one in every two voters because they challenged the authoritarian legacy of the empire, rejected the class-based vision of Social Democrats and Communists, and both honored the solidarity and upheld the chauvinism of the nation at war. They thus twisted together strands from the political Left and the political Right without being loyal to the precepts of either camp. Mobilizing enormous energies and profound expectations for a new beginning, reimagining the nation as a new, fiercely nationalistic body politic, and willing to bloody the streets to realize their aims, the Nazis seized power in January 1933 in what amounted to a national revolution.

May 1933

The Nazi May Day on Tempelhof Field, Berlin, 1 May 1933

Photo credit: Ullstein Bilderdienst

Sausages, beer, an airshow followed by fire-
works—the festivities in the German capital had all the trappings of a fun-filled spring holiday in the middle of the twentieth century. Yet the ruling National Socialist German
Workers' Party sought much more than family entertainment.
Declared by the new regime as a "Feiertag der nationalen Arbeit"—a celebration of national work—1 May 1933 was carefully choreographed to honor workers and to demonstrate the
national sense of purpose that was now said to animate the
German people. May Day was appropriated from the socialist
repertoire in order to reenact fundamental operations of National Socialism: the vernacularization of German nationalism
so that it was the worker, the artisan, and the farmer who stood
for the greater whole; and the nationalization of what had been
international symbols of class uplift and social reform. The
message of this May Day was that the economic well-being
and social recognition that workers and especially socialist
workers had sought for so long were inextricably tied to the
nation. Compared to the mood of resistance and defiance with
which Social Democrats and Communists had very separately
demonstrated on 1 May 1932, as in previous years, the contrast
could not have been greater. In place of the language of class
struggle there was a rhetoric of national belonging; in place of
the gestures of alienation, the motions of reconciliation.

Just how credible this Nazi rendition of May Day really was
remained unclear, however. As workers marched down Berlin's
streets to the fairgrounds near Tempelhof Airport wearing
their distinctive work clothes, organized in groups according

to factory and trade as if they constituted separate links in a chain of national productivity, it was apparent that many were playing their prescribed roles with considerable unease. Only a thinning line of bystanders stretched along parts of the parade route. On this May Day at least, the theatrical nature of Nazi political production was too apparent. For many observers, it was obvious that the streets were but stage scenery, the blue smocks simply costumes, the gestures and speeches awkwardly followed scripts, and the audience insufficiently animated.

The coercive aspects to the role-playing on this day became very explicit on the next, when the Nazis physically invaded and assumed control over the buildings of and suppressed the entire socialist trade-union organization. It was not long before the Nazis erected their own German Labor Front under the leadership of Robert Ley. The first of May was very much a set-up for the second of May. And yet the May Day ceremony was not entirely a charade, since, however heavy-handed the choreography, it corresponded in a rough way to emotionally resonant ideas that many workers shared about the nation. May Day 1933 previews both the genuine support and the sheer terror that composed public life in the Third Reich. This day is therefore an appropriate moment to explore the credibility of the National Socialist revolution.

The "star" formation of the marchers was familiar to workers, since it followed the basic format of all big assemblies that had taken place during the Weimar Republic: the monster demonstration to protest the murder of Foreign Minister Walther Rathenau in June 1922, for example, or the huge gathering in the Lustgarten in opposition to fascism in January

1933. From points all around the working-class periphery of the city, paraders made their way to a central point. From Charlottenburg's Westend, from the south—Wilmersdorf, Schöneberg, Marienfelde, and Neukölln—from Friedrichshain in the east and Prenzlauer Berg and Wedding in the north, columns of 50,000 workers each marched to the great graded plain at Tempelhof, where they assembled on designated blocks—I, II, III, IV, V, VI, VII, VIII, IX, and X. Altogether more than one million Germans—workers, employees, young people—gathered at Tempelhof. Berlin's subways and trams and buses moved over two million people on 1 May.[1]

On this occasion, however, the working-class crowds did not occupy the arena as they saw fit, with pals and neighbors, roaming around, singing, or speech-making, as had been the case during May Day celebrations in the Weimar period. Instead, participants reported to work before getting the day off, marched with their factory mates, and observed exemplary shopfloor discipline, arranging themselves into teams, lines, and squares, following directions, signals, and cordons: I, II, III, IV, V, VI, VII, VIII, IX, X. Everybody else had to pay two marks to get onto the Tempelhof grounds.

At first glance, the serried ranks assumed an almost military-like formation in which spontaneity and liberty appeared to have been banished. What better expressed the totalitarian nature of the regime than these blocks composed of workers who had been pulled out of their proletarian neighborhoods, dressed up like so many guild members, and reassembled to hear the "Führer" speak until he was hoarse? Public ceremonies such as this one composed the dream world of National Socialism in which the "Volk" was present, completely united and perfectly synchronized. Yet suspicion, apathy, and fear lingered behind the facade of May Day ceremonies, Nuremberg rallies, and other acclamatory spectacles of the Third Reich. Participants often cut the line. "As the parade passed a pissoir, I said to myself: 'in you go,'" remembered one worker on the way to Tempelhof. "As I stepped out of line, the guy next to me followed, and when we were done, we ran home."[2] The story was the same elsewhere. May Day parades were skipped and other Nazi functions perfunctorily visited. A picture of this twentieth-century dictatorship of virtue begins to emerge: neighbors preferred to stay at home rather than participate in the strenuous social life that had been imposed by National Socialism. It follows that whatever bold promises the Nazis made before 1933, the regime did not generate genuine consensus and its opportunism left sympathizers disappointed. Historians agree: indifference to public events and withdrawal into private arenas characterized much of everyday life in Germany after 1933.[3]

Given the martial and authoritarian nature of the Nazi regime, this retreat into private life makes sense. It appeals to the best opinions we have of ourselves and of the multitude of "decent Germans." Yet it is starkly at odds with the highly charged political mobilization before 1933 and may well be exaggerated. The Gebenslebens and the Rauchs, young and old nationalists who have appeared in the folds of this story, certainly continued to take part in regime activities as enthusiastic volunteers, recruits, wardens, and soldiers. Indeed, by their own testimony, the two workers who ducked out of line to take a pee returned to their flats in a proletarian district (Friedrichshain) to find that neighbors had draped tenement facades with Nazi flags. They had ably circumvented party officials at work, yet "nearly fell over" at the sight of so many ordinary Hitlerites at home. Though hardly objective, Nazi newspapers made pointed reference to the swastikas flying in "knallrot" (totally red; that is, Communist) strongholds: Wedding, Spandau, and even in the *Laubenkolonien*, the garden plots that so many workers tended.[4] Obviously, May Day 1933 was more complicated than the black-and-white scheme of oppressive National Socialist order versus spunky working-class liberty.

What is more, it is difficult to accept at face value the notion that ordinary Germans were indifferent to fascist spectacle. To be sure, many workers detested the Nazis. Even groups who had voted for the Nazis inevitably grew tired of the ceaseless parading. There is no doubt that the inevitable relaxation of political tensions after 1933 left party officials frustrated: "Every member must look upon it as a duty to attend," they insisted time and again in Northeim: "No citizen must be allowed to stay at home."[5] Nonetheless, the despondency these exhortations imply fails to convince because it summarily depoliticizes the large number of Germans who had been so active throughout the 1920s. Did Nazi supporters really suddenly withdraw into private life? Given the wide appeal of resurgent patriotism and ideas of national solidarity, it does not make sense that so many Germans entered the public square quite so reluctantly. What happened to the appealing idea of "National Revolution"? A closer look suggests that there was considerable enthusiasm for the Nazi cause long after the seizure of power in January 1933. While the Social Democratic underground assembled evidence that many workers stayed clear of official May Day events in 1933 and in the years that followed, the fact was, as informants invariably noted: "Once again Tempelhof was full."[6] This conclusion that Nazism continued to enjoy a broadening base of support despite certain disappointments is an unhappy one, but it fits the facts better than any other.

Why was it that workers and, in even greater numbers, the middle classes filled Tempelhof again and again? In the first place, the festivities were hardly as oppressive as some of the geometric images of mass discipline circulated in the media would have suggested. On the edges of the assembly, families did picnic and children did play. People meandered forth and back behind the lines, enjoying the day off work, drinking beer, eating sausages, and, in the evening, marveling at the fireworks that followed the Führer's speech. May Day in Nazi Germany thus smudged the boundary between summer carnival and political rally. For both participants and organizers, the effect of one did not cancel out the other. Indeed, recreation and discipline may have fit together rather well, insofar as the post–civil war mood of fun and games seemed to rest on the political hygiene that the Nazis had achieved.

The symbolic gestures of the regime also mattered. To workers who had watched Social Democrats fight long and hard and always unsuccessfully to persuade the Reichstag to recognize 1 May as an official holiday, the authoritative National Socialist declaration in April 1933 must have made quite an impression. What is more, in a country where redundant workers had been brushed aside by a state unable to maintain unemployment benefits and where those workers who still clung to jobs knew that their children had little prospect for social advancement as a result of deep and persisting class prejudices, Hitler made an impact simply by honoring so publicly the contributions of manual laborers. His gestures were unprecedented, even if they remained gestures. It is revealing that in April 1933 socialist Free Trade Union leaders warmly acknowledged the embrace of the newly proposed Volksgemeinschaft and urged members to participate in the official ceremonies the Nazis had planned.[7]

Social Democrats always pointed out that it was workers who mined the coal, manufactured the iron and steel, and assembled the machinery that had made Germany a world power; and the National Socialists proceeded to commemorate just that on May Day. Workers' delegations from around the country, and from the (French-occupied) Saar, the free city of Danzig (another creature of Versailles), and Austria (already symbolically admitted into the Third Reich), were flown into the capital as special guests of the government. As part of its special May Day broadcast, German radio carried live their red-carpet arrival at the airport (1:00 PM) and later their audience with Reichspräsident Hindenburg and Reichskanzler Hitler (5:30 PM). All day long, as the crowds made their way to Tempelhof, the radio played the songs of "miners, farmers, and soldiers," broadcast a "symphony of work" composed by Hans-Jürgen Nierentz and Herbert Windt, and featured interviews with (specially selected) ordinary fellows: a dockworker from Hamburg, an agricultural laborer from East Prussia, a metalworker from the Saar, a miner from the Ruhr, and a vintner from the Mosel Valley. Again and again, various (male) parts were made to represent the whole: workers from different regions and diverse trades were the links that composed the great chain of German being. On this May Day, workers did not enter the public sphere as a class apart, as proletarians struggling against adversity. They did so as recognizable and skilled professionals who belonged to the nation.

May Day was also an unabashed celebration of German nationalism, in which German workers played major roles. When "workers' poets" read from their work (3:05 PM), they articulated the "authentic" voice of the "man on the street" who had made his peace with National Socialism, and they thereby broadcast German nationalism in an appealing vernacular. With these readings the Nazis hoped to revive the blue-collared patriotic culture that had flourished during World War I when workers' poets such as Karl Bröger and Heinrich Lersch first found a national audience. Later in the afternoon the essayist Eugen Diesel—son of the great engineer—opened up a treasure chest of enchanting words to describe the hand-built landscape of power lines, factories, and fields that corresponded so well to the muscular vitality of the Third Reich (6:20 PM).

All the while, squadrons of Junker airplanes overflew Tempelhof. Among the featured pilots was the ever popular Ernst Udet, whom Social Democrats would have instantly recognized since he had frequently performed in republican ceremonies. For one hour in the afternoon Germany's new ocean-crossing 236-meter zeppelin circled over the city as it proceeded on its spectacular twenty-six-hour tour of the nation. The airshow was a favorite item in working-class circles, for it not only displayed the manufacturing skills of German workers but incorporated them into a wider spectacle of national purpose and national identity. Even before Hitler mounted the stage (8:00 PM), the choreography of May Day had fastened the links between workers and the nation, between machinists and machine-age dreams, between technical mastery and national prowess.[8] After a speech by Adolf Hitler, a collective singing of the national anthem, and a fireworks display, 1933's May Day came to an end shortly before midnight. The next day the *Berliner Morgenpost*, just three months earlier a newspaper inclined to the Social Democrats, happily gushed: "the biggest demonstration of all times."[9]

The media's representation of the big day embellished nationalist themes. Cutting, splicing, and editing the pictures of the assembly, the illustrated magazines (the top-selling *Berliner Illustrirte Zeitung*, the more conservative *Die Woche*, and the Nazis' own *Illustrierte Beobachter*) depicted a triumphant gathering in which disorderly masses had congealed into a coherent Volksgemeinschaft. Spread across two pages of the *Berliner Illustrirte* was the familiar shot of the Graf Zeppelin casting its shadow over the densely packed crowd. It was a stunning photograph in which the people were framed by one of the technological and military symbols of the nation. Images of a nation reunited retold the story of the day and thereby allowed readers to recognize themselves and then insert themselves in the collective destiny. The fact that the definition of German was being reworked to exclude Jewish citizens was passed over. What was reproduced and what stood out in collective memory was the crowd assembled in the frame of the nation.

Later in the 1930s film cameras would recreate what the individual—waiting, standing, peeing—had not been able to experience: the synchronized movement of masses around the pivot of leadership in what amounted to choreographed plebiscites. The spectacle itself was subordinated to its mechanical reproduction. Thanks to weekly newsreels and especially to Leni Riefenstahl's *Triumph of the Will*, the cinematic rendition of the 1934 party rally in Nuremberg which played to packed theaters across Germany, the tentative, awkward movements of individual Germans could be screened as comprehensible national history.[10] In the end what Nazi spectacle sought to recreate for every person was the experience of Adolf Hitler when he stepped into the patriotic crowd on Munich's Odeonsplatz on 2 August 1914 and recognized the correspondence of his personal identity with Germany's national identity.

A word of caution is in order. Public spectacles such as May Day and the Nuremberg Rallies did not create Nazis out of Germans. Social identities cannot be fashioned on a potter's wheel. Many Germans remained skeptical about the social conventions and the authoritarian structures of the Third Reich. Slack business turnover and larger economies of scale, especially as rearmament lifted Germany out of the depression, meant that middle-class shopkeepers and artisans continued to moan and groan, even though the Nazis had cleansed the country of Marxists. For their part, workers surely enjoyed full employment by 1936 but suffered longer working hours and generally inelastic wages. Neighbors from all social backgrounds also grew to despise the "little Nazis," the local party bosses whose venality and corruption reached unparalleled heights. There is plenty of evidence that prominent Nazis fashioned themselves into a new, very dislikable elite: the opulence in which labor leader Robert Ley or Air Minister Hermann Goering lived attested to that. In light of this it is no wonder that a measure of apathy greeted the regime's political spectacles. Also, for all the joyous celebration that accompanied

Hitler's great foreign policy successes—remilitarization of the Rhineland, Anschluss with Austria, the "return" of the Sudetenland, and the quick military victories against the Reich's archenemies Poland and France—German solidarities wore thin once victories gave way to defeats after 1942.[11]

The much-vaunted Volksgemeinschaft in the Third Reich was dubious and tentative in many aspects. Yet it should not be dismissed out of hand as invalid or illegitimate. For all the evidence that money and birth still mattered in Nazi Germany, there was a broad discussion about the continuing validity of codes of etiquette and privileges of status and the importance of recognizing merit. Far more people were involved in renovating the nation and felt the emotional pull of the nation in the 1930s than had been the case half a century earlier. A psychological enfranchisement followed the regime's emphasis on national solidarity and racial elitism. It is worth recalling how the *Berliner Morgenpost* anticipated the first Nazi May Day on Tempelhof: "All German classes are jumbled up" on the field, "jumbled up and intermingling." And "they see not what separates them, but what unites them."[12] A new political quality was in the making.

Press reports are not in themselves accurate, though it is striking to see how quickly liberal newspapers such as the *Morgenpost* and the *Berliner Tageblatt* took up the Nazi message, but they hint at an enormous hunger for wholeness, which surely moved ordinary Germans. As a result, for many citizens, National Socialism "felt" more democratic than Weimar and certainly than Wilhelmine Germany.[13] A historical break had been made with old German conservatism; recognizing that, millions of Germans, particularly younger ones, were increasingly at home in the Third Reich. At the same time, the vast effort to rearm and reequip the nation offered unprecedented opportunities for social mobility. Workers as a class suffered, but those individuals who accepted the premises of an achievement-oriented consumer society (bent on war) could anticipate rewards. Numerous scholars also remind us to take seriously Nazi claims to honor workers and argue that efforts to integrate labor into the national community were not without effect. The German Labor Front, in particular, has been credited with improving the status of workers. Similar analyses of the Hitler Youth and the social service of middle-class activists suggest that the domestic policies of the regime enjoyed substantial support. The National Socialists were popular insofar as they were identified with a new national mood that emphasized national integration, social reform, and economic prosperity.[14]

In the end what the Nazis achieved was not the creation of a new type of German but rather the validation of new social roles which more and more Germans tried on. Although these roles were not comprehensive and did not regulate all or even most of the exchanges that people had with one another, they created expectations and presumptions. Much of the Nazi phenomenon took place in the subjunctive tense. It offered the promise and possibility of a renovated social sphere that retained considerable appeal until the very end. In the years 1933–1945 Germans lived in two worlds. In the midst of the familiar universe of stable links to family, region, and social milieu, the Nazis constructed a "second world" out of "a network of organizations" in which "the traditional criteria of social worth and social placement had no validity."[15]

Although many fascist precepts remained merely a "happy illusion"—*schöner Schein*—they also moved the population in new and demonstrable ways. "Jumbled up and intermingling"—the *Berliner Morgenpost's* description of May Day—is altogether too cheery, but nonetheless captures the way Germans began to move in the public sphere during the Nazi period. Thousands upon thousands of Berliners tramped to Tempelhof on May Day, over one million volunteers participated in the Reich's annual *Winterhilfe* charity drive, several million more young people were recruited into the Hitler Youth, more than two million workers enrolled in apprenticeship programs run by the German Labor Front, as many as eight million Germans joined local civil-defense leagues, and an astonishing fifty-four million had, in just the year 1938, participated in some sort of Nazi-sponsored leisure activity *(Kraft durch Freude)*.[16] Nazis promoted, and Germans were drawn to, participation in the creative act of building a national community. While this commitment offered particular social rewards, it appealed to strongly held conceptions of public idealism as well.

Wartime service after 1939 only strengthened the role of National Socialist institutions in daily life. The war allowed the Nazis to actualize their ideas about national mobilization and racial hierarchy. To enter the war zone was to enter a newly constructed world organized around race. The brutal fighting on the eastern front, for example, appeared to establish the validity of the party's unsparing contempt for Slavic "subhumans."[17] The extraordinary effort to root out Jewish life and finally to exterminate Jews themselves sharpened the indistinct anti-Semitism that so many Germans had learned at home.

During the war the Nazi world view had become in large measure the world in view. Without relinquishing ties to family, workmates, and neighbors, Germans moved relatively easily from one to the other social context, adopting as they did the vocabulary of national integration, the messianism of the Führer cult, the terms of constant struggle, and eventually the identities of Aryan overlords vis-à-vis conquered European civilians and foreign workers.[18]

That so many ordinary Germans were complicit in the murder of Jews and other so-called undesirables was not so much the function of a genocidal anti-Semitism which they shared in uncomplicated fashion with Nazi leaders; rather, over the course of the twelve-year Reich, more and more Germans came to play active and generally congenial parts in the Nazi revolution and then subsequently came to accept the uncompromising terms of Nazi racism. Indeed, it was the ease with which Germans enrolled themselves in the national destiny that made it possible for the Nazis to prepare a new round of increasingly fierce mobilizations which, in turn, strengthened the national community of fate and led it ever closer to complete annihilation. National solidarity ultimately rested on war to the point that community became inextricably linked to its antithesis, which was death. At the cost of millions of innocent lives, Nazism self-destructed in the most terrible racial war of modern times, but not before having demonstrated just how compelling national reassembly was to the twentieth-century imagination. It is this mobilization of violence in the name of populism and ethnic nationalism that is the searing, burning impression of the years 1914–1945, Germany's twentieth-century revolution.

National reassembly—this is the key motion of National Socialist politics. The appeal of the movement rested on a vision of the nation that recognized and enfranchised the people on the basis of what they did for the Volk rather than who they were according to scales of status and one that promised social reform and economic stability. It premised this renovation on a radical break with the political traditions of the past. There is no doubt that the regime fell short of its goals, but not so far short that it did not enjoy considerable legitimacy throughout German society. Moreover, the legitimacy of the Third Reich rested on more than simply the benefits that accrued to individual Germans. To examine the social achievements in the years 1933–1945 as if they were items on an balance sheet assumes that the seizure of power in 1933 was some sort of gigantic gamble that caught Germans a bit by surprise and would remain acceptable only if it continued to generate winnings (wages, turnover, tax relief). In my view, the "national socialist" consensus was not nearly so circumstantial. It had deeper ideological roots, connecting the leaders in power to the aspirations of citizens and giving the policies of the regime a fair degree of familiarity and pertinence.

In 1933 millions of Nazi sympathizers could point to long records of political activism in which they had confronted Communist and Social Democratic opponents or battled conservative elites, even if they had done so not as Nazis but as some sort of radical nationalists or vaguely spiritual socialists. Over the course of the 1920s voters abandoned those parties judged to be unpatriotic or insufficiently social reformist or lacking a popular touch. In election after election, in each of which as much as one-quarter of the electorate switched party allegiances, a "national socialist" plurality gradually took shape. This dynamic ultimately favored the National Socialists more than any other political grouping, though the German National People's Party, the Stahlhelm, and the Landvolk were initial beneficiaries. In sum, the Nazis were not political aliens.

My argument that National Socialism was the result of broad trends in German politics since the onset of World War I leads me to reject explanations that are either overly circumstantial or overly consensual. In the first place, I have shown that the Nazis were not creatures of extraordinary crisis. Their appeal cannot be explained by pointing to vague resentments that the German people held against the Allies or against the Treaty of Versailles. There were enough parties to vigorously attack Germany's international position after World War I; the National Socialist German Workers' Party did not occupy otherwise empty space on that issue. Moreover, while Hitler's movement owed much of its insurgent momentum to the economic catastrophe of the Great Depression, German politics was extremely roiled by political newcomers before New York's stock market crash in 1929. The established middle-class parties that had administered the German Reich since unification in 1871 were already in a state of advanced decay, and the electorate had responded repeatedly to those "national-social" initiatives which proposed a more inclusive, solidaristic society along the lines imagined in August 1914. Factor out the Great Depression; German politics was still headed in an illiberal and rather unconventional direction. Some sort of ambitious military regime, if not a fascist-like new community, could well be expected to appear at the end of the road.

Second, I reject the idea that the Nazis simply put into

operation cultural prejudices held in common by most Germans. Anti-Semitism was certainly current in Weimar Germany, probably more so than in the prewar years, but it does not explain why people voted for Hitler or even why the majority of activists joined the party. Jewish Germans did not figure in the divisive issues that the Nazis raised against other political groups or in the dramatic motions of partisan activity in which so many citizens were engaged. Nor do alleged antidemocratic or militaristic proclivities among Germans tell us why these proclivities should have helped the Nazis, instead of traditional authoritarians. To make sense of these years we have to keep in mind the millions of Germans who abandoned older political loyalties and claimed new ones. What this volatility validates as politically salient are the differences among partisan groups, not any common cultural code. It is therefore important to take seriously National Socialist claims to be a revolutionary movement that did not seek legitimacy from the past.

National Socialism proposed to regenerate the nation, although the appeal of this renovation was not the same for every German. Precisely because the intention was to renovate, the Nazis repudiated older, purportedly less forthcoming political traditions. Most obviously, they were implacable opponents of the Social Democrats and the ultimate victors in an overtly ideological contest with the Left. At the same time, the Nazis broke with liberal state administrators, social conservatives, and traditional authoritarians. They had as little affection for the Kaiserreich as they had for the Weimar Republic. In short, the Nazis were ideological innovators. The National Socialist German Worker's Party effectively responded to popular demands for political sovereignty and social recognition and insisted that these could only be achieved through national union, which would provide Germans with an embrasive sense of collective identity and a strong role in international politics.

It was this far-reaching program of renovation that made the Nazis stand out and made them attractive to a plurality of voters. If Hitler and his followers had simply recirculated the anti-Semitism of Anton Drexler's German Workers' Party or blustered on about the shameless Treaty of Versailles or devoted all their energies to combatting the Social Democrats and other treasonous "November criminals," the movement would have stalled completely. This is exactly what happened to Wolfgang Kapp and the Freikorpsmen of 1919–1920 and also explains the demise of Alfred Hugenberg and the German Nationalists in 1924–1930. Instead, attacks on conservatives as well as Marxists, denunciations of local power arrangements as well as the national parliament, and an affirmative vision of a prosperous, technologically advanced nation gave the Nazis a sharp ideological edge.

At a time when so much civic strife is defined in terms of cultural affinities it is all the more important, if sometimes difficult, to recall the force of ideology. Long-standing ethnic hatreds, religious fundamentalisms, and transnational "civilizations" dominate contemporary discussions about instability and unrest, which are frequently understood in terms of the friction between basically essential cultural qualities that have come into contact with one another. However, the Nazi phenomenon was not a hyperventilated expression of German values, even as it pronounced the allegedly superior quality of the German people. Nor was it the pathological result of economic hard times. Instead National Socialism comprised a program of cultural and social regeneration premised on the superordination of the nation and the Volk and modeled very much on the public spirit and collective militancy of the nation at war.

This made it a distinctive and disruptive political contender, which threatened to overturn the privileged position of social elites while co-opting the gains made by the working-class movement. National Socialism was rooted in the imagination because it appealed to populist aspirations that had been frustrated since German unification and to solidaristic virtues newly kindled by World War I. Mustering broad support, it also challenged well-defined political groups and rejected the civic claims of citizens who would not or could not belong to the newly stylized national community. Thus, even as the Nazis upheld an integral, almost redemptive nationalism, they created new categories of outsiders, enemies, and victims. Nazism was neither accidental nor unanimous.

Notes

Introduction

1. Rudolf Herz and Dirk Halfbrodt, *Fotografie und Revolution* (Munich, 1988), pp. 279, 281; Heinrich Hoffmann, *Hitler wie ich ihn sah: Aufzeichnungen seines Leibfotografen* (Munich, 1974), p. 32.
2. Richard Hanser, *Putsch: How Hitler Made Revolution* (New York, 1971), pp. 76–77.
3. Adolf Hitler, *Mein Kampf*, trans. John Chamberlain et al. (New York, 1941), pp. 210–211.
4. *Mein Kampf* quoted in J. P. Stern, *Hitler: The Führer and the People* (Berkeley, 1975), p. 54. See also *Illustrierter Beobachter*, no. 31, 2 Aug. 1930.
5. I disagree with Daniel Jonah Goldhagen's conclusions in *Ordinary Germans: Hitler's Willing Executioners* (New York, 1996), but share his emphasis on desire and ideology in understanding Nazism.

July 1914

1. "Berliner Beobachter," *Berliner Lokal-Anzeiger*, no. 374, 26 July 1914.
2. "Österreichfreundliche Kundgebungen in Berlin," *Berliner Tageblatt*, no. 374, 26 July 1914. I am much indebted to the detailed studies by Jeffrey Verhey, "The 'Spirit of 1914': The Myth of Enthusiasm and the Rhetoric of Unity in World War I Germany" (Ph.D diss., University of California, Berkeley, 1991); and Jeffrey Smith, "A People's War: The Transformation of German Politics, 1913–1918" (Ph.d diss., University of Illinois, 1997). Translations are my own unless otherwise noted.

3. "Das Strassenbild am Sonntag," *Vossische Zeitung*, no. 375, 27 July 1914.

4. "Das Aufflammen des nationalen Hochgefühls in Berlin," *Kreuz-Zeitung*, no. 346, 27 July 1914.

5. See Verhey, "Spirit of 1914," pp. 105–107.

6. *Frankfurter Zeitung* quoted in ibid., p. 3.

7. "Zweite Balkonrede des Kaisers, 1. August 1914," in Ulrich Cartarius, ed., *Deutschland im Ersten Weltkrieg* (Munich, 1982), p. 15.

8. Modris Eksteins, *Rites of Spring: The Great War and the Birth of the Modern Age* (Boston, 1989), p. 61.

9. Fritz Fischer, *Germany's War Aims in the First World War* (New York, 1967); Hans Ulrich Wehler, *The German Empire, 1871–1918*, trans. Kim Traynor (Leamington Spa, 1985).

10. Verhey, "Spirit of 1914," p. 141. See also Wolfgang Kruse, *Krieg und nationale Integration: Eine Neuinterpretation des sozialdemokratischen Burgfriedensschlusses 1914/15* (Essen, 1994), pp. 30–38.

11. Both cited in Verhey, "Spirit of 1914," pp. 163–164.

12. Siegfried Jacobsohn, *Die ersten Tage* (Konstanz, 1916), pp. 30–31, cited in Bernd Ulrich, "Die Desillusionierung der Kriegsfreiwilligen von 1914," in Wolfram Wette, ed., *Der Krieg des kleinen Mannes: Eine Militärgeschichte von unten* (Munich, 1992), pp. 111–112.

13. Smith, "A People's War," ch. 2.

14. Peter Fritzsche, *Reading Berlin 1900* (Cambridge, 1996), pp. 165–169.

15. Smith, "A People's War," ch. 3; Belinda Davis, "Reconsidering Habermas, Gender, and the Public Sphere: The Case of Wilhelmine Germany," in Geoff Eley, ed., *Society, Culture and the State in Germany, 1870–1930* (Ann Arbor, 1996), p. 408.

16. "Erste Balkonrede Kaiser Wilhelms II, 31. Juli 1914," in Cartarius, ed., *Deutschland im Ersten Weltkrieg*, pp. 12–13.

17. See, e.g., Bernd Weisbrod, "German Unification and the National Paradigm," *German History* 14 (1996), pp. 193–203; Eksteins,

Rites of Spring; Liah Greenfield, *Nationalism: Five Roads to Modernity* (Cambridge, 1992).

18. *Berliner Lokal-Anzeiger,* no. 398, 8 Aug. 1914, cited in Laurence Moyer, *Victory Must Be Ours: Germany in the Great War, 1914–1918* (New York, 1995), p. 88.

19. Friedrich Meinecke, *The German Catastrophe* (Boston, 1963), p. 25.

20. Ernst Glaeser, *Class of 1902,* trans. Willa and Edwin Muir (New York, 1929), pp. 213–214.

21. Johanna Boldt to Julius Boldt, 27 Aug. and 3 Sept. 1914, cited in Edith Hagener, *"Es lief sich so sicher an Deinem Arm": Briefe einer Soldatenfrau 1914* (Weinheim, 1986), pp. 41, 48–49.

22. Philip Scheidemann quoted in Cartarius, ed., *Deutschland im Ersten Weltkrieg,* p. 23. See also Jagow, "2. Stimmungsbericht," 26 Aug. 1914 and "4. Stimmungsbericht," 2 Sept. 1914, in Ingo Materna and Hans-Joachim Schreckenbach, eds., *Berichte des Berliner Polizeipräsidenten zur Stimmung und Lage der Bevölkerung in Berlin 1914–1918* (Weimar, 1987), pp. 4, 6.

23. Cited in Ute Daniel, *Arbeiterfrauen in der Kriegsgesellschaft: Beruf, Familie und Politik im Ersten Weltkrieg* (Göttingen, 1989), p. 23.

24. Karl Kraus, "Kriegssegen," *Die Fackel* 27 (Dec. 1925), pp. 29–42; Hermann Bahr, *Kriegssegen* (Munich, 1915), pp. 19–33; Ernst Toller, *Eine Jugend in Deutschland* (Munich, 1978), p. 53.

25. Glaeser, *Class of 1902,* pp. 214, 327, 350.

26. Hagener, *"Es lief sich so sicher an Deinem Arm,"* p. 39.

27. Volker Ullrich, "Kriegsalltag. Zur inneren Revolutionierung der Wilhelminischen Gesellschaft," in Wolfgang Michalka, *Der Erste Weltkrieg: Wirkung, Wahrnehmung, Analyse* (Munich, 1994), p. 604.

28. Lothar Burchardt, "Die Auswirkungen der Kriegswirtschaft auf die deutsche Zivilbevölkerung im Ersten und im Zweiten Weltkrieg," *Militärgeschichtliche Mitteilungen* 1 (1974), pp. 66–69.

29. Volker Ullrich, *Kriegsalltag: Hamburg im ersten Weltkrieg* (Cologne, 1982), pp. 41, 43.

30. In addition to Ullrich, *Kriegsalltag*, see Klaus-Deiter Schwarz, *Weltkrieg und Revolution in Nürnberg: Ein Beitrag zur Geschichte der deutschen Arbeiterbewegung* (Stuttgart, 1971), esp. p. 131; Karl-Ludwig Ay, *Die Entstehung einer Revolution: Die Volksstimmung in Bayern während des Ersten Weltkrieges* (Berlin, 1968); and Manfred Faust, *Sozialer Burgfrieden im Ersten Weltkrieg: Sozialistische und christliche Arbeiterbewegung in Köln* (Essen, 1992), esp. pp. 67–68.

31. Hagener, *"Es lief sich so sicher an Deinem Arm,"* p. 68. The names of the dead are taken from "Verlustliste Nr. 8," *Berliner Tageblatt*, no. 429, 25 Aug. 1914. They served in Königsberg's Grenadierregiment Nr. 1; Gumbinnen's Füsslierregiment Nr. 33; and Pillau's Infanterieregiment Nr. 43.

32. Letters of 3 Aug. 1914 and 9 Sept. 1914 in A. F. Wedd, *German Students' War Letters* (New York, 1929), pp. 1, 3. See also Ulrich, "Desillusionisierung," in Wette, ed., *Krieg des kleinen Mannes*, pp. 113–114.

33. Ulrich, "Desillusionisierung," in Wette, ed., *Krieg des kleinen Mannes*, pp. 116–117.

34. Ullrich, "Kriegsalltag," in Michalka, ed., *Der Erste Weltkrieg*, p. 606.

35. Wilhelm Deist, "Verdeckter Militärstreik im Kriegsjahr 1918?" in Wolfram Wette, ed., *Der Krieg des kleinen Mannes: Eine Militärgeschichte von unten* (Munich, 1992).

36. Elisabeth Domansky, "Der Erste Weltkrieg," in Lutz Niethammer et al., eds., *Bürgerliche Gesellschaft in Deutschland* (Frankfurt, 1990), pp. 287, 290.

37. Anthony Powell quoted in Eksteins, *Rites of Spring*, p. 178.

38. Richard Bessel, *Germany after the First World War* (Oxford, 1993), pp. 5–8.

39. Jürgen Kocka, *Klassengesellschaft im Krieg*, 2nd rev. ed. (Göttingen, 1978), p. 13.

40. Faust, *Sozialer Burgfrieden im Ersten Weltkrieg*, p. 55.

41. Ernst Kaeber, *Berlin im Weltkriege: Fünf Jahre städtischer Kriegsarbeit* (Berlin, 1921), p. 397.

42. Karl Retzlaw, *Spartakus. Aufstieg und Niedergang. Erinnerungen eines Parteiarbeiters* (Frankfurt, 1971), p. 72.

43. Carl Busse, ed., *Deutsche Kriegslieder 1914/16* (Bielefeld, 1916), p. vi.

44. Bernd Ulrich, "Feldpostbriefe im Ersten Weltkrieg—Bedeutung und Zensur," in Peter Knoch, ed., *Kriegsalltag: Die Rekonstruktion des Kriegsalltags als Aufgabe der historischen Forschung und der Friedenserziehung* (Stuttgart, 1989), p. 43.

45. Letter of 2 Sept. 1914 in Hagener, *"Es lief sich so sicher an Deinem Arm,"* p. 48.

46. Ulrich, "Feldpostbriefe," in Knoch, ed., *Kriegsalltag*.

47. Ay, *Die Entstehung einer Revolution*, p. 25; Schwarz, "Bericht der Abteilung VII, Exekutive, 3. Kommissariat an den Polizeipräsidenten Berlin," 4 Mar. 1915, in Materna and Schreckenbach, eds., *Berichte*, p. 47; Ulrich, "Desillusionisierung," in Wette, ed., *Krieg des kleinen Mannes*, p. 117.

48. *Illustrirte Zeitung*, no. 3711, 13 Aug. 1914; no. 3712, 20 Aug. 1914.

49. Verhey, "Spirit of 1914," p. 262, 270–271; Philipp Witkop, *Kriegsbriefe deutscher Studenten* (Gotha, 1916). An American version of the expanded German edition appeared as A. F. Wedd, *German Students' War Letters* (New York, 1929). See also Ulrich, "Feldpostbriefe," in Knoch, ed., *Kriegsalltag*, p. 40; and Manfred Hettling and Michael Jeismann, "Der Weltkrieg als Epos. Philipp Witkops 'Kriegsbriefe gefallener Studenten,' " in Gerhard Hirschfeld and Gerd Krumeich, eds., *"Keiner fühlt sich hier mehr als Mensch . . .": Erlebnis und Wirkung des ersten Weltkriegs* (Essen, 1993), pp. 175–198.

50. Gunther Mai, " 'Aufklärung der Bevölkerung' und 'Vaterländischer Unterricht' in Württemberg 1914–1918: Struktur, Durchführung und Inhalte der deutshen Inlandspropaganda im Ersten Weltkrieg," *Zeitschrift für Württembergische Landesgeschichte* 36 (1977), pp. 199–235, here 202.

51. Ibid., p. 215.

52. Moyer, *Victory Must Be Ours*, p. 99.

53. Nigel Hamilton, *The Brothers Mann: The Lives of Heinrich and Thomas Mann, 1871–1950 and 1875–1955* (New Haven, 1979), p. 166.

54. Ulrich, "Desillusionisierung," in Wette, ed., *Krieg des kleinen Mannes*, p. 114.

55. See entries 6 Aug. 1914, 10 Aug. 1914, 23 Aug. 1914, 24 Aug. 1914; and 15 Aug. 1915 in *Käthe Kollwitz. Die Tagebücher*, ed. Jutta Bohnke-Kollwitz (Berlin, 1989).

56. For Berlin, Irene Stoehr and Detel Aurand, "Frauen im Ersten Weltkrieg: Opfer oder Täter?" *Courage* (1982), p. 46; for Frankfurt, Verhey, "Spirit of 1914," p. 221.

57. Heinrich Haacke, *Barmen im Weltkrieg* (Barmen, 1929), pp. 42–44. See also Elaine Catherine Boyd, " 'Nationaler Frauendienst: German Middle-Class Women in Service to the Fatherland, 1914–1918" (Ph.D diss., University of Georgia, 1979). On Social Democratic volunteers see Faust, *Sozialer Burgfrieden im Ersten Weltkrieg*, p. 146; and Jagow, "2. Stimmungsbericht," 26 Aug. 1914, in Materna and Schreckenbach, *Berichte*, p. 5.

58. Anneliese Seidel, *Frauenarbeit im Ersten Weltkrieg als Problem der staatlichen Sozialpolitik. Dargestellt am Beispiel Bayerns* (Frankfurt, 1979), p. 107; *Nationaler Frauendienst in Berlin, 1914–1917* (Berlin, 1917), p. 41.

59. Christiane Eifert, "Frauenarbeit im Krieg: Die Berliner 'Heimatfront' 1914 bis 1918," *Internationale Wissenschaftliche Korrespondenz zur Geschichte der deutschen Arbeiterbewegung* 21 (1985), p. 285; Anne Roerkohl, *Hungerblockade und Heimatfront: Die kommunale Lebensmittelversorgung in Westfalen während des Ersten Weltkrieges* (Stuttgart, 1991), pp. 204–205.

60. Haacke, *Barmen*, pp. 52, 154–155.

61. "Berliner Kriegsküchen," *Berliner Tageblatt*, no. 247, 16 May 1915.

62. Moyer, *Victory Must Be Ours*, p. 95.

63. Roerkohl, *Hungerblockade*, p. 201.

64. Jagow, "10. Stimmungsbericht," 5 Oct. 1914, in Materna and

Schreckenbach, eds., *Berichte*, p. 15; von Kessel to Kaiser Wilhelm II, 3 Dec. 1914, ibid., p. 30; Verhey, "Spirit of 1914," p. 221.

65. *Vorwärts*, no. 19, 19 Jan. 1915; *Berliner Tageblatt*, no. 37, 21 Jan. 1915.

66. "Die Wollberge am Königsplatz," *Berliner Tageblatt*, no. 39, 22 Jan. 1915; Haacke, *Barmen*, p. 67.

67. Haacke, *Barmen*, pp. 68, 112.

68. Ibid., p. 168; Roerkohl, *Hungerblockade*, p. 52; Klaus Saul, "Jugend im Schatten des Krieges: Vormilitärische Ausbildung— Kreigswirtschaftlicher Einsatz—Schulalltag in Deutschland 1914–1918," *Militärische Mitteilungen* 34 (1983), p. 174n173. On socialist support for the collections, see *Vorwärts*, no. 21, 21 Jan. 1915.

69. Moyer, *Victory Must Be Ours*, p. 162.

70. Roerkohl, *Hungerblockade*, pp. 53–54.

71. Haacke, *Barmen*, pp. 167–168; Roerkohl, *Hungerblockade*, p. 54.

72. Saul, "Jugend im Schatten des Krieges," p. 113.

73. Rudy Koshar, *Social Life, Local Politics, and Nazism: Marburg, 1880–1935* (Chapel Hill, 1986), pp. 127–150; Peter Fritzsche, *Rehearsals for Fascism: Populism and Political Mobilization in Weimar Germany* (New York, 1990), pp. 76, 250n1; Renate Mayntz, "Die Vereine als Produkt und Gegenwicht sozialer Differenzierung," in Gerhard Wurzbacher, ed., *Das Dorf im Spannungsfeld industrieller Entwicklung* (Stuttgart, 1954).

74. Ignaz Jastrow, *Gut und Blut fürs Vaterland* (Berlin, 1917), p. 87; Robert Knauss, *Die deutsche, englische und französische Kriegsfinanzierung* (Berlin, 1923), pp. 150–174; Gerald D. Feldman, *The Great Disorder: Politics, Economics, and Society in the German Inflation, 1914–1924* (New York, 1993), pp. 42–43.

75. "Der Hindenburg-Tag," *Vossische Zeitung*, no. 452, 4 Sept. 1915.

76. "Der Hindenburg von Berlin," *Berliner Tageblatt*, no. 452, 4 Sept. 1915; "Bei Hindenburg auf dem Königsplatz," ibid., no. 453, 5 Sept. 1915; "Die Enthüllung des 'Eisernen Hindenburg' in Berlin," *Norddeutsche Allgemeine Zeitung*, no. 246, 5 Sept. 1915.

Whatever happened to the "Iron Hindenburg"? Apparently he was never completely clad with nails and as the war dragged on fewer patriots came to put down a few marks to pick up a hammer. The scaffolding was stolen during the revolution and municipal authorities quickly dismantled Hindenburg and used his parts for firewood so all that remained was the massive head, which police detectives stumbled upon in a shed in north Berlin in 1938. Too large to put into a museum, this patriotic ironwork found a final resting place in the old Lehrter train station, where it was destroyed during the war. See Paul Weiglin, *Berlin im Glanz. Bilderbuch der Reichshauptstadt von 1888 bis 1918* (Cologne, 1954), p. 146.

77. Paul Singer, *SPD-Parteitagsprotokoll* (Berlin, 1892), p. 131.

78. Konrad Hänisch, *Die deutsche Sozialdemokratie in und nach dem Weltkriege* (Berlin, 1916), p. 144.

79. Eksteins, *Rites of Spring*, p. 100.

80. *Rheinische Zeitung* (Cologne), 28 Aug. 1914, cited in Faust, *Sozialer Burgfrieden im Ersten Weltkrieg*, p. 162.

81. Kruse, *Krieg und nationale Integration*, pp. 91–92, 106.

82. Bieber, *Gewerkschaften in Krieg*, pp. 122–123.

83. Dittmann, "Bericht der Abteilung VII. Exekutive, 3. Kommissariat an den Polizeipräsident Berlin," 15 Feb. 1915, in Materna and Schreckenbach, eds., *Berichte*, p. 43.

84. Schwarz, *Weltkrieg und Revolution*, pp. 115–116.

85. Faust, *Sozialer Burgfrieden im Ersten Weltkrieg*, p. 155; Frauke Bey-Heard, *Hauptstadt und Staatsumwälzung—Berlin 1919: Problematik und Scheitern der Rätebewegung in der Berliner Kommunalverwaltung* (Stuttgart, 1969), pp. 47–51, 54–59.

86. Gunther Mai, "Burgfrieden und Sozialpolitik in Deutschland in der Anfangsphase des Ersten Weltkrieges (1914/15)," *Militärgeschichtliche Mitteilungen* 20 (1976), pp. 21–50; Mai, *Das Ende des Kaiserreichs: Politik und Kriegführung im Ersten Weltkrieg* (Munich, 1987), pp. 88–95; Hans-Joachim Bieber, *Gewerkschaften in Krieg und Revolution: Arbeiterbewegung, Industrie, Staat und Militär in Deutschland 1914–1920* (Hamburg, 1981), pp. 116–121.

87. *Berliner Morgenpost*, no. 288, 17 Oct. 1915.

88. Mai, *Das Ende des Kaiserreichs*, pp. 95–105; Klaus Schönhoven, "Die Kriegspolitik der Gewerkschaften," in Michalka, ed., *Der Erste Weltkrieg*, pp. 682–683; and Wilhelm Deist, "Armee und Arbeiterschaft 1905–1918," *Francia* 2 (1974), pp. 474–477.

89. Robert Sigel, *Die Lensch-Cunow-Haenisch-Gruppe: Eine Studie zum rechten Flügel der SPD im Ersten Weltkrieg* (Berlin, 1976), pp. 55, 100–101; Faust, *Sozialer Burgfrieden im Ersten Weltkrieg*, pp. 156–157.

90. Mai, " 'Verteidigungskrieg' und 'Volksgemeinschaft,' " in Michalka, ed., *Der Erste Weltkrieg*, pp. 590–592.

91. Cited in Verhey, "Spirit of 1914," p. 308.

92. Stolle, "13. Stimmungsbericht," 26 Oct. 1914, in Materna and Schreckenbach, eds., *Berichte*, p. 20; Jagow, "18. Stimmungsbericht," 30 Nov. 1914, ibid., p. 27; von Kessel to Kaiser Wilhelm II, 3 Dec. 1914, ibid., p. 30.

93. "Nachts vorm Schloss," *Tägliche Rundschau*, no. 356, 1 Aug. 1914.

94. Albrecht Mendelssohn-Bartholdy, *The War and German Society: The Testament of a Liberal* (New York, 1971), p. 57.

95. See the citations in Verhey, "Spirit of 1914," pp. 297–298.

96. Hettling and Jeismann, "Der Weltkrieg als Epos," in Hirschfeld and Krumeich, *Keiner fühlt sich hier mehr als Mensch*.

97. Detlev J. K. Peukert, *The Weimar Republic: The Crisis of Classical Modernity*, trans. Richard Deveson (New York, 1993), p. 27.

98. Verhey, "Spirit of 1914," pp. 375–377; Wolfgang J. Mommsen, *Max Weber and German Politics, 1890–1920*, trans. Michael S. Steinberg (Chicago, 1984), pp. 244–252; Ludwig Bergsträsser, *Die preussische Wahlrechtsfrage im Kriege und die Entstehung der Osterbotschaft 1917* (Tübingen, 1929), pp. 125–129, 161; Ute Frevert, *Women in German History: From Bourgeois Emancipation to Sexual Liberation*, trans. Stuart McKinnon-Evans (New York, 1989), p. 162.

99. Reinhard Rürup, "Der 'Geist von 1914' in Deutschland: Kriegsbegeisterung und Ideologisierung des Krieges im Ersten Welt-

krieg," in Bernd Hüppauf, ed., *Ansichten vom Krieg: Vergleichende Studien zum Ersten Weltkrieg in Literatur und Gesellschaft* (Königstein, 1984), pp. 1–30, esp. 16. See also Rudolf Kjellen, *Die Ideen von 1914—Eine Weltgeschichtliche Perspektive* (Leipzig, 1915); Johann Plenge, *1789 und 1914: Die symbolischen Jahre in der Gesichchte des politischen Geistes* (Berlin, 1916).

100. Wolfgang Kapp, "The National Groups and the Imperial Chancellor," 20 May 1916, rpt. in Ralph Laswell Lutz, ed., *Fall of the German Empire, 1914–1918* (New York, 1969), pp. 81–106, esp. 82–84.

101. "Warum muss ich der Vaterlandspartei beitreten," cited in Verhey, "Spirit of 1914," p. 418.

102. Karl Wortman, *Geschichte der Detuschen Vaterlands-Partei 1917–1918* (Halle, 1926), p. 7.

103. Dirk Stegmann, "Zwischen Repression und Manipulation: Machteliten und Arbeiter- und Angestelltenbewegung 1910–1918. Ein Beitrag zur Vorgeschichte der DAP/NSDAP," *Archiv für Sozialgeschichte* 12 (1972), pp. 351–432.

104. Reports from 18 and 19 July 1916 cited in Materna and Schreckenbach, eds., *Berichte*, pp. 140–141.

105. Lewald, "Bericht des Polizeipräsidenten Berlin-Lichtenberg an den Polizeipräsidenten Berlin," 16 Oct. 1915, in Materna and Schreckenbach, eds., *Berichte*, p. 89. Belinda Davis, in "Home Fires Burning: Politics, Identity and Food in World War I Berlin" (Ph.D diss., University of Michigan, 1992), p. 184n45, raises the possibility that Assmann's was a Jewish firm, but finds no evidence of the anti-Semitism that played a role in later incidents.

106. *Berliner Morgenpost*, no. 288, 17 Oct. 1915.

107. Burchardt, "Die Auswirkungen der Kriegswirtschaft," *Militärgeschichtliche Mitteilungen*, pp. 68–69, 74.

108. Cited in Ullrich, *Kriegsalltag*, p. 65.

109. Kuhlmann, "Bericht des Polizeipräsidenten Berlin-Lichtenberg an den Polizeipräsidenten Berlin," 4 July 1917, in Materna and Schreckenbach, eds., *Berichte*, p. 210.

110. Ullrich, *Kriegsalltag*, p. 70; Roerkohl, *Hungerblockade*, p. 323.

111. Ay, *Die Entstehung einer Revolution*, pp. 35–36.

112. Ibid., pp. 178–183. See also Clara Viebig, *Töchter der Hekuba* (Berlin, 1917), pp. 92–93.

113. Ute Daniel, *Arbeiterfrauen in der Kriegsgesellschaft: Beruf, Familie, und Politik im Ersten Weltkrieg* (Göttingen, 1989), pp. 126, 168–169.

114. Jürgen Kocka, *Facing Total War: German Society, 1914–1918* (Cambridge, 1984), p. 190n59.

115. Ibid., p. 158.

116. Schwarz, *Weltkrieg und Revolution*, p. 158; Ay, *Die Entstehung einer Revolution*, pp. 162–164, 177–178.

117. Jagow, "38. Stimmungsbericht," 1 May 1915, in Materna and Schreckenbach, eds., *Berichte*, pp. 58–59; Dittmann, "Bericht der Abteilung VII, Exekutive, 3. Kommissariat an den Polizeipräsidenten Berlin," 17 May 1915, ibid., pp. 60–61.

118. *Berliner Morgenpost*, no. 179, 29 June 1916.

119. Glaeser, *Class of 1902*, p. 350.

120. Arthur Holitscher, *Mein Leben in dieser Zeit. Der "Lebensgeschichte eines Rebellen"* (Potsdam, 1928), cited in Dieter and Ruth Glatzer, *Berliner Leben 1914–1918: Eine historische Reportage aus Erinnerungen und Berichten* (Berlin, 1983), pp. 146–147.

121. See Davis, "Home Fires Burning."

122. This point is made forcefully by Faust in *Sozialer Burgfrieden im Ersten Weltkrieg*, pp. 148, 243.

123. Schwarz, *Weltkrieg und Revolution*, pp. 164, 174–176.

124. Kocka, *Facing Total War*, pp. 91–111; Robert G. Moeller, *German Peasants and Agrarian Politics, 1914–1924: The Rhineland and Westphalia* (Chapel Hill, 1986), pp. 61–67; Andreas Kunz, *Civil Servants and the Politics of Inflation in Germany, 1914–1924* (Berlin, 1986), pp. 112–131.

125. See Kocka, *Facing Total War*, and Gerald D. Feldman, *Army, Industry and Labor in Germany, 1914–1918* (Princeton, 1966). For a resume of the contemporary mood, Otto Baumgarten,

"Der sittliche Zustand des deutschen Volkes unter dem Einfluss des Krieges," *Geistige und sittliche Wirkungen des Krieges in Deutschland* (Stuttgart, 1927), pp. 1−88.

126. Walther Lambach, *Ursachen des Zusammenbruchs* (Hamburg, 1919), esp. p. 59.

127. Bessel, *Germany after the First World War*, p. 45.

128. Richard Wall and Jay Winter, eds., *The Upheaval of War: Family, Work, and Welfare in Europe, 1914−1918* (Cambridge, Eng., 1988).

129. Bethmann-Hollweg cited in Hans-Joachim Bieber, *Bürgertum in der Revolution: Bürgerräte und Bürgerstreiks in Deutschland 1918−1920* (Hamburg, 1992), p. 40.

November 1918

1. Cited in Dieter and Ruth Glatzer, eds., *Berliner Leben 1914−1918: Eine historische Reportage aus Erinnerungen und Berichten* (Berlin, 1983), pp. 434−435.

2. Heinrich August Winkler, *Von der Revolution zur Stabilisierung: Arbeiter und Arbeiterbewegung in der Weimarer Republik 1918 bis 1924* (Berlin, 1984), pp. 45, 55; A. J. Ryder, *The German Revolution of 1918: A Study of German Socialism in War and Revolt* (Cambridge, 1967), p. 155.

3. "Scheidemann ruft die Republik aus, 9.11.1918," in Gerhard A. Ritter and Susanne Miller, eds., *Die deutsche Revolution 1918−1919: Dokumente*, 2nd rev. ed. (Hamburg, 1975), pp. 77−78.

4. Entries for 9 and 12 Nov. 1918, Harry Kessler, *In the Twenties: The Diaries of Harry Kessler* (New York, 1971), pp. 7−10.

5. *Berliner Tageblatt*, no. 576, 10 Nov. 1918.

6. See, e.g., Hans Goslar, "Revolution," *Deutsche Allgemeine Zeitung*, no. 581, 14 Nov. 1918; Oskar Müller, Revolution und Parteien," ibid., no. 586, 17 Nov. 1918; Müller, "Bilanz der Revolution," ibid., no. 611, 1 Dec. 1918.

7. *Schleswig-Holsteinische Volkszeitung*, 5 Nov. 1918, cited in

Koppel S. Pinson, *Modern Germany: Its History and Civilization* (New York, 1966), p. 357.

8. Ryder, *German Revolution*, p. 138.

9. Winkler, *Von der Revolution*, p. 45; Ryder, *German Revolution*, p. 143.

10. Prince Max von Baden, *Erinnerungen und Dokumente*, ed. Golo Mann and Andreas Burckhardt (Stuttgart, 1968), p. 588.

11. Winkler, *Von der Revolution*, pp. 42–43. See also Susanne Miller, *Die Bürde der Macht: Die deutsche Sozialdemokratie 1918–1920* (Düsseldorf, 1978), p. 82.

12. Hans-Joachim Bieber, *Gewerkschaften in Krieg und Revolution: Arbeiterbewegung, Industrie, Staat und Militär in Deutschland 1914–1920* (Hamburg, 1981), p. 574.

13. Martin Müller-Aenis, *Sozialdemokratie und Rätebewegung in der Provinz: Schwaben und Mittelfranken in der bayerischen Revolution 1918–1919* (Munich, 1986), p. 109.

14. Ryder, *German Revolution*, p. 150.

15. *Goslarsche Zeitung*, no. 264, 8 Nov. 1928. In general, Hans-Joachim Bieber, *Bürgertum in der Revolution: Bürgerräte und Bürgerstreiks in Deutschland 1918–1920* (Hamburg, 1992), pp. 50–51.

16. Cited in Bieber, *Bürgertum in der Revolution*, p. 50.

17. *Deutsche Zeitung*, 13 Nov. 1918, ibid., p. 52.

18. On reformism in the November Revolution see Müller-Aenis, *Sozialdemokratie und Rätebewegung;* Barrington Moore, *Injustice: The Social Bases of Obedience and Revolt* (White Plains, 1978); and Wolfgang J. Mommsen, "The German Revolution, 1918–1920: Political Revolution and Social Protest Movement," in Richard Bessel and E. J. Feuchtwanger, eds., *Social Change and Political Development in Weimar Germany* (Totowa, N.J., 1981), pp. 21–54.

19. Käthe Kollwitz, entry for 9 Nov. 1918, in *Die Tagebücher*, ed. Jutta Bohnke-Kollwitz (Berlin, 1989), pp. 378–379.

20. *Illustrierte Geschichte der Deutschen Revolution* (Berlin, 1929), pp. 201, 207.

21. Kessler, diary entry for 12 Nov. 1918, *In the Twenties*, p. 10; Bieber, *Bürgertum in der Revolution*, pp. 126, 132, 135.

22. Bieber, *Bürgertum in der Revolution*, pp. 145–146.

23. Ibid., pp. 100–101, 104, 176.

24. *Berliner Tageblatt*, no. 606, 27 Nov. 1918; Bieber, *Burgertum in der Revolution*, pp. 100, 103.

25. *Berliner Tageblatt*, no. 590, 18 Nov. 1918; no. 592, 19 Nov. 1918.

26. Stefan Grossmann, "Gegen die Redewut," *Vossische Zeitung*, no. 586, 15 Nov. 1918.

27. *Berliner Tageblatt*, no. 590, 18 Nov. 1918; no. 596, 21 Nov. 1918; no. 604, 26 Nov. 1918; no. 608, 28 Nov. 1918; no. 615, 2 Dec. 1918; no. 621, 5 Dec. 1918.

28. Diary entry for 15 Nov. 1918, Kessler, *In the Twenties*, p. 13.

29. See esp. Manfred Faust, *Sozialer Burgfrieden im Ersten Weltkrieg: Sozialistische und christliche Arbeiterbewegung in Köln* (Essen, 1992), pp. 302–306.

30. *Berliner Tageblatt*, no. 651, 10 Dec. 1918.

31. Entry for 12 Dec. 1918, Kollwitz, *Die Tagebücher*, p. 389.

32. Ernst von Salomon, *Die Geächteten* (Berlin, 1930), pp. 26–35, cited and translated in Robert G. L. Waite, *Vanguard of Nazism: The Free Corps Movement in Postwar Germany, 1918–1923* (Cambridge, 1952), pp. 43–44.

33. Diary entry for 18 Dec. 1918, Kessler, *In the Twenties*, p. 37

34. Diary entry for 22 Dec. 1918, ibid., p. 39. See also Ulrich Kluge, *Soldatenräte und Revolution: Studien zur Militärpolitik in Deutschland 1918/19* (Düssseldorf, 1975), pp. 219–220.

35. Waite, *Vanguard of Nazism*, pp. 12–16, 35–37.

36. Max Hildebert Boehm, "Nationalversammlung und Parteien," *Grenzboten* 77, no. 4 (1918), p. 197; Eugen Diederichs cited in Gary Stark, *Entrepreneurs of Ideology: Neoconservative Publishers in Germany, 1890–1933* (Chapel Hill, 1981), p. 155.

37. Heinrich Kessler, *Wilhelm Stapel als politischer Publizist* (Nuremberg, 1967), p. 37.

38. Cited in Bieber, *Bürgertum in der Revolution*, pp. 115–116.

39. Karl Brammer, *Das Gesicht der Reaktion, 1918–1919* (Berlin,

1919), pp. 13–15; Friedrich Meinecke, *Nach der Revolution: Geschichtliche Betrachtungen über unsere Lage* (Munich, 1919); Peter Fritzsche, "Breakdown or Breakthrough? Conservatives and the November Revolution," in Larry Eugene Jones and James Retallack, eds., *Between Reform, Reaction, and Resistance: German Conservatism in Historical Perspective* (Providence, 1993), p. 302.

40. *Cellesche Zeitung*, no. 265, 11 Nov. 1918; Ulrich Popplow, "Göttingen in der Novemberrevolution, 1918/19," *Göttinger Jahrbuch* (1976), p. 219.

41. Müller-Aenis, *Sozialdemokratie und Rätebewegung*, p. 215.

42. Bertha Haedicke-Rauch to Minna von Alten-Rauch, 28 Nov. 1918, in Hedda Kalshoven, ed., *Ich denk so viel an Euch. Ein deutsch-holländischer Briefwechsel, 1920–1949* (Munich, 1995), p. 49.

43. St. [Stapel], "Wohin geht die Fahrt?" *Deutsches Volkstum*, 12, no. 1 (Jan. 1919), pp. 1–3.

44. Brammer, *Gesicht der Reaktion*, pp. 13, 22.

45. Bertha Haedicke-Rauch to Minna von Alten-Rauch, 20 Jan. 1919, in Kalshoven, ed., *Ich denk so viel an Euch*, p. 52.

46. Bieber, *Gewerkschaften in Krieg und Revolution*, p. 583.

47. Bieber, *Bürgertum in der Revolution*, pp. 104–105.

48. William L. Patch Jr., *Christian Trade Unions in the Weimar Republic, 1918–1933: The Failure of "Corporate Pluralism"* (New Haven, 1985), p. 48.

49. Jonathan Osmond, *Rural Protest in the Weimar Republic: The Free Peasantry in the Rhineland and Bavaria* (New York, 1993), p. 3.

50. Robert G. Moeller, *German Peasants and Agrarian Politics, 1914–1924: The Rhineland and Westphalia* (Chapel Hill, 1986), p. 79.

51. Calculated from Heinrich August Winkler, *Mittelstand, Demokratie und Nationalsozialismus: Die politische Entwicklung von Handwerk und Kleinhandel in der Weimarer Republik* (Cologne, 1972), pp. 225n124, 229n43, 232n4.

52. *Nachrichten für Stadt und Land* (Oldenburg), no. 6, 7 Jan. 1919; no. 23, 24 Jan. 1919; no. 39, 30 Jan. 1919; no. 161, 16 Aug. 1919.

53. *Deutsche Handelswacht*, no. 18, 26 Oct. 1920. See also Bieber, *Bürgertum in der Revolution*, p. 145.

54. Bieber, *Bürgertum in der Revolution*, p. 100; Peter Fritzsche, *Rehearsals for Fascism: Populism and Political Mobilization in Weimar Germany* (New York, 1990), p. 43; Moeller, *German Peasants and Agrarian Politics*, p. 76.

55. Fritzsche, *Rehearsals for Fascsim*, pp. 39–54; Larry Eugene Jones, *German Liberalism and the Dissolution of the Weimar Party System, 1918–1933* (Chapel Hill, 1988), pp. 28–29, 96; Andreas Kunz, *Civil Servants and the Politics of Inflation in Germany, 1914–1924* (Berlin, 1986), pp. 153–154; Moeller, *German Peasants and Agrarian Politics*, p. 92; Michael Prinz, *Vom neuen Mittelstand zum Volksgenossen: Die Entwicklung des sozialen Status der Angestellten von der Weimarer Republik bis zum Ende der NS-Zeit* (Munich, 1986), pp. 50–51. In general, Thomas Childers, *The Nazi Voter: The Social Foundations of Fascism in Germany, 1919–1933* (Chapel Hill, 1983).

56. Fritzsche, *Rehearsals for Fascism*, p. 44.

57. *Nachrichten für Stadt und Land* (Oldenburg), no. 284, 18 Oct. 1920; *Nordwestdeutsche Handwerkszeitung*, no. 27, 5 July 1923.

58. On the Free Peasantry, see Osmond, *Rural Protest*.

59. Spengler quoted in Kurt Sondheimer, *Antidemokratisches Denken in der Weimarer Republik: Die Ideen des deutschen Nationalismus zwischen 1918 und 1933* (Munich, 1968), p. 265.

60. Lederer cited in James Sheehan, *German Liberalism in the Nineteenth Century* (Chicago, 1978), p. 250. For the inflation see Gerald D. Feldman, *The Great Disorder: Politics, Economics, and Society in the German Inflation, 1914–1924* (New York, 1993).

61. Waite, *Vanguard of Nazism*, p. 40.

62. There are important exceptions, but consider the publication dates of standard works such as Alfred Brackmann, ed., *Baltische Lande* (Leipzig, 1939); Claus Grimm, *Jahre deutscher Entscheidung im Baltikum 1918–1919* (Essen, 1939); Curt Hotzel, ed., *Deutscher Aufstand: Die Revolution des Nachkrieges* (Stuttgart, 1934); Friedrich Wilhelm von Oertzen, *Die deutschen Freikorps, 1918–*

1923 (Munich, 1939); Hans Roden, ed., *Deutsche Soldaten vom Frontheer und Freikorps über die Reichswehr zur neuen Wehrmacht* (Leipzig, 1935); Ernst von Salomon, ed., *Das Buch vom deutschen Freikorpskämpfer* (Berlin, 1938); and *Die Wirren in der Reichshauptstadt und im nördlichen Deutschland 1918–1920* (Berlin, 1940).

63. Carl Schmitt, *Political Romanticism*, trans. Guy Oakes (Cambridge, 1986 [1919]).

64. Quoted in Hagen Schulze, *Freikorps und Republik 1918–1920* (Boppard, 1969), p. 56.

65. Quoted ibid., p. 328.

66. Waite, *Vanguard of Nazism*, p. 165.

67. John H. Morgan quoted in Schulze, *Freikorps und Republik*, p. 66.

68. Waite, *Vanguard of Nazism*, p. 164.

69. Schulze, *Freikorps und Republik*, p. 59.

70. James M. Diehl, *Paramilitary Politics in Weimar Germany* (Bloomington, 1977), p. 62.

71. Fritzsche, *Rehearsals for Fascism*, pp. 58–61; David Clay Large, "The Politics of Law and Order: A History of the Bavarian *Einwohnerwehr*, 1918–1921," *Transactions of the American Philosophical Society* 70, pt. 2 (1980), pp. 34, 46–47.

72. Cited in Waite, *Vanguard of Nazism*, p. 142.

73. *Goslarsche Zeitung*, no. 64, 19 Mar. 1920; Helge Matthiesen, "Zwei Radikalisierungen—Bürgertum und Arbeiterschaft in Gotha 1918–1923," *Geschichte und Gesellschaft* 21 (1995), p. 47.

74. Martin Broszat, *Hitler and the Collapse of Weimar Germany*, trans. V. R. Berghahn (New York, 1987), p. 40.

75. Rudy Koshar, *Social Life, Local Politics, and Nazism: Marburg, 1880–1935* (Chapel Hill, 1986), pp. 130, 127–150.

76. Fritzsche, *Rehearsals for Fascism*, p. 77.

77. Adelhein von Saldern, "Sozialmilieus und der Aufstieg des Nationalsozialismus in Norddeutschland (1930–1933)," in Frank Bajohr, *Norddeutschland im Nationalsozialismus* (Hamburg, 1993), pp. 35–36, 39–40.

78. Elisabeth Gebensleben-von Alten to Irmgard Gebensleben, 27 Apr. 1924 and 2 May 1924; Irmgard Gebensleben to Elisabeth Gebensleben-von Alten, 2 July 1924; Elisabeth Gebensleben-von Alten to Irmgard Gebensleben, 27 Aug. 1924 and 9 Sept. 1924, in Kalshoven, ed., *Ich denk so viel an Euch*, pp. 68–69, 73.

79. Diehl, *Paramilitary Politics*, p. 294.

January 1933

1. *New York Times*, 31 Jan. 1933.

2. André François-Poncet, *The Fateful Years: Memoirs of a French Ambassador in Berlin, 1931–1938*, trans. Jacques LeClerq (New York, 1949), p. 48.

3. *Der Angriff*, no. 26, 31 Jan. 1933.

4. Entry for 30 Jan. 1933 in Elke Fröhlich, ed., *Die Tagebücher von Joseph Goebbels*, pt. 1, vol. 2 (Munich, 1987), p. 358.

5. Herbert Seehofes, "Das erwachte Berlin marschiert," *Völkischer Beobachter*, no. 31, 31 Jan. 1933; Elisabeth Gebensleben-von Alten to Irmgard Gebensleben, 3 Feb. 1933, in Kalshoven, ed., *Ich denk so viel an Euch*, p. 161.

6. "Farmer, politician," aged 34, quoted in Walter Kempowski, *Did You Ever See Hitler?* (New York, 1975), p. 33.

7. François-Poncet, *The Fateful Years*, p. 49.

8. As it turns out, Maikowski may well have been shot by a renegade SA man who sympathized with the Communists, a turn of events that does not change the fact that local Communists confronted Maikowski's troop and were ready to fight. See Jay W. Baird, *To Die for Germany: Heroes in the Nazi Pantheon* (Bloomington, 1990), pp. 94, 97–98.

9. Ralf Georg Reuth, *Goebbels*, trans. Krishna Winston (New York, 1993), p. 164.

10. Dietrich Orlow, *The History of the Nazi Party: 1919–1933* (Pittsburgh, 1969), p. 239n1.

11. *Frankfurter Zeitung*, no. 83, 31 Jan. 1933.

12. William Sheridan Allen, *The Nazi Seizure of Power: The Expe-*

rience of a Single German Town, 1922–1945, rev. ed. (New York, 1984), pp. 153–154.

13. Hsi-Huey Liang, *The Berlin Police Force in the Weimar Republic* (Berkeley, 1970), pp. 71, 84–85.

14. Richard Bessel, *Political Violence and the Rise of Nazism: The Storm Troopers in Eastern Germany, 1925–1934* (New Haven, 1984), p. 100.

15. Baird, *To Die for Germany,* pp. 95–96.

16. *Der Angriff,* no. 35, 10 Feb. 1933.

17. Quoted in Johannes Steinhoff, Peter Pechel, and Dennis Showalter, *Voices from the Third Reich: An Oral History* (Washington, 1989), p. xxxvii.

18. J. P. Stern, *Hitler: The Führer and the People* (Berkeley, 1975), p. 168.

19. Sebastian Haffner, *Anmerkungen zu Hilter* (Munich, 1978), p. 46, cited by a more skeptical Ian Kershaw in *The "Hitler Myth": Image and Reality in the Third Reich* (Oxford, 1987), p. 1, who provides a masterly survey of the subject.

20. *Berliner Tageblatt,* 16 Sept. 1930, cited in Martin Broszat, *Hitler and the Collapse of Weimar Germany,* trans. V. R. Berghahn (New York, 1987), p. 16.

21. Knowlton L. Ames Jr., *Berlin after the Armistice* (n.p., 1919), p. 77. See also Friedrich Meinecke, *Nach der Revolution: Geschichtliche Betrachtungen über unsere Lage* (Munich, 1919), pp. 2, 11.

22. H. R. Knickerbocker, *The German Crisis* (New York, 1932), pp. 42–43, 76, 94, 97, 206–207, 209.

23. See, e.g., Allen, *Nazi Seizure of Power,* p. 322.

24. Erich Matthias, "The Influence of the Versailles Treaty on the Internal Development of the Weimar Republic," in Anthony Nicholls and Erich Matthias, eds., *German Democracy and the Triumph of Hitler* (London, 1970), pp. 13–28; Otmar Jung, "Plebiszitärer Durchbruch 1929? Zur Bedeutung von Volksbegehren und Volksentscheid gegen den Young Plan für die NSDAP," *Geschichte und Gesellschaft* 15 (1989), pp. 506–507.

25. Cited in Heinrich August Winkler, *Der Weg in die Katastrophe: Arbeiter und Arbeiterbewegung in der Weimarer Republik 1930 bis 1933* (Berlin, 1987), p. 45.

26. Hans Fallada, *Kleiner Mann—was nun?* (Berlin, 1932).

27. Knickerbocker, *German Crisis*, p. 50. See also Graf Alexander Stenbock-Fermor, *Deutschland von unten: Reise durch die proletarische Provinz* (Stuttgart, 1931).

28. Theodor Geiger, *Die soziale Schichtung des deutschen Volkes: Soziographischer Versuch auf statistischer Grundlage* (Stuttgart, 1932), p. 86; Winkler, *Weg in die Katastrophe*, p. 39.

29. Winkler, *Weg in die Katastrophe*, p. 43; Knickerbocker, *German Crisis*, pp. 51–52.

30. Broszat, *Hitler*, p. 50.

31. Allen, *Nazi Seizure of Power*, pp. 72–73; Theodor Geiger, "Panik im Mittelstand," *Die Arbeit* 7 (1930), pp. 637–659.

32. *Frankfurter Zeitung*, no. 86, 1 Feb. 1933; Allen, *Nazi Seizure of Power*, p. 84. See also Geoffrey Pridham, *Hitler's Rise to Power: The Nazi Movement in Bavaria, 1923–1933* (New York, 1973), p. 237.

33. Klaus Fischer, *Nazi Germany: A New History* (New York, 1995), pp. 234, 256.

34. Jürgen Falter, "The Two Hindenburg Elections of 1925 and 1932: A Total Reversal of Voter Coalitions," *Central European History* 23 (1990), pp. 225–241; idem, *Hitlers Wähler* (Munich, 1991), pp. 123–125.

35. Helmut Heiber, *Die Republik von Weimar* (Munich, 1966), p. 172.

36. Broszat, *Hitler*, p. 67.

37. Bessel, *Political Violence and the Rise of Nazism*, p. 25.

38. *Volksfreund* (Braunschweig), no. 85, 11 Apr. 1925.

39. Peter Fritzsche, "Presidential Victory and Popular Festivity in Weimar Germany: Hindenburg's 1925 Election," *Central European History* 23 (1990), pp. 212–216; Ernst Glaeser, *The Last Civilian*, trans. Gwenda David and Eric Mosbacher (New York, 1935).

40. Fritzsche, "Presidential Victory and Popular Festivity," pp. 214–215. For Saxony, see Benjamin Lapp, *Revolution from the Right: Politics, Class and the Rise of Nazism in Saxony, 1919–1933* (Atlantic Highlands, N.J., 1997), pp. 142–143.

41. Fritzsche, "Presidential Victory and Popular Festivity," pp. 217–218.

42. *Weser Zeitung* (Bremen), no. 247, 7 May 1927.

43. *Deutsche Allgemeine Zeitung*, no. 461, 2 Oct. 1927.

44. *Braunschweigische Neuste Nachrichten*, no. 200, 27 Aug. 1926; *Pirnaer Anzeiger*, 25 Sept. 1926, cited in Lapp, *Revolution from the Right*, p. 148.

45. Gerhard Stoltenberg, *Politische Strömungen im schleswig-holsteinischen Landvolk 1918–1933* (Düsseldorf, 1962), p. 111; Erwin Topf, *Die Grüne Front: Der Kampf um den deutschen Acker* (Berlin, 1933), p. 5.

46. Lapp, *Revolution from the Right*, p. 168.

47. *Nachrichten für Stadt und Land* (Oldenburg), no. 5, 6 Jan. 1928.

48. Stoltenberg, *Politische Strömungen;* Fritzsche, *Rehearsals for Fascism*, pp. 114–118; Rudolf Heberle, *From Democracy to Nazism: A Regional Case Study in Political Parties in Germany* (Baton Rouge, 1945); Jürgen Bergmann and Klaus Megerle, "Protest und Aufruhr der Landwirtschaft in der Weimarer Republik (1924–1933). Formen und Typen der politischen Agrarbewegung im regionalen Vergleich," in Bergmann et al., eds., *Regionen im historischen Vergleich: Studien zu Deutschland im 19. und 20. Jahrhundert* (Opladen, 1989), pp. 200–287; Lapp, *Revolution from the Right*, p. 168.

49. *Anzeiger für Harlingerland* (Aurich), no. 5, 6 Jan. 1928; *Täglicher Anzeiger* (Holzminden), no. 65, 16 Mar. 1928.

50. Cited in Jeremy Noakes, *The Nazi Party in Lower Saxony, 1921–1933* (Oxford, 1971), p. 119.

51. *Emder Zeitung*, no. 11, 13 Jan. 1928; Herbert Volck, *Rebellen um Ehre* (Berlin, 1932), p. 251.

52. Quotations are all from the foreword of Walter Luetgebrune's *Neu-Preussens Bauernkrieg: Entstehung und Kampf der Land-*

volkbewegung (Hamburg, 1931). The song is cited in Topf, *Grüne Front*, p. 40. See also novels by Hans Fallada, *Bauern, Bonzen und Bomben* (Berlin, 1931); Ernst von Salomon, *Die Stadt* (Berlin, 1932); and Bodo Uhse, *Söldner und Soldat* (Paris, 1935).

53. Fritzsche, *Rehearsals for Fascsim*, p. 199.

54. *Anzeiger für Harlingerland* (Aurich), no. 5, 6 Jan. 1928.

55. Fritzsche, *Rehearsals for Fascism*, pp. 191–193, 197, 200.

56. Ibid., pp. 207–208; Lapp, *Revolution from the Right*, p. 205.

57. Thomas Childers, "Interest and Ideology: Anti-System Politics in the Era of Stabilization, 1924–1928," in Gerald D. Feldman, ed., *Die Nachwirkungen der Inflation auf die deutsche Geshichte 1924–1933* (Munich, 1985), pp. 1–20.

58. Orlow, *History of the Nazi Party*, p. 47–48; Klaus Fischer, *Nazi Germany: A New History* (New York, 1995), pp. 126–131.

59. Orlow, *History of the Nazi Party*, p. 90; Gerhard Paul, *Aufstand der Bilder: Die NS-Propaganda vor 1933* (Bonn, 1990), pp. 36–38; Karlheinz Schmeer, *Die Regie des öffentlichen Lebens im Dritten Reich* (Munich, 1956), pp. 11–12.

60. Fischer, *Nazi Germany*, p. 179.

61. Geoffrey Pridham, *Hitler's Rise to Power: The Nazi Movement in Bavaria, 1923–1933* (New York, 1973), p. 79.

62. Orlow, *History of the Nazi Party*, p. 53; Joachim C. Fest, *Hitler*, trans. Richard and Clara Winston (New York, 1975), p. 226.

63. Fritzsche, *Rehearsals for Fascism*, p. 202; *Deutsches Volkstum* 12 (1927), p. 953.

64. On the role of newspapers, see Richard F. Hamilton, *Who Voted for Hitler?* (Princeton, 1982); Falter, *Hitlers Wähler*, pp. 334–339; Klaus Wernecke, "Die Provinzpresse am Ende der Weimarer Republik. Zur politischen Rolle der bürgerlichen Tageszeitungen am Beispiel der Region Ost-Hannover," in *Presse und Geschichte* (Munich, 1987); Adelheid von Saldern, "Sozialmilieus und der Aufstieg des Nationalsozialismus in Norddeutschland (1930–1933)," in Frank Bajohr, ed., *Norddeutschland im Nationalsozialismus* (Hamburg, 1993), p. 37; Lapp, *Revolution from the Right*, pp. 202, 207–209.

65. Karl Dietrich Bracher, *The German Dictatorship: The Origins, Structure, and Effects of National Socialism*, trans. Jean Steinberg (New York, 1970), pp. 133, 179; Conan Fischer, *The Rise of the Nazis* (Manchester, 1995), p. 172.

66. Rudy Koshar, "Contentious Citadel: Bourgeois Crisis and Nazism in Marburg/Lahn, 1880–1933," in Childers, ed., *Formation of the Nazi Constituency*, pp. 23–24; Saldern, "Sozialmilieus und der Aufstieg des Nationalsozialismus," pp. 33, 49n74; Zdenek Zofka, *Die Ausbreitung des Nationalsozialismus auf dem Lande: Eine regionale Fallstudie zur politische Einstellung der Landbevölkerung in der Zeit des Aufstiegs und der Machtergreifung der NSDAP, 1928–1933* (Munich, 1979), p. 140n1; Roger Chickering, "Political Mobilization and Associational Life: Some Thoughts on the National Socialist German Workers' Club (e.V.)," in Larry Eugene Jones and James Retallack, eds., *Elections, Mass Politics, and Social Change in Modern Germany* (Cambridge, 1992), p. 314.

67. Zofka, *Die Ausbreitung des Nationalsozialismus auf dem Lande*, pp. 81, 142–143; Noakes, *Nazi Party in Lower Saxony*, p. 146; Allen, *Nazi Seizure of Power*.

68. Elisabeth Gebensleben-von Alten to Irmgard Gebensleben, 15 Sept. 1930, in Kalshoven, ed., *Ich denk so viel an Euch*, p. 99.

69. Respondent in Theodor Abel, *The Nazi Movement: Why Hitler Came to Power* (New York, 1966), p. 88.

70. Allen, *Nazi Seizure of Power*, p. 30.

71. Jung, "Plebiszitärer Durchbruch 1929?" pp. 504–506.

72. Lapp, *Revolution from the Right*, p. 208. Klaus Wernecke cites similar praise in Lüneburg. See "Die konservative Faschisierung der protestantischen Provinz: Bürgerliche Öffentlichkeit und Nationalsozialismus," in Lüneburger Arbeitskreis, "Machtergreifung," *Heimat, Heide, Hakenkreuz: Lünebergs Weg ins Dritte Reich* (Hamburg, 1984), pp. 53–81.

73. Bessel, *Political Violence and the Rise of Nazism*, p. 153.

74. Conan Fischer, *Stormtroopers: A Social, Economic and Ideological Analysis, 1929–1935* (London, 1983), pp. 118–119, 122.

75. Lapp, *Revolution from the Right*, p. 208; Noakes, *Nazi Party in Lower Saxony*, p. 216.

76. Lapp, *Revolution from the Right*, p. 198; Hamilton, *Who Voted for Hitler*, pp. 320–325.

77. Noakes, *Nazi Party in Lower Saxony*, p. 216.

78. Schmeer, *Die Regie des öffentlichen Lebens*, pp. 12–16.

79. Allen, *Nazi Seizure of Power*, p. 32. See also Gerhard Paul, *Aufstand der Bilder: Die NS-Propaganda vor 1933* (Bonn, 1990); Zofka, *Die Ausbreitung des Nationalsozialismus auf dem Lande*, pp. 80–81.

80. Elisabeth Gebensleben-von Alten to Irmgard Gebensleben, 18 Oct. 1931, in Kalshoven, ed., *Ich denk so viel an Euch*, p. 123.

81. Glaeser, *The Last Civilian*.

82. See Broszat, *Hitler*, p. 92; Zofka, *Die Ausbreitung des Nationalsozialismus auf dem Lande*, p. 115; Noakes, *Nazi Party in Lower Saxony*, pp. 248–249; von Saldern, "Sozialmilieus und der Aufstieg des Nationalsozialismus," p. 30.

83. Ute Frevert, *Women in German History: From Bourgeois Emancipation to Sexual Liberation*, trans. Stuart Mckinnon-Evans (New York, 1989); Claudia Koonz, *Mothers in the Fatherland: Women, the Family, and Nazi Politics* (New York, 1987), pp. 21–123.

84. Hamilton, *Who Voted for Hitler*, pp. 87–89; Winkler, *Weg in die Katastrophe*, pp. 109–111.

85. A white-collar worker in Abel, *Nazi Movement*, p. 128.

86. Fritzsche, *Rehearsals for Fascism*, p. 224.

87. Falter, *Hitlers Wähler*, pp. 111, 199–228.

88. Karl Rohe, *Das Reichsbanner Schwarz-Rot-Gold: Ein Beitrag zur Geschichte und Struktur der politischen Kampfverbände zur Zeit der Weimarer Republik* (Düsseldorf, 1966), pp. 126–158, 245–266; Conan Fischer, "Workers, the Middle Classes, and the Rise of National Socialism," *German History* 9 (1991), pp. 357–373. See also Shlomo Avineri, "Marxism and Nationalism," in Jehuda Reinharz and George L. Mosse, eds., *The Impact of Western Na-*

tionalism: Essays dedicated to Walter Z. Laqueur on the Occasion of His 70th Birthday (London, 1992), pp. 283–303.

89. Udo Kissenkoetter, *Gregor Strasser und die NSDAP* (Stuttgart, 1978), pp. 83–122; Gregor Strasser, *Arbeit und Brot* (Munich, 1932).

90. Allen, *Nazi Seizure of Power*, p. 32; Broszat, *Hitler*, p. 91.

91. Donna Harsch, *German Social Democracy and the Rise of Nazism* (Chapel Hill, 1993), pp. 190, 239; Wolfram Pyta, *Gegen Hitler und für die Republik: Die Auseinandersetzung der deutschen Sozialdemokratie mit der NSDAP in der Weimarer Republik* (Düsseldorf, 1989), p. 236.

92. See, e.g., the conclusion of Heinrich August Winkler, *Weimar 1918–1933: Die Geschichte der ersten deutschen Demokratie* (Munich, 1993).

93. Pyta, *Gegen Hitler und für die Republik*, p. 366.

94. Fischer, *Rise of the Nazis*, p. 54.

95. See the overviews in Falter, *Hitlers Wähler*, and Saldern, "Sozialmilieus und der Aufstieg des Nationalsozialismus," pp. 20–52.

96. Hamilton, *Who Voted for Hitler?*

97. See Thomas Childers, "The Limits of National Socialist Mobilization: The Elections of 6 November 1932 and the Fragmentation of the Nazi Constituency," in Childers, ed., *Formation of the Nazi Constituency*, pp. 232–259.

98. The most effective counterargument that draws attention to the blunders paving the way for Hitler's seizure of power is provided by Henry Ashby Turner in *Hitler's Thirty Days of Power* (Reading, Mass., 1996).

99. Ian Kershaw, "Hitler and the Germans," in Richard Bessel, ed., *Life in the Third Reich* (New York, 1987), pp. 45–46.

100. Kershaw, "*Hitler Myth*," p. 5.

101. Sarah Gordon, *Hitler, Germans, and the "Jewish Question"* (Princeton, 1984).

102. Elisabeth Gebensleben-von Alten to Irmgard Brester-Gebensle-

ben, 21 Jan. 1930, in Kalshoven, ed., *Ich denk so viel an Euch,*
p. 93, on having attended "The Threepenny Opera"; ibid., 6
April 1933, pp. 189–191, on the anti-Jewish boycott.

103. Geoff Eley, "What Produces Fascism: Pre-Industrial Traditions or
a Crisis of the Capitalism State," in idem, *From Unification to
Nazism: Reinterpreting the German Past* (Boston, 1986), p. 270.

104. Quoted in Peter Gay, *Weimar Culture* (New York, 1968), p. 70.
See also the cover illustration to the American paperback edition
of Detlev J. K. Peukert, *The Weimar Republic: The Crisis of Classical Modernity* (New York, 1993).

105. *Vorwärts,* no. 50, 30 Jan. 1933.

106. Martin Broszat, "Die Struktur der NS-Massenbewegung," *Vier-
teljahrshefte für Zeitgeschichte* 31 (1983), p. 72.

107. Thomas Childers, *The Nazi Voter: The Social Foundations of Fascism in Germany, 1919–1933* (Chapel Hill, 1983), pp. 268–269.

May 1933

1. *Berliner Tageblatt,* no. 202, 2 May 1933.

2. Cited in Wieland Elfferding, "Von der proletarischen Masse zum
Kriegsvolk: Massenaufmarsch und Öffentlichkeit im deutschen
Faschismus am Beispiel des 1. Mai 1933," in *Inszenierung der
Macht: ästhetische Faszination im Faschismus* (Berlin, 1987),
p. 24n2. For similar incidents, see William Sheridan Allen, *The
Nazi Seizure of Power: The Experience of a Single German
Town, 1922–1945,* rev. ed. (New York, 1984), pp. 229, 232, 254–
255; Barbara Dorn and Michael Zimmermann, *Bewährung-
sprobe: Herne und Wanne-Eickel 1933–1945. Alltag, Widerstand, Verfolgung unter dem Nationalsozialismus* (Bochum,
1987), pp. 113, 118, 125; Hans-Josef Steinberg, "Die Haltung der
Arbeiterschaft zum NS-Regime," in Jürgen Schmädeke and Peter Steinbach, eds., *Der Widerstand gegen den Nationalsozialismus: Die deutsche Gesellschaft und der Widerstand gegen Hitler* (Munich, 1985), p. 870.

3. See, e.g., Detlev Peukert, "Working-Class Resistance: Problems

and Options," in David Clay Large, ed., *Contending with Hitler: Varieties of German Resistance in the Third Reich* (Cambridge, 1991), p. 45; Allen, *Nazi Seizure of Power*, pp. 254–255, 283; Ian Kershaw, *Popular Opinion and Political Dissent in the Third Reich: Bavaria, 1933–1945* (Oxford, 1983), p. 314.

4. *Völkischer Beobachter*, no.121/122, 1/2 May 1933. See also *Berliner Morgenpost*, no. 104, 2 May 1933, on Wedding's Sperrplatz.

5. Allen, *Nazi Seizure of Power*, p. 255.

6. Sopade report cited in Elfferding, "Von der proletarischen Masse zum Kriegsvolk," p. 24n2.

7. Heinrich August Winkler, *Der Weg in die Katastrophe: Arbeiter und Arbeiterbewegung in der Weimarer Republik, 1930 bis 1933* (Berlin, 1987), pp. 921–923. See also the remarks of various prominent labor leaders, "Deutscher Arbeit zur Ehre: Stimmen zum 1. Mai," *Berliner Tageblatt*, no. 200, 30 Apr. 1933.

8. The radio broadcast for May Day can be found in Elfferding, "Von der proletarischen Masse zum Kriegsvolk," p. 26. On aviation and nationalism, Peter Fritzsche, *A Nation of Fliers: German Aviation and the Popular Imagination* (Cambridge, 1992), pp. 162–170.

9. *Berliner Morgenpost*, no. 104, 2 May 1933.

10. See, e.g., Brigitte Bruns, "Neuzeitliche Fotografie im Dienste der nationalsozialistischen Ideologie. Der Fotograf Heinrich Hoffmann und sein Unternehmen," in Diethart Krebs et al., eds., *Die Gleichschaltung der Bilder: Zur Geschichte der Pressefotografie 1930–36* (Berlin, 1983); Klaus Kreimeier, *The Ufa Story: A History of Germany's Greatest Film Company, 1918–1945*, trans. Robert and Rita Kimber (New York, 1996).

11. See, e.g., Richard Grunberger, *The 12-Year Reich: A Social History of Nazi Germany, 1933–1945* (New York, 1971).

12. *Berliner Morgenpost*, no. 103, 30 Apr. 1933.

13. Stanley G. Payne, *A History of Fascism, 1914–1945* (Madison, 1996), pp. 194–195.

14. Rüdiger Hachtmann, "Thesen zur 'Modernisierung' der Industriearbeit in Deutschland 1924 bis 1944," in Frank Bajohr, ed., *Norddeutschland im Nationalsozialismus* (Hamburg, 1993),

pp. 414–451; John Gillingham, "The 'Deproletarianization' of German Society: Vocational Training in the Third Reich," *Journal of Social History* 19 (1986), pp. 423–432. The popularity of the regime among workers is discussed in Gunther Mai, "Arbeiterschaft zwischen Sozialimus, Nationalismus und Nationalsozialismus," in Uwe Backes, Eckhard Jesse, and Rainer Zitelmann, eds., *Die Schatten der Vergangenheit: Impulse zur Historisierung des Nationalsozialismus* (Frankfurt, 1990), pp. 195–217; Ulrich Herbert, "Arbeiterschaft im 'Dritten Reich'. Zwischenbilanz und offene Fragen," *Geschichte und Gesellschaft* 15 (July–Sept. 1989), pp. 320–360; and Alf Lüdtke, "'Ehre der Arbeit': Industriearbeiter und Macht der Symbole. Zur Reichweite symbolischer Orientierungen im Nationalsozialismus," in Klaus Tenfelde, ed., *Arbeiter im 20. Jahrhundert* (Stuttgart, 1991), pp. 343–392. See also Arno Klönne, *Jugend im Dritten Reich* (Düsseldorf, 1982); Herwart Vorländer, *Die NSV: Darstellung und Dokumentation einer nationalsozialistischen Organisation* (Boppard, 1988); Claudia Koonz, *Mothers in the Fatherland: Women, the Family, and Nazi Politics* (New York, 1987); Peter Fritzsche, "Where Did All the Nazis Go? Reflections on Collaboration and Resistance," *Tel Aviver Jahrbuch für deutsche Geschichte* 23 (1994), pp. 191–214.

15. Jens Alber, "Nationalsozialismus und Modernisierung," *Kölner Zeitschrift für Soziologie und Sozialpsychologie* 41 (June 1989), p. 348, elaborates on this point, which was first raised in David Schoenbaum, *Hitler's Social Revolution: Class and Status in Nazi Germany, 1933–1939* (New York, 1966), pp. 283–288.

16. Ronald Smelser, *Robert Ley: Hitler's Labor Front Leader* (New York, 1988), pp. 191–216; Vorländer, *Die NSV*.

17. Omer Bartov, *Hitler's Army: Soldiers, Nazis, and War in the Third Reich* (New York: Oxford University Press, 1991).

18. Smelser, *Robert Ley*, pp. 302–303; Ian Kershaw, *The "Hitler Myth": Image and Reality in the Third Reich* (Oxford, 1987); Detlev Peukert, *Inside Nazi Germany: Conformity, Opposition and Racism in Everyday Life*, trans. Richard Deveson (New Haven, 1987), pp. 125–155; Bartov, *Hitler's Army*, esp. pp. 144–178.

Index